DATE DUE

SE 19 '96			
DE 2 '96			
MR 4 97			
AP 8 '99			
MY 27 '99			
AUG 05 1999			
DE 4 01			
DE 19 01			
DE 9 02			
DE 18 03			
DE 8 '05			
MY 7 07			
OC 15 09			

DEMCO 38-296

MEN WHO BEAT THE MEN WHO LOVE THEM: BATTERED GAY MEN AND DOMESTIC VIOLENCE

David Island, PhD
Patrick Letellier, MA

SOME ADVANCE REVIEWS

"I applaud the publication of this book for it breaks the silence surrounding gay men's (and lesbian) domestic violence (DV). Presented herein is a comprehensive, thoughtful analysis and plan to provide the services for victims/survivors of gay DV. This book is a welcome addition to the Battering Syndrome library and the challenges that gay and lesbian DV poses to the field."

Naomi Lichtenstein, MSW, CSW
Director of Client Services
NYC Gay and Lesbian Anti-Violence Project
New York, New York

"[*Men Who Beat the Men Who Love Them*] rips away the myth that states that gay men are not and cannot be victims of abuse in their intimate relationships. From defining the abuse and violence to suggesting methods of intervention and treatment, this book educates, stimulates, provokes, and challenges us all to take the next step(s). It is exhilarating to finally see the publication of a book that so clearly addresses one of the most serious problems facing the gay community today."

Ned Farley, MA, CMHC
Clinical Director
Seattle Counseling Service for Sexual Minorities

Men Who Beat the Men Who Love Them

Battered Gay Men and Domestic Violence

HAWORTH Gay & Lesbian Studies
John P. De Cecco, PhD
Editor-in-Chief

New, Recent, and Forthcoming Titles:

Gay Relationships edited by John De Cecco

Perverts by Official Order: The Campaign Against Homosexuals by the United States Navy by Lawrence R. Murphy

Bad Boys and Tough Tattoos: A Social History of the Tattoo with Gangs, Sailors, and Street-Corner Punks by Samuel M. Steward

Growing Up Gay in the South: Race, Gender, and Journeys of the Spirit by James T. Sears

Homosexuality and Sexuality: Dialogues of the Sexual Revolution, Volume I by Lawrence D. Mass

Homosexuality as Behavior and Identity: Dialogues of the Sexual Revolution, Volume II by Lawrence D. Mass

Understanding the Male Hustler by Samuel M. Steward

Sexuality and Eroticism Among Males in Moslem Societies edited by Arno Schmitt and Jehoeda Sofer

Men Who Beat the Men Who Love Them: Battered Gay Men and Domestic Violence by David Island and Patrick Letellier

Men Who Beat the Men Who Love Them
Battered Gay Men and Domestic Violence

David Island, PhD
Patrick Letellier, MA

The Haworth Press
New York • London • Sydney

The Haworth Press, Inc., 10 Alice Street, Binghamton, NY 13904-1580
EUROSPAN/Haworth, 3 Henrietta Street, London WC2E 8LU England
ASTAM/Haworth, 162-168 Parramatta Road, Stanmore (Sydney), N.S.W. 2048 Australia

Library of Congress Cataloging-in-Publication Data

Island, David.
    Men who beat the men who love them : battered gay men and domestic violence / David Island, Patrick Letellier.
        p. cm.
    Includes bibliographical references and index.
    ISBN 1-56024-112-8 (alk. paper)
    1. Gay men—United States—Abuse of. 2. Family violence—United States. I. Letellier, Patrick. II. Title.
HQ76.3.U5I69 1991
362.82'92—dc20
                                           91-4631
                                         CIP

I dedicate this book

to my sons
Timothy Joel Island
and
Tobin Christopher Island
two nonviolent men
whose love and acceptance
serve as an example
for children of gay fathers everywhere

*   *   *

I dedicate this book

to the memory of my mother
Margo Hobert Letellier
whose laughter and smiles
will always warm my heart

to the memory of my grandmother
Clare Hobert Haskell
whose love knew no bounds

to Sharon Silverstein
who was always there

CONTENTS

Lenore E. Walker, EdD, ABPP
Tom L. Rhodus, MA

ABOUT THE AUTHORS

David Island, PhD, is Senior Consultant at Trial Behavior Consulting, Incorporated, a professional business in San Francisco that offers social science consulting and research services to trial lawyers and law firms. He is also the principal in David Island and Associates, a communications consulting firm in San Francisco offering mediation services to gay men. A former professor on the graduate faculty at the University of Washington in Seattle and faculty member at California State University in Sacramento, he has also been a junior high and high school teacher and counselor. In recent years he has served as President and Board Member of the American Society of Trial Consultants, been a member of the Roseville, California Community Hospital Board of Directors, served as an arbitrator and trainer for the American Arbitration Association, and been a trainer of mediation skills for California Lawyers for the Arts. David co-conducted with Patrick Letellier many workshops on gay male battering at numerous conferences, including the 1990 Second National Conference of the National Lesbian and Gay Law Association and the 1991 annual conference of the National Organization of Victim Assistance. He is currently active in the National Lesbian and Gay Health Foundation in Washington, DC, having served to coordinate and organize institutes, presentations, and plenary sessions on gay and lesbian domestic violence at the NLGHF Annual Conferences of 1989, 1990, and 1991.

Patrick Letellier, MA, recently completed his Master's Degree in Counseling at the University of San Francisco. A former victim of a violent partner, Patrick has spent the past three years researching and working in the domestic violence field. He has worked at the San Francisco Family Violence Project, providing counseling and advocacy to battered women, and volunteered at the Community United Against Violence in San Francisco. He has collaborated with David Island on numerous published articles, presentations, seminars, and speeches on the subject of gay men's domestic violence. He and David Island are co-editors of the National Lesbian and Gay Domestic Violence Network Newsletter, the only national publication serving the movement to stop gay and lesbian domestic violence. Patrick's papers on gay men's domestic violence have been presented at the 1989, 1990, and 1991 National Lesbian and Gay Health Foundation Annual Conferences.

Acknowledgments

We would like to thank Sharon Silverstein, who was the coordinator of the Gay Men's Domestic Violence Project at Community United Against Violence in San Francisco, in 1987. Sharon was an invaluable source of support and information to Patrick and provided a lot of Kleenex. You were tremendously helpful, Sharon. This book would not exist without you.

We are also grateful to Jesse Gutierrez, PhD, and Philip Steigerwald, MSW. These two skilled therapists provided countless hours of emotional support to Patrick (and other victims) through individual and group support for battered gay men. Jesse and Philip were available at all hours of the day and night and were instrumental in Patrick's transition away from his violent lover and into safety and security. We recall the night Philip rearranged his living room furniture for Patrick, who needed to talk but was afraid to sit near a window. You are both valued friends and colleagues. Thank you.

We would also like to thank the six other men in Patrick's support group. Their love, understanding, support, and humor made life bearable then. Thanks to all of you.

We cannot thank Rick Collins enough for his legal expertise. Rick has been Patrick's attorney and friend since the beginning and never asked for a penny. Rick, your time, energy, and brainpower are all greatly appreciated. Your willingness to get involved and your boundless support made all the difference. Thank you very much.

Stasi Martin immediately became a pillar of strength and support at Patrick's workplace. You are wonderful, Stasi, and the hugs in the back stairwell were life savers. We are also grateful to Tom Staats, Patrick's boss, who took Patrick seriously and helped to make work a safe place for him. Thank you to Mario, Kim, Jeff, and everyone else at The Fresh Market for your support and encouragement. A special thank you to Lorrie Toy who has been a loving and supportive friend throughout Patrick's escape from violence and through the writing of this book. Also, a special thank you to Atheria Smith, who has become a major source of encouragement and has been a lot of fun, too. Thanks, girl!

We are grateful to Nello Carlini, whose home became Patrick's new home. Thank you, Nello, for providing a safe and comfortable place to live, for hours of conversations about domestic violence, and for all the hugs. We love you.

Thank you to Lyndall Nipps, who was there from the beginning. Lyndall believed what Patrick said about the violence the night before he escaped, and he has been a steadfast friend ever since. Thank you for being there (at those crazy rendezvous spots, too), when it seemed that everyone else had gone away.

Peter Flanders deserves a thank you and a huge round of applause. Peter has been a great friend and housemate of David's since we started the book. He prepared countless gourmet dinners for us, and he never complained when the conversation inevitably turned to domestic violence. He also has not seemed to mind that the creation of this book took over their home on a thousand different occasions. Instead, warm humor, quick repartee, and cartoon-character tip-toeing around the apartment were his fine points. Thank you, Peter! We love you.

Tom Hollis was a creative help in the early stages of writing. Tom read the manuscript with care, and helped to make it much more readable, particularly the narratives. We are grateful for Tom's hilarious, incisive comments.

Phyllis Frank, the Katherine Hepburn of the domestic violence movement, how can we thank you! You do not know how important the long distance contact with you has been. Your no-nonsense approach to batterers and to the whole topic of domestic violence continues to inspire us. We are grateful for your generosity with your written work, allowing us to tailor it to apply to gay men. You are an admired and respected leader in the movement, Phyllis. Thank you for all your help and encouragement.

John De Cecco, our acquisition editor for The Haworth Press and a professor at San Francisco State University, was a pleasure to work with. John praised our work and explained how it could fit into the Haworth gay and lesbian series as soon as he saw it! Some say that getting a book published is painful and frustrating. John, you helped eliminate almost all of the negative from the process. Thank you very much.

Jack Huberman, our copy editor, was thorough and detailed. Thanks to his work, our writing was improved. To all of the people at The Haworth Press, especially Bill Cohen for his encouragement and good humor, we thank you.

To the National Lesbian and Gay Health Foundation in Washington, D.C., we owe a big debt. This organization, particularly the efforts of Ellen Ratner, Michael Weeks and Bill Scott in 1989 and 1990, provided the fledgling Gay and Lesbian Domestic Violence Movement with a forum from which we have reached out across the entire nation to find friends and colleagues. As a result, a large network of concerned people now exists, and they provide the national leadership for ending domestic violence in gay America. Thank you NLGHF.

Thank you to all the people at the Family Violence Project of San Francisco who taught Patrick about the criminal justice system as it applies to domestic violence. Rosalind Nalls, Jacqueline Agtuca, Maria Ramos, Lisa Swanson, Susan Breall, and Donna Lee, thank you all for your time, patience, and instruction. Your hard work in the movement to stop domestic violence is greatly appreciated. A special thanks to Roz, who has been a great supervisor and colleague.

San Franciscan Rik Isensee, author of *Love Between Men,* reviewed a later version of the manuscript and offered detailed and insightful criticism of it, as well as encouragement. Rik, you will see the results of your painstaking work in this book.

To Mark King in San Francisco, and Dawn and Mary at the Paper Clip in Tahoe City, we thank you for your complaint-free translations of our often unreadable rough drafts into typed copy.

Linda Allen is a literary agent in San Francisco who, while not our agent, took us under her wing anyway to offer assistance and advice whenever we needed it. You supported this project, Linda, and you made us feel important and competent. We did it! Thank you.

Jerry Leverson, attorney, caterer, and friend assisted us at several points along the way, particularly in working out our agreements with each other and in contract negotiations with our publisher. You were a big help, Jerry. Thank you.

David's sons, Tim and Toby Island, were always supportive and encouraging, urging us to carry on with the project. When we decided to do our own word processing, Toby became a major consultant to the production. Late-night crisis calls were handled with his usual calm when the bombs went off in our computer.

We would also like to thank John Linder, who simply "expected" us to turn out a fine manuscript. He was a cheerleader and critic without peer, always there with encouragement and enthusiasm. And, to Sean Hoag, Wendell, David, Stacey and Bruce, the Sea Ranch Weekend boys, we thank you for your feedback on the manuscript.

All of the folks at David's business, Trial Behavior Consulting, Incorporated, in San Francisco, encouraged our efforts. We used TBCI's typewriters, copy machine, postage meter, and Fed Ex account on many occasions. Thank you TBCI. John Sheridan, thank you for your independently contracted time with us to word process the earliest version of the book, those tapes of the narratives.

Clare Sartor, Patrick's sister, has been excited and enthusiastic about this project for a long time. Thank you, Clare, for your love and support, especially over the past year. It has been great to share this project with you.

Sheila and Patrick Kelly, and JoAnn Holland were also the most supportive friends imaginable. Thanks to you for your openness, for your desire to understand gay men's domestic violence, and for those wild dinners! Max Kincora, Phil Sciaroni, Nute Meeker, and Mike Medieros were wonderful sources of support and fun. Thanks to each of you. Also, thank you to Dr. Marjorie Mosick-Feldis for being good at what you do.

We are thrilled and proud that Lenore E. Walker, the world's foremost authority on heterosexual battering, and her colleague Tom L. Rhodus, wrote the foreword to our book, endorsing our primary purposes. Dr. Walker, through her advocacy for abused women in her three important books and by daily example in her life work in their behalf, has taught us much of what we know about domestic violence. Her commitment to stop domestic violence is an inspiration to all women and men who are repulsed by its presence in our culture. Tom Rhodus recognized the significance of our message to gay men, and, over a period of time spanning many months and two versions of our manuscript, orchestrated the foreword project and then co-wrote it with Lenore Walker. Tom and Lenore, we prize your contribution to our book, and we thank you!

David Island, PhD
Patrick Letellier, MA

Foreword

The exposure of domestic violence in the heterosexual community shocked the sensibilities of the general public as well as professionals who were never trained to deal with the victims and perpetrators of abuse. Now you will learn about another type of domestic violence — the battering of men by other men in the gay community. Like those in the woman's movement who used first-person stories to force us to look at the devastation, David Island and Patrick Letellier share personal stories. Reading Patrick's narrative of his own abuse experiences is chilling. You may be shocked and offended by the personal accounts of violence, and you might want to put this book down. Don't do it!

Violence in any relationship spills out into the streets and poisons us all. Men rarely talk about being victims for a variety of reasons, not the least of which is the fear that they will be feminized for admitting they have been hurt. But, Patrick and David first put forth the idea that men can be victims and then go about proving their treatise. There is no other book like this one in the domestic violence literature. It challenges us to look at men as victims. In fact, Patrick and David believe that lesbian and gay battering challenge the current thinking in the domestic violence field by extending analysis of power dynamics in relationships beyond the traditional male/female dyad. Power, not gender, underlies gay male abuse. Yet, we must not forget that most gay men and lesbians were raised in heterosexual homes where power differences between men and women fueled the sex role socialization patterns that they model in their own relationships.

Stories about violence are ugly. Those of us who work in the field and hear them daily must deal with our own feelings of outrage. It is not surprising that most mental health professionals are uncomfortable with talking about violence. Most refuse to believe what they hear. There are barriers to services for abuse victims throughout the system. Patrick and David point out that there are no services or shelters for gay men who are battered. Police must be trained to take gay battering seriously. Just as when women first demanded validation for their pain and trauma, law enforcement must learn to see male violence against one another as more than two men wrestling, scuffling, or playing around.

Codependency, the label given to partners in a dysfunctional relationship who cannot seem to terminate with each other, has nothing to contribute to the field of domestic violence. Labeling the abuse victim as codependent continues to *blame the victim* for his own abuse, even if he is seen as trying to control the violence. Patrick points out the futility of the battered person trying to control the batterer's behavior with the example of the "Carrots Incident," involving himself and Stephen. Like other attacks from Stephen, this one came unprovoked. Patrick stayed together with Stephen for all the many reasons battered persons stay with an abusive partner, but particularly since he realized that leaving does not stop the abuse. Staying is a coping strategy; it does not make him *codependent*.

Domestic violence is wrong, it is criminal and it must stop. Models for stopping the violence come from the battered woman's movement and can be applied in the gay community. Clearly, it will be up to the gay community to inform others: the mental health professionals, lawyers, advocates, and concerned citizens. As the gay community took on the challenge of AIDS, so must it take on another one. When you finish this book, you will be convinced that domestic violence is lethal, too.

Lenore E. Walker, EdD, ABPP
Tom L. Rhodus, MA

Preface

On September 8, 1987, my lover attacked me for the last time. On that sunny afternoon, he locked our apartment door and threatened to sort me out "once and for all." This time, I did not let him. Using a plan I developed that morning, I escaped through a window of our second story apartment, ran down the fire escape and jumped to the street. He chased me, but I outran him. Two days later I said "Goodbye Stephen," and I have not spoken to him since that day.

* * *

On September 8, 1987, my telephone rang. It was Patrick, out of breath, calling from a public phone. It had happened again, he said, but this time he had escaped. He was okay, he added, but could he come over for a couple of hours to talk and figure out what to do? I drove to where he was hiding, picked him up and brought him to my home. As it turned out, Patrick stayed for four months, using my home as a "safe house." His lover did not know me and, therefore, he did not know where Patrick was. That night I learned from Patrick what I had not known about him before.

I learned that he was a battered gay man. The last two years of his four-year relationship with his lover Stephen had been typified by bruises, humiliation, and psychological abuse. Stephen had kicked, struck, punched, and slapped him. He had shoved and thrown Patrick up against walls and down onto closet floors. From ridicule and harassment, Patrick knew guilt, shame, confusion, and loneliness. Stephen had threatened to kill him more than once. Patrick's happy upbringing in a small town in Connecticut had served him well in most every area of his life – a college degree, trust in people, a sunny disposition, a big Irish extended family, excellent communication skills and lots of friends – but it had not prepared him for this devastating reality: at age 24, Patrick was a victim of gay men's domestic violence.

* * *

Even though he has a PhD in educational psychology and had been a university professor for years, David knew nothing of gay men's domestic violence before that day. In fact, he had never even heard of it. David had spent his time raising two sons, Tim and Toby, now both in college. He started a small San Francisco business that grew and grew. He ran some, read a lot, and avidly followed the 49ers. He led a relatively conventional life as a gay man in San Francisco.

David has his not-so-conventional side, too. He blasts through San Francisco traffic in his Bronco/tank, accosting all the lousy drivers. He microwaves his ice cream so it's "soft enough to eat."(!) And he knows more about geography and high-altitude gardening than anyone else alive. David has also spent a long time training therapists, which has made him an expert on helping people in crisis. He knows how to listen, how to be supportive, and how to unfold and examine personal difficulties. David knew exactly how to deal with me.

* * *

During the time that Patrick stayed at my home, we talked about him as a victim, Stephen as a batterer, and the violence. We began to think and talk about domestic violence in gay male relationships and quickly realized that few people knew anything about it. There was no information available, and there were no books or resources. Worse yet, nobody in the gay community ever talked about it.

* * *

On Christmas Day, 1987, I sat down with a Dictaphone and began recording my experience as a victim of gay men's domestic violence. It is from that original tape that the idea for this book came to us.

* * *

The idea was that a book exploring this topic was desperately needed to advocate victim's needs, teach about the phenomenon, speak to therapists, send a message to batterers and alert our brothers in the gay community.

So we read everything we could get our hands on. We talked to therapists, police officers, politicians, and domestic violence experts all over the country. We gave speeches, listened to seminar presentations, and debated with friends and strangers. We became victim advocates.

What we learned we now submit to you in this first book on the taboo subject of gay men's domestic violence.

Introduction

Gay men's domestic violence is not a new problem, just a newly recognized problem. It has existed ever since gay men began coupling and living together. What is new is that abused gay men all over the United States are starting to come forward seeking help, as victims of domestic violence. Their lovers are violent men, and the victims are being battered. As these battered men emerge from their "inner closets," they face a gay community and a society at large that is unprepared and ill-equipped to help them.

Domestic violence is a big problem for America's 9.5 million adult gay men. We estimate that as many as 500,000 gay men are victims, and, of course, equal numbers are also perpetrators. Thus, only substance abuse and AIDS adversely affect more gay men, making domestic violence the third largest health problem facing gay men today. We believe the problem is too brutally realistic to be ignored any longer.

A total of no more than 20 professionals, scattered in four American cities (Seattle, New York, Minneapolis, and San Francisco) are adequately experienced or trained to deal effectively with victims. Even more alarming is the near-total absence of agencies set up to provide services to gay male batterers. Thus, the state of the art and of the knowledge about gay men's domestic violence is pitifully elementary, about where the heterosexual battered women's movement was 20 years ago.

No literature exists about this problem. No research has been done. Since the gay community is only just beginning to learn about the problem, ignorance is widespread, outreach to victims is scarce, and few services are provided. Education about gay men's domestic violence is urgently needed, since lack of information helps perpetuate the problem.

In this first book on gay men's domestic violence, we hope to open some closet doors, to generate awareness about the phenomenon, and to start the educational process. This book marks a turning point in the movement to stop gay men's domestic violence. As a community, we must wake up, learn about domestic violence occurring in our midst, unambiguously condemn it, and start to work to eradicate it. We must end the violence.

This book, paradoxically, validates gay relationships and gay coupling by demonstrating through an intelligent analysis of this problem that gay men are subject to the same problems that heterosexuals are. The time has come for a book written by gay men that takes gay coupling seriously, while at the same time forthrightly examining the severe problem of domestic violence without blaming the dominant, homophobic, and homohating culture for it. Its publication marks the maturing of the reality of gay life in America.

We hope that our discussion of gay men's domestic violence will help to translate some of the theory, practice, and politics of the earlier battered women's movement (and the more recent movement to stop lesbian battering) into workable strategies for gay men. The book draws on all domestic violence literature to date, finding validity in much of it. However, many theoretical, treatment-related, and political positions taken by the heterosexual domestic violence pioneers do not work for gay men, and moreover, we think some are a hindrance to ending all domestic violence. Thus, we challenge several fundamental premises in the literature, and we depart from tradition frequently and unabashedly.

Domestic violence is not a gender issue, since both men and women can be either batterer or victim. Domestic violence is a crime, and perpetrators are criminals. Individual acts of domestic violence are not caused by a victim's provocation, not by a violent, patriarchal society, not by alcohol or by any other excuse or rationalization one could dream up. Domestic violence is caused by individual, violent people. Because domestic violence is a decision made by a batterer, a batterer's violent actions are premeditated. Abusers *intend* to harm their lovers. Therefore, domestic violence is an enormous mental health problem in America. A batterer cannot possibly be seen as a mentally healthy, well-functioning member of a domestic couple. In fact, in this book we show that batterers suffer from a diagnosable, progressive mental disorder in their domestic setting, with their partners as the targets of their unhealthy condition, manifested most clearly just before, during, and after one of their violent attacks. Batterers do not voluntarily seek help, cannot and do not fix themselves magically, and become increasingly abusive over time. Batterers have learned to be violent, evidencing both a disorder which is correctable through treatment and behavior which is punishable by law. Both consequences must follow for batterers.

Victims, by and large, are normal people who are unfortunately in relationships with violent partners. Couple counseling is inappropriate and unethical as treatment, and victims unequivocally are not codependent. The only effective method known so far to stop violence in the lives of victims is for the victim to get out of the relationship, stay out, and have no further contact with their former abusive partners.

We want gay men's domestic violence to end. Our passion for that goal is evident in this book, a comprehensive exploration of the entire topic.

Chapter I provides an explanation of what gay men's domestic violence is and is not. An analytic approach is used to describe the scope of the problem, and the myths and misconceptions about domestic violence are refuted. Starting in this chapter and continuing throughout the book at the beginning of each chapter, Patrick Letellier writes personal narratives, bringing vividly to life some of the brutality he experienced as a victim of an abusive partner.

Chapter II is a critical examination of why gay men's domestic violence occurs more than once and what reinforces it. This chapter outlines the first detailed theory on the subject, suggesting that repeated instances of gay men's domestic violence can best be explained by known psychosocial principles, including positive reinforcement, negative reinforcement, punishment dynamics, and the lack of disincentives for battering.

Chapters III and IV describe the profiles of batterers and victims in significant detail, offering a theory to explain the behavior of each. Extensive discussions about why batterers batter and why victims stay underscore the analysis of many of the roots of the problem of domestic violence. Since so few batterers receive any treatment today, the psychological and psychiatric communities are petitioned in Chapter III to develop new pathology nomenclature for abusive personality disorders for all batterers, in order to encourage entrepreneuring clinicians to treat more batterers, and get paid for it, and to increase the availability of treatment in general for batterers.

In Chapter V, the difficulties that victims have in getting out of relationships with violent men are addressed. Specific tips and ideas are presented to encourage gay male victims to leave their destructive partners. This chapter and Chapter VI are "self-help" oriented with practical information for gay male victims who want to leave and stay away from their violent partners.

In Chapter VI, issues of staying out are analyzed. Ideally, victims of gay men's domestic violence should *stay out of* relationships with violent men from the first time they first leave. Tips are offered to victims on how to stay out, and a checklist is provided to help gay men spot and avoid potential batterers.

Chapter VII outlines the difficult topic of how to help a friend or relative who wants to leave or who has just left a relationship with an abusive man. Friends too often try to act as mediators to help both parties, an action that is bound to fail. Detailed basic and sophisticated advice is offered to friends and relatives on how to focus their helping efforts successfully on the victim to aid him in staying safely and permanently out. This chapter is also useful to experienced professionals since it contains insightful counseling advice.

Chapter VIII examines possible intervention strategies for professionals who work with victims of gay men's domestic violence. Suggestions are made about what kinds of help victims need and what kinds of skills the service providers ought to possess. Competency criteria for therapists who treat gay male victims are suggested, as are treatment methods and outcome measures. Victims are given advice and direction on what to look for in a therapist and are encouraged to seek both individual and group therapy. An overall theory of community intervention is presented, including specific suggestions for law enforcement, the judicial system, community support, and safe houses.

Chapter IX is comprised of eight essays that elucidate the complex and unusual psychology of domestic violence, describing issues and phenomena with which victims and society must contend. The roles that AIDS, drugs and alcohol, and "provocation" play in wrongly excusing batterer conduct are described. Codependency and gender are dismissed as invalid causes of domestic violence, and the importance of understanding how batterer and victim have distinctly separate psychologies is argued. The difficulty gay male victims face in having their violent partners arrested is explored, in addition to the difficulty everyone has in understanding victims' inherently paradoxical situations.

Finally, Chapter X spells out the pressing need for government action, education, community support, and publicity about gay men's domestic violence. It provides a political and community blueprint for change. New laws and revisions to existing policies are demanded and defined in order to further criminalize domestic violence. The book concludes with a challenge to the academic, corporate, civic, and gay communities to begin educating the public, conducting research, providing greater funding, and offering broader services to solve the rapidly emerging, serious mental health, medical, and legal problems of gay men's domestic violence.

Chapter I

Is This Violence?

THE CARROTS INCIDENT

Stephen and I are in our kitchen in the Castro in San Francisco, cooking dinner. The music is on, the windows are open, and we're chatting and bopping around. It's an average day. Stephen turns to me and says, "Patrick, will you cut the carrots?" And I say, "Sure, how do you want them?" Stephen answers, "Oh, any way. It doesn't matter." I continue my talking and dancing and the carrots are cut, and I am ready to do whatever is next . . . the tomatoes? the chicken?

Stephen is suddenly angry.

*"Oh, honestly. Look at **these**!" he shouts. "These are no good!" He is clenching his fists. "I can't believe you!" he shouts. "What am I supposed to do with these?!!"*

It's the carrots. He doesn't like the way the carrots are cut. "Stephen, you said it didn't matter how I cut them. They're fine."

*Stephen shouts back, "I'll **tell** you! They're **not** fine!" With one swipe of his hand the carrots are off the cutting board and onto the floor.*

"Oh, Stephen, come on, what d'ya do that for?"

"Don't tell me to 'come on,' do you hear!?"

POW – a fist on the side of my head. POW – another fist, this one in the ribs. I am pushed up against the wall. Again he yells, "Don't tell me to 'come on'!!"

I shout, "Get off me, you fucker," and I push him away, livid. He pummels me in the head, in the face, in the chest. I'm thrown against the wall again. I run out of the room, terrified. Angry. Shocked. Sad. What did I do? Why does this happen? What am I doing wrong? I run into the bedroom.

Stephen stays behind to clean up the carrots and to continue cooking. He comes into the bathroom ten minutes later, where,

shirtless, I am washing my face and neck and chest. "Let me see,"
he says, gently taking my chin in his hand and turning my face
towards his. He eyes my cut lip and some marks on my neck and
chest. I'm still shaking. I start crying.
  Stephen says, "Oh my darling. How can I do this to you? I love
you so much . . . come here . . ." And, he hugs me and rocks me as
I cry. "You've got to help me Patrick. I don't like hitting you . . ."

As the "Carrots Incident" clearly shows, violence in the home
can happen with lightning speed. Within 45 seconds, Patrick has
been shouted at, threatened, pushed up against the wall, punched in
the ribs, hit with a fist on the side of his head, and struck in the face
and chest. And, the perpetrator of all the violence is his lover.

The "Carrots Incident" also demonstrates how ordinary domestic violence situations may be. Here, Patrick is abused while preparing dinner. We are not describing sado-masochism, nor a "fair
fight" between equals, nor a drunk or drug-crazed man blindly battering his lover, nor an extreme case of domestic violence as reported in the news, where one man is beaten to death by his lover.
Domestic violence is not necessarily extreme and not always physical. Domestic violence most often occurs in ordinary household
settings between ordinary gay men.

"Carrots" further shows that domestic violence can happen without warning and without a build-up of tension to a crisis. This violence
took Patrick completely by surprise. No one could have predicted it.

Of serious importance in this narrative is its ending. Stephen becomes the provider of comfort to Patrick, an unhealthy development
for Patrick. When a batterer soothes his victim, a confusing and complex psychological phenomenon occurs. The result is that Patrick suc-
cumbs to Stephen, the only source of solace available, in order to
receive the support he needs, and in so doing, he becomes even more
vulnerable to Stephen's future efforts to control and intimidate him.

HOW MANY GAY MEN ARE VICTIMS
OF DOMESTIC VIOLENCE?

Domestic violence because of carrots: clear, stark, and unmistak-
able. Right now, at this very moment, it is happening in households
all over the United States. Men are bashing their wives; some

women are abusing their husbands. And, lesbians and gay men are battering their lovers. Yet, while millions of Americans, straight and gay, are affected every year by domestic violence, the topic remains shrouded in secrecy, swept under the rug, "closeted."

All of us have relatively clear ideas about *some types* of violence. We all know that murder is a violent crime, that riots are violent, that rape is a crime of violence, and that if you are attacked by a mugger, you have experienced violence. However, once we shift our focus into that domain known as a household and observe people in their at-home, domestic settings, our once-clear ideas about what violence is become blurry and seem to be harder to define. Further, if the people in this domestic setting are lovers, the ability to identify and label their behavior as "violence" diminishes markedly. When what is known as violence occurs between lovers, it becomes easier to excuse it, justify it, look the other way and pretend it did not happen, blame the victim for causing it, or trivialize it.

The conspiracy of silence around violent, criminal conduct by members of a family, such as child abuse, incest, and partner battering, is well-documented throughout history. Even today, a large percentage of Americans actually condone violence in the family by their belief that such matters are private.

The point is that domestic violence is just that: violence. When the two people involved are gay men, we have Gay Men's Domestic Violence. It is that simple.

Of course, no one knows for sure how prevalent violence is among gay male couples. Such statistics are hard to come by and do not yet exist in any organized sense. Only since 1987 have any statistics on gay men's domestic violence appeared. In that year, the San Francisco police responded to no fewer than 100 calls per month for gay and lesbian domestic violence. We learned from the early days of reporting the battering of heterosexual women not to rely only on the violence reported to the police since that would result in a ridiculously low estimate of actual violence. But, it is a start. The San Francisco police data indicate the tip of an iceberg. Those data are a warning, a sign that domestic violence must be a big problem if 100 calls every month are made to the police about gay domestic violence in San Francisco alone. The uncomfortable truth is that there are thousands upon thousands of victims of gay men's domestic violence in the United States each month.

WHY IS IT SO HARD TO FIND OUT HOW MANY GAY MEN ARE BATTERED BY THEIR MATES?

Domestic violence is a taboo topic. Few government bureaus and few cities have the political integrity to investigate the incidence of gay men's domestic violence. One need think back only a few years to remember the official disinterest shown when indications began to surface about the extent of heterosexual battering. Domestic violence was then and remains now a taboo topic. Today, most people know that domestic violence exists, but few want details and even fewer want to do anything about it. The very topic makes people nervous. For cities, law enforcement agencies, and governments to show interest in gay men's domestic violence would mean that something would have to be done in response. This issue is further compounded for the authorities because gay men's domestic violence involves *gay* men. Why should society address domestic violence among gay couples, when sodomy is still considered a crime or a deviance by many states, and when street violence against gays by non-gays (gay bashing) is completely ignored, if not encouraged, by those in authority? The taboo overlay of "gay" onto already taboo "domestic violence" explains a basic reason why no useful statistics have ever been gathered on gay men's domestic violence.

Inadequate reporting. If a victim of gay men's domestic violence chooses not to call the police, whom else does he notify? In most communities in the United States, there is no one to notify. The New York City Gay and Lesbian Anti-Violence Project, San Francisco's Community United Against Violence, The Community University Health Care Center in Minneapolis, and the Seattle Counseling Service for Sexual Minorities are among the rarest exceptions to this void. Reluctance to call the police is commonplace. Only the strongest of victims will call the police and only then for the most severe of incidents. While being forced by your lover to have sex against your will is certainly domestic violence, it nonetheless is not the kind of violent incident that would bring the police to your door in most communities, even if you are a heterosexual woman. Spousal rape should be a crime, no matter what the gender of the abuser or victim. In the absence of an agency to notify, or proper laws directing police conduct, then, that kind of gay men's domestic violence will go unreported. Unquestionably, virtually all incidents of gay men's domestic violence are not reported because there is no adequate reporting mechanism in our society.

The gay community avoids the problem. Some members of the gay community believe that information about gay male domestic violence, if widely known, would merely fuel the fires of anti-gay discrimination from the heterosexual world. Armed with such information, it is reasoned, gay-haters would have one more weapon to use to further degrade the public reputation of gay relationships. Other gay people feel that such knowledge would be just plain bad press for gays and that all bad news needs to be suppressed. Many also feel that gay men have a self-proclaimed image to maintain. Gay men, generally, believe they are more affluent than their straight brothers, are better educated, are in better physical shape, and make a significant effort to lead a more enlightened lifestyle. But, if the gay community really did take its own domestic violence seriously, it would mean that gays themselves would have to recognize that gay men truly are not only ordinary people, but also have a proportionate share of violent individuals in their midst who bash other gay men in startlingly high numbers. One very important reason why it is so hard to find out how many gay men are battered by their mates is that the gay community would rather not know. (See Chapter II for a more thorough analysis of this problem.)

No one has tried to find out. No systematic, scientific study has ever been conducted to ascertain the number of victims of gay men's domestic violence.

Some victims seek help and tell authorities the real reason. A very small percentage of gay men who are victims of domestic violence call the police, appear at hospitals, make appointments with psychologists, or seek help at community-run projects that offer assistance to battered people. These are the men who tell authorities the real reason they want help. It is from these few, brave victims that the Gay Men's Domestic Violence Movement has emerged. They alone have shouldered the burden of responsibility to alert our society about a problem that rightfully should be shared by all. But, to calculate the actual number of victims from only the total represented by these admitted victims is to mistakenly represent reality.

Some victims seek help but don't tell authorities the real reason. Many victims of gay men's domestic violence seek appropriate help from legal, medical, and psychological professionals but do not disclose what brought them in for help. Broken arms are said to have been caused by "falls." Anxiety is said to have been caused by "job stress." Police are told that an "accident" occurred. Such disguises are understandable in our heterosexist, homophobic, and religiously hypocritical nation that reserves compassion, caretaking, full civil rights, and justice for the straight, white, middle-class dominant culture.

Most victims don't tell anyone at all. This group of victims is undoubtedly the largest. They are a major reason so little is known about the incidence of gay men's domestic violence. This group is comprised of one-time victims, first-time victims, or, even more likely, chronic victims who have chosen to stay with an abusive partner. This group of victims is also made up of those men who trivialize violence ("It wasn't that bad"), or those who think that because bones were not broken, their experience of violence does not warrant the attention of anyone. Finally, this group of victims includes men whose abusive lovers have convinced them that they do not need help and that they should not tell anyone what happened. Shame, denial, and fear of further violence propel these men into silence.

The authorities fail to ask. Physicians, nurses, and emergency room medical personnel are reluctant to inquire about, acknowledge, and address the causes of injuries from domestic violence. Poorly designed medical forms, fragmentary medical shorthand, and the near-total absence of proper inquiry by all medical personnel preclude accurate identification of injury caused by battering. After treatment, most victims are discharged without regard to the life-threatening conditions to which they return (Randall, 1990, pp. 939-940). Even if medical authorities fail to ask the right questions as they should, all domestic violence victims must tell medical authorities about the exact causes of their injuries, insist that the real cause is properly documented and demand that their safety become a primary consideration of health care providers.

Nearly 100% of batterers do not tell anyone and do not seek help voluntarily. With only the rarest exceptions batterers never admit to their problem and even fewer seek the help they desperately need. Of the few who appear for treatment or are mandated by the courts to do so, most drop out quickly or remain unaffected by the treatment. Gay male domestic violence occurs because a gay male batterer abuses his mate. We do not know the extent of this problem mainly because these abusive men remain silent and choose to hide.

Though there is no parallel at all between the disorders of alcoholics and those of batterers, we now know that the extent of alcoholism in America was largely unknown until alcoholics came out of their closets by the millions and owned up to their problem. Until batterers do the same, we are left with only estimates of their numbers.

BEST ESTIMATES

The pros know. The few agencies and service providers who deal directly with victims of lesbian and gay men's domestic violence provide a valid look at the real extent of domestic violence. These community workers and professional helping people know first-hand how many victims and batterers alike walk into their offices for help. All of these professional community workers assert that they see only a few of a much larger, invisible group of victims and batterers in the gay community.

The Coordinator of Domestic Violence Services at the New York City Gay and Lesbian Anti-Violence Project states that between 12 and 15 percent of the people who contact their agency are domestic violence cases. Approximately 150 individuals per year, about half lesbian and half gay male, receive agency services for domestic violence reasons. The Lesbian and Gay Counseling Program at Family and Children's Service in Minneapolis served about 100 lesbians, in groups and individual therapy, for domestic violence reasons in 1988 and 1989. Neither the New York nor the Minneapolis official has estimated overall prevalence statistics.

The Director of the Gay Men's Domestic Violence Project at the Community United Against Violence (CUAV) in San Francisco stated that domestic violence may affect and poison as many as 50 percent of gay male couples. Over a two-year period from the spring of 1987 to the spring of 1989, CUAV served more than 700 victims. If that agency estimate is correct, San Francisco would count approximately 20,000 victims of gay men's domestic violence each year. Since the San Francisco police respond to only 1,200 calls per year, it is clear that the other 18,800 incidents of violence are unreported.

Incidence of heterosexual battering. Because domestic violence in heterosexual relationships has been a source of governmental concern for over 20 years, reliable statistics are now available about heterosexual battering. New York State probably has the most advanced approach in the nation, as it is the only state with a permanent office devoted to the problem of domestic violence, the Office for Prevention of Domestic Violence. That office's predecessor, the New York Governor's Commission on Domestic Violence, determined that approximately 6,000,000 wives and 300,000 husbands are abused each year in the United States. In addition, it is known that 2,750,000 wives experience physical violence three or four times per year. Husbands use knives or guns against 110,000 wives each year with 2,000 to 4,000 killed and beaten to death annually by family members. These are the generally accepted figures now used in most of the domestic violence literature.

In 1990, there were 250,000,000 people in the United States. Subtracting the 60,000,000 children under 18, there remain 190,000,000 adults. Assuming that 10 percent of the adult population is homosexual (19,000,000), there then remain 171,000,000 straight adults, 85.5 million men and 85.5 million women. American adults currently marry, or couple, at a rate of 64 percent. Thus, there are 55,000,000 wives and 55,000,000 husbands in America today.

The 6,000,000 wives who are abused by their husbands represent 10.9 percent of the total number of wives, and that is the incidence of heterosexual domestic violence committed by husbands on their wives. Many experts believe that even 11 percent is too low, and that it should more accurately be placed at around 20 percent, or one in five marriages.

Using the 6,000,000 battered wives and the 300,000 battered husbands figures, we note that 95 percent of battering in heterosexual couples is committed by males.

500,000 gay male victims each year. There is no reason at all to believe that the incidence of gay men's domestic violence is any less than that in the heterosexual community. Alas, as discussed further in this section, we postulate that gay men's domestic violence may occur at a rate *greater* than domestic violence in the heterosexual community.

The incidence of gay men's domestic violence can best be calculated from the known rate of domestic violence among heterosexuals. In 1990, there are 9,500,000 adult gay males in the United States. If adult gay males couple at the same rate as heterosexuals (64 percent), then 6,000,000 gay men are coupled, with half of each couple (3,000,000) representing potential victims. Multiplying 3,000,000 times the 10.9 percent heterosexual battering rate yields a figure of 330,000 gay male victims of domestic violence each year. This is the figure that we propose as the *lowest* estimate of the number of battered gay men in America each year.

The 330,000 victim figure may be too low for several reasons. Men in heterosexual couples commit 95 percent of the battering. But, there are two men present in a gay couple, which means that *either member* has the same probability of being a batterer. Therefore, the probability of violence occurring in a gay couple is mathematically double the probability of that in a heterosexual couple.

Second, one of the members in a gay male couple is *not* a woman. Despite the fact that American society is violent, there still exists a strong ethic *not* to hit women. Thus, even though as many as 20 percent of the men in America batter their wives, the vast majority of men do not hit women. Not so with men, however. Men hit men with alacrity in America.

Third, there is no evidence to show that gay men are any less violent or any less prone to violence than straight men.

It is possible, therefore, and likely for all of the above reasons, that the incidence of domestic violence among gay men is nearly double that in the heterosexual population. Because of that possibility, we believe that as many as 650,000 gay men may be victims of domestic violence each year in the United States. This is the figure that we propose is at the *high end* of the range of the estimated number of battered gay men in America each year.

We emphasize that the 650,000 victim figure is the high estimate. We are interested in proposing an accurate, conservative estimate. We have no desire to exaggerate the estimated number of victims and would prefer that the number of victims of gay men's domestic violence were zero. But, it is not. It is a big number, somewhere between 350,000 and 650,000 men per year.

One fact that may operate to lower the high-end figure toward some midpoint is that gay men may couple at a lower rate than heterosexuals. The only known statistic on coupling among gay men was derived by a 1989 *San Francisco Examiner* national survey of gay America, which showed that 60 percent of the gay men in their sample were coupled, a figure close to the 64 percent in the heterosexual community (Yollin, 1989, p. 18). But the coupling rate among gay men remains uncertain.

A second fact which also may operate to lower the high-end figure is that the longer a couple is together, the higher the probability for violence. Gay male relationships may be shorter in term than heterosexual relationships, thereby lowering the likelihood of domestic violence.

In conclusion, we believe that a midpoint estimate of 500,000 annual victims of gay men's domestic violence represents a likely, reasonable, and non-speculative estimate. We hope that it is too high, but we suspect that it is right on the mark.

MYTHS AND MISCONCEPTIONS

Since I left my ex-lover, I have been both amazed and quite distressed by the prejudices I have encountered as an ex-victim of gay men's domestic violence. It is a topic surrounded by myths and misconceptions. Eventually I came to accept the idea that even among my gay male friends, few people understand domestic violence in gay relationships. In fact, most people, straight and gay alike, are walking around with myths firmly held in their heads.

Victims of domestic violence are the people who suffer most from the myths surrounding it. These myths keep people from recognizing and labeling domestic violence even as it looms before them. They keep us all from taking any responsibility and any appropriate action to help victims and to stop the violence. Finally, these myths serve as powerful forces that may keep gay men with abusive partners, where both the frequency and the severity of the violence escalates over time.

MYTH ONE: Only Straight Women Get Battered; Gay Men Are Never Victims of Domestic Violence

This is not true. The Gay Men's Domestic Violence Project at the Community United Against Violence (CUAV) in San Francisco estimates that for every police incident report on gay men's domestic violence that CUAV receives, there are between 10 and 20 incidents that go unreported. Clearly, not only are gay men victims of domestic violence, but they are being battered at an alarming rate.

This myth hits on one of the cornerstones of denial about gay men's domestic violence: that men are never victims. This idea is both sexist and dangerous. Just as lesbian battering forces us to admit that some women batter their partners, gay men's domestic violence forces us to look at some men as *victims*, which contradicts all the stereotypes we have in our society about men. Domestic violence is not a gender issue. It is a power issue, a legal issue, and a mental health issue. The truth is that men can be victims of domestic violence.

MYTH TWO: Domestic Violence is More Common in Straight Relationships Than in Gay Male Relationships

This is not true. There is no reason to assume that gay men are less violent than heterosexual men. We estimate that at least 500,000 gay men are abused by their lovers each year in the United States. With two men in a relationship it is possible that domestic violence occurs more frequently in the gay male community than in straight America. One thing is certain: Domestic violence is acknowledged, talked about, and dealt with more in straight relationships than in gay male relationships.

MYTH THREE: Gay Men's Domestic Violence Is a "Fight," and When Two Men Fight, It Is a Fair Fight Between Equals

This is not true. This myth draws on our inability or unwillingness to look at violence between two people of the same sex, particularly men, as a violent situation where one person is clearly a victim. This is referred to as the "Boxing Ring" myth, based on the idea that domestic violence is two men battling it out, and that it is "fair." This myth also falsely assumes that *both* men are ready and willing to be physically violent with each other. There is nothing fair about domestic violence: Being knocked against a wall and punched in the face by your angry lover does not entail fairness.

Furthermore, this myth completely overlooks psychological abuse and material destruction. You do not have to be hit to be a victim of domestic violence, and one should not underestimate the damage that psychological abuse can cause.

My bruises healed about a week after I left my ex-lover, but two years later I was still dealing with the traces of his constant criticism and the erosion of my self-esteem.

MYTH FOUR: It Is Not Really Violence When Two Men Fight; It Is Normal; It Is Boys Being Boys

This is not true. This myth addresses the larger societal attitude that exists about male violence: that it is acceptable for men to be violent; that it is normal; that it is, somehow, okay.

There is nothing normal about domestic violence. The "boys being boys" idea may have been harmless when we were all six years old, but when a man is 26 years old, is in the hospital with broken bones, and his lover broke them, this is not normal! This is much more than boys being boys. It is violence. Unfortunately, this myth is pervasive in the gay male community. With few positive relationship role models available, many gay men tend to view and accept violence by their partners as the norm.

MYTH FIVE: Gay Men's Domestic Violence Is Just a Lovers' Quarrel

This is not true. There is a tremendous difference between a lovers' quarrel and domestic violence. All lovers and all couples have quarrels. It is a normal and healthy part of human relationships. Violence, however, is not an acceptable way to resolve a lovers' quarrel, no matter how severe or intense the disagreement.

In addition, dismissing domestic violence as "just" a lovers' quarrel is to say that violence between two people who are in a relationship together is acceptable. We contend, of course, that violence is never acceptable.

This myth also fails to take into account psychological abuse, which is a large part of the domestic violence picture. Being harassed on the telephone at work, having your lover threaten suicide if you leave him, and being continually shouted at are some of the psychologically destructive forces at work in domestic violence, making it much more than "just a lovers' quarrel."

MYTH SIX: The Batterer Will Always Be Bigger and Stronger; the Victim Will Always Be Smaller and Weaker

This is not true. A man who is 5'7", prone to violence, and very angry can do a lot of damage to someone who is 6'2", twenty pounds heavier, and a non-violent person. Size, weight, butchness, queeniness, or any other physical attribute or role are not good indicators of whether or not a man will be a victim or a batterer.

Again, this myth focuses only on the physical aspects of domestic violence. A batterer does not need to be built like a linebacker to smash your compact discs, cut up all your clothing, or threaten to tell everyone at work that you are really a "queer." Violence is a matter of personal choice, not body size.

MYTH SEVEN: Men Who Are Abusive While Under the Influence of Drugs or Alcohol Are Not Responsible for Their Actions

This is not true. Drugs and alcohol are *excuses* for violence, and this myth takes responsibility off the batterer for his violent behavior and puts it on drugs and/or alcohol. The truth is that violence is a choice, and the responsibility for making that choice is the batterer's.

It is important not to underestimate the degree to which people cling to this myth to excuse or justify violence or to blur the responsibility for it. This myth is so widely held in the gay community, that many gay men believe that their gay brothers (unlike heterosexual men, evidently) do not batter their partners, but if it happens, surely drugs and alcohol are involved. If a person who batters is also on drugs or alcohol, that person has two separate and serious problems.

Violence is a choice, and many gay men who are violent with their lovers are men who do not drink or use drugs. *My ex-lover was a prime example.*

MYTH EIGHT: Gay Men's Domestic Violence Has Increased as a Result of the AIDS Epidemic, Alcoholism, and Drug Abuse

This is not true. AIDS, drugs, alcohol, the devil, or any other problem, condition, or dilemma a gay man finds himself in does not cause domestic violence. Because perpetrators decide to be violent, their own conscious intent is the cause of every violent act they commit.

This is one of the most tenacious myths because many people attribute outside forces as the cause of behavior. Such outside forces may well be correlated with certain conduct, but they do not cause the conduct. For example, alcohol does not cause traffic fatalities, drunk drivers cause them.

The stress of AIDS and the abuse of drugs do not cause increases in domestic violence. Violent men cause increases in domestic violence. (For a further discussion of the relationship between AIDS, alcohol, drugs, and domestic violence see Chapter IX.)

MYTH NINE: Gay Men's Domestic Violence Is Sexual Behavior, a Version of Sado-Masochism; the Victims Actually Like It

This is not true. Domestic violence is not sexual behavior. Domestic violence and sado-masochism (S&M) are entirely different. In S&M relationships, there is usually some contract or agreement about the limits or the boundaries of the behavior in which each person is willing to partake, even when pain is involved. Domestic violence entails no such contract. There is nothing fun or exciting about being punched in the ribs while watching TV, or about being told repeatedly you are so ugly that nobody else would want you. Domestic violence is abuse, manipulation and control that is *unwanted* by the victim.

As for victims of domestic violence "liking" the violence, the following questions are posed: Do victims of any violent crime enjoy the violence? Do people who are raped or mugged enjoy it? If you were to be attacked by two gay-bashers with baseball bats, would anyone assume that you enjoyed the violence? Like victims of other violent crimes, victims of domestic violence do not enjoy the violence they experience.

Unfortunately, this myth is also pervasive within the gay male community, where it allows gay men to dismiss or trivialize domestic violence, or to deny its existence. And again, as with some of the other myths, victims are the people who suffer most from this false belief that they enjoy the violence. When they finally come out and start telling people that they are being abused by their lovers, they are often ridiculed, or teased about enjoying pain, or simply not believed. Belief in this myth allows the gay community to ignore the cries of victims of domestic violence and do nothing to help them.

MYTH TEN: The Law Does Not and Will Not Protect Victims of Gay Men's Domestic Violence

This is not true everywhere. Unfortunately, it depends entirely on where you live in the United States, and on what particular police officer responds to your call. People living in states that have sodomy laws, or who live in rural areas of the country, may have much more difficulty with the police and the legal system than men who live in other regions. In some cities great strides have been made in sensitizing and educating the police about both gay relationships and about domestic violence. Seattle, for example, has a judicial system in which gay and lesbian batterers can be arrested and court-ordered into treatment programs designed specifically for homosexual batterers (Farley, 1990). This, of course, is no guarantee that the police officer who arrives at your front door will not be a homo-hating bigot, no matter where you live. In many areas of the country, however, the police can and will help victims of gay men's domestic violence.

This myth rests on the premise that because you are gay, the entire legal system, and perhaps the police in particular, will not help you. Indeed, many victims of domestic violence have experienced further victimization and homophobia in dealing with the legal bureaucracy. What always needs to be kept in mind, however, is that heterosexuality is not a criterion for protection under the law. As gay people we often have to *demand* our rights, and one of those rights is protection under the law from a violent person, regardless of the nature of our relationship with that person.

In San Francisco, the police, the courts, and the entire legal system are all on the side of the victim. A difficulty in the past has been getting the police to acknowledge the existence of gay men's domestic violence when filling out their incident reports. That is, the police have been unwilling to even acknowledge gay male relationships, and their inability or unwillingness to see men as *victims* has influenced their underreporting of gay men's domestic violence. Until just recently, most cases of gay domestic violence have been reported as "mutual combat," going right back to the "Fair Fight Between Equals" myth.

Battery is a crime. Thus, while it may take the police a while to recognize gay men's domestic violence, they must always be on the side of a victim.

People who work with victims of gay men's domestic violence are advised to investigate the local legal channels themselves, so that with some degree of confidence they can encourage male victims to take advantage of the help the police can provide. At the very least, medical personnel and therapists should be able to help victims prepare for possible homophobia and further victimization by police in their state, county, and precinct. Victims of gay men's domestic violence are encouraged to contact the police not only because of the invaluable help and security they can provide, but also so that we move beyond the long history of animosity that has existed between the police and the gay community.

Finally, keep in mind that victims do not have to "come out" when they contact the police. In many places when you call the police it may be best not to tell them that the man attacking you is your boyfriend or lover. Tell them only that you are being attacked and need help. Later, when filling out police reports, you may decide it is safe to identify your attacker as your partner.

Overall, my experience with the San Francisco Police as an openly gay male victim of domestic violence was very positive. Only once did I experience blatant homohatred, when two policewomen refused to file an incident report about a restraining order violation and referred to me as "she" and "this woman" to each other and to other officers in my presence. (Eventually I had to go to another station to file the report.) Since I left Stephen, he has violated two Restraining Orders a total of 11 times, and I have made countless trips to police stations. In almost all instances, when I told the police that the man I was trying to protect myself from was my ex-lover, they were generally more cooperative and seemed to take me more seriously.

MYTH ELEVEN: Victims Often Provoke the Violence Done to Them; They Are Getting What They Deserve

This is not true. This myth perpetuates the idea that the victims are responsible for the violence done to them, that somehow victims *cause* batterers to be violent. Again, violent behavior is solely the responsibility of the violent person. The victim is responsible for staying in the relationship, but that does not make him responsible for the violence.

This myth is common among both batterers and victims of domestic violence, and believing in it may be one of the forces that keeps a victim in a relationship with a violent partner. If victims believe that they are the cause of and are deserving of the violence, they may not make the necessary efforts to get out of the relationship.

MYTH TWELVE: Victims Exaggerate the Violence That Happens to Them; If It Were Really Bad, They Would Just Leave

This is not true. In fact, the exact opposite is true. Most victims tend to trivialize and minimize the violence that happens to them. One reason for minimization is that there is a tremendous amount of guilt, shame, and self-blame associated with being a victim of domestic violence. Since victims are ashamed of what they have experienced, they downplay how bad the violence has actually been.

A second, and perhaps more powerful reason for the trivialization of violence, is that when gay men "come out" as victims of domestic violence to their friends and family and begin telling people about the abuse they have experienced, often they are not believed. Victims are accused of making it up, of "making a big deal" out of it, or of simply exaggerating the violence. Victims quickly learn to avoid the unpleasant denial, criticism, and blame by telling people few details of the violence they have experienced and downplaying its severity.

As for "if it were really bad, victims would just leave," keep in mind that it may actually be harder for the victim to leave the relationship than it is to stay. He may be threatened with more harassment or violence or murder if he tries to leave. Leaving his batterer may mean leaving his home and all of his things behind. It may mean dealing with friends and family and co-workers who do not believe him or blame him for the violence. It means dealing with scores of people, some counselors included, who encourage him to return, to "stop provoking" the abuser, to try to change and to try to work it out. And it may mean dealing with the police, medical, legal, and social services that are perceived as, and may very well be, homophobic.

MYTH THIRTEEN: *It Is Easier for Gay Male Victims of Domestic Violence to Leave Their Violent Partners Than It Is for Heterosexual Battered Women*

This is not true. This myth is based on many false assumptions and prejudices about gay men and their love relationships, such as the myth that gay men flit from lover to lover, or that gay male relationships are sexual but not emotional. Gay couples are as intertwined and involved in each other's lives as straight couples. Similar to many straight battered women, many battered gay men are raising children, are financially dependent on their violent partners, and feel that a failed relationship represents their failure as a person.

Unlike straight women, however, many gay men are alienated from their families of origin due to homophobia and heterosexism. Thus, they may place even greater value on their love relationship, as it may be their only family, their only source of support. Living in a homohating society, many gay couples also describe their relationships as having an "us-against-the-world" quality, further unifying the two men, and making it more difficult for the victim to extricate himself.

It is naive or ignorant to assume that it is easier for gay men to leave their violent partners than it is for anyone else to do so.

MYTH FOURTEEN: Gay Men's Domestic Violence Occurs Primarily Among Men Who Hang Out in Bars, Are Poor, or Are People of Color

This is not true. Domestic violence crosses all racial, ethnic, religious, educational, and class boundaries. It is a non-discriminatory phenomenon. This myth grows out of the higher visibility in the social services that some disenfranchised groups have, as well as the assumption that domestic violence is an alcohol-related phenomenon. The gay community needs to recognize that wealthy, white, educated, "politically correct" gay men batter their lovers as much as does any other group in our society.

MYTH FIFTEEN: Victims of Domestic Violence Are Codependent

This is not true. There is little, if anything, in the codependency literature that is helpful in understanding the dynamics of domestic violence. (Codependency is more fully addressed in Chapter IX.) Domestic violence is not a relationship problem. Victims are not "partners in dependency" with their batterers. The two have separate psychological problems: The batterer is violent, and the victim is in a relationship with a violent man.

This myth is based on a complete lack of understanding of domestic violence. For example, because victims use many coping strategies to survive in life-threatening situations, their behavior may appear to be like that of a so-called "codependent." Their adaptive behaviors in a dangerous situation are mislabeled codependency.

Victims of domestic violence do not meet the codependent profile criteria. Labeling them codependent is yet another attempt to blur responsibility for the violence and take it off the shoulders of the batterer.

IS THIS VIOLENCE?

The following list of Acts of Violence is included to help make clear what the term "Domestic Violence" means. The term may appear ambiguous to some, but we think it is possible to be concrete and definite about it. As in the "Carrots Incident," most of the violence here is easy to recognize.

It is necessary to include on this list some of the less obvious, and probably more widely occurring, acts of psychological violence and material destruction. For many people, the concept of domestic violence brings to mind the extreme cases of physical abuse and vicious brutality presented in the media, such as in the TV movie, "The Burning Bed," or in the Joel Steinberg trial. While these are both indeed gruesome examples of physical abuse, unfortunately such emphasis on sensational cases detracts attention from the *psychological* abuse these and most other victims of domestic violence experience. The debilitating effects of such psychological abuse as continual ridicule, humiliation, and threats of physical violence should not be underestimated.

In addition to helping to clarify what domestic violence is, the following list also demonstrates how wide the scope of behavior is that domestic violence includes.

When reviewing the list of violent acts below, keep several things in mind. First, gay men's domestic violence involves at least one angry man, or, as is more likely the case, one *very* angry man. Thus, violent acts are frequently committed in anger: Hair pulling is not a gentle tug or pull, but a yank that hurts the victim who does not want or deserve to be hurt!

Has your boyfriend ever flipped his dinner plate in your face in anger? Does he intentionally break things that you value, to "show you who's boss"? Does he threaten to kill himself if you leave him?

These are all acts of violence and abuse, and they differ markedly from similar, but nonabusive behavior. Of course, you can grab someone nonviolently or humorously threaten to keep someone in line. With domestic violence, however, anger and intent to harm are typically present and are used by one man to coerce, control, manipulate, or injure the other.

A second factor to keep in mind is that it should *always* be the victim who decides if abuse is occurring. The phrase, "Oh, I didn't hit you that hard,'' is said all too commonly by batterers. It is the victim who should decide if he has been hurt, physically or psychologically. The definition of Gay Men's Domestic Violence, presented in the next section, incorporates this crucial concept of the victim as the decision maker.

The list is divided into three separate sections: physical violence, psychological violence, and material or property destruction. As you read the list, think carefully about your relationships and check off which acts have been committed against you and which ones you have committed yourself.

ACTS OF VIOLENCE

PHYSICAL VIOLENCE

- GRAB
- PULL HAIR
- KICK
- SLAP
- CHOKE
- PUNCH
- HOLD DOWN, TIE, OR PHYSICALLY RESTRAIN
- BITE
- HIT WITH OBJECT OR WEAPON
- PUSH OR SHOVE
- CLAW OR SCRATCH
- SIT OR STAND ON
- RAPE
- FORCE ANAL, ORAL, GENITAL CONTACT
- FORCE S&M, 3-WAYS, BONDAGE
- FORCE SCAT
- STAB OR CUT
- FORCE TO GROUND OR FLOOR
- THROW
- THROW OBJECTS AT
- FORCE INTO PROSTITUTION
- FORCE TO HAVE SEX WITH ANYONE
- DRIVE OVER WITH VEHICLE
- LOCK OUT OF HOUSE
- HOLD UNDERWATER
- BANG HEAD OR BODY AGAINST WALL OR FLOOR
- IMPRISON, LOCK UP OR DETAIN
- SHOOT
- EXPLOIT IN ANY MANNER

PSYCHOLOGICAL VIOLENCE

- ISOLATE
- HUMILIATE
- RIDICULE
- IGNORE, NEGLECT
- THREATEN PHYSICAL ABUSE
- THREATEN SEXUAL ABUSE
- HARASS
- PUBLICLY EMBARRASS
- FOLLOW
- THREATEN TO LEAVE
- REFUSE TO WORK
- WITHHOLD LOVE OR APPROVAL
- POUND FISTS IN ANGER
- MAKE DENIGRATING SEXUAL REMARKS
- PUT DOWN SEXUALLY
- THREATEN TO DESTROY OBJECTS OR FURNITURE
- CRITICIZE
- LIE TO
- MOCK
- INSULT
- THREATEN TO KILL SELF, VICTIM, OTHERS
- THREATEN TO REVEAL SEXUAL ORIENTATION
- CALL NAMES
- BLAME
- THREATEN TO ABUSE, FAMILY, FRIENDS, PETS
- HARM OR NEGLECT PET
- MANIPULATE
- "PUNISH"
- SEXUALLY HUMILIATE
- RIDICULE FOR SEXUAL INADEQUACY

MATERIAL OR PROPERTY DESTRUCTION

•HIT OBJECTS
•BURN CLOTHING
•DISCARD CLOTHING
•CUT UP CLOTHING
•DESTROY CLOTHING
•HIT FURNITURE
•BREAK FURNITURE
•THROW FURNITURE
•DESTROY VEHICLE

•DESTROY VALUABLES
•STEAL BELONGINGS
•SELL BELONGINGS
•HIDE BELONGINGS
•BREAK WINDOWS
•DAMAGE VEHICLE
•THROW OBJECTS
•BURN BELONGINGS

VIOLENCE IS THIS

If you are a reader who is wondering whether or not abuse or violence is happening to you in your relationship, the fact that you are asking the question suggests that the answer is "yes."

However, to help you to be sure and to give a clear, easy-to-remember definition of gay men's domestic violence, we suggest the following parsimonious wording.

Gay Men's Domestic Violence is:

- • Any
- • Unwanted
  - • Physical Force
  - • Psychological Abuse
  - • Material or Property Destruction
- • Inflicted by One Man
- • On Another.

These words are carefully chosen.

"Any" means just that: Any.

"Unwanted" means that YOU do not want it and that you have made your feelings known to your batterer. It means you have the right to say "stop" to your partner and expect him to stop. If you do not want it, then it is unwanted.

"Physical Force" means that it probably hurts. And, YOU decide if it hurts or not. There is nothing ambiguous about pain.

"Psychological Abuse" means that mental games are being played. It means that threats or intimidation or manipulation is occurring. Fear and trepidation are your best indicators of whether or not psychological abuse is occurring. Again, YOU are the judge of its existence.

"Material or Property Destruction" means your belongings or property are being destroyed. You are the judge of the value of your possessions.

"Inflicted by One Man" means that the abuser has been identified.

"On Another" means that the victim has been identified.

Domestic violence assumes that the two individuals involved have some sort of relationship involvement with each other. The men may be lovers, may be dating, or, may or may not be living together. They do function as a couple, however, no matter how informal that coupling is.

Gay Men's Domestic Violence is ANY UNWANTED PHYSICAL FORCE, PSYCHOLOGICAL ABUSE, OR MATERIAL OR PROPERTY DESTRUCTION INFLICTED BY ONE MAN ON ANOTHER.

A central element to this, and any, definition of domestic violence is *power*. Abuse and violence, in whatever form, are used by the batterer to maintain power and control over the victim. Through the intentional use of violence, or even the intentional threat of violence, the batterer creates an atmosphere of fear and intimidation in which he is able to get his partner to do what he wants.

Gay men's domestic violence is more than just the acts of violence a man commits against his lover. It is also the power imbalance in the relationship that is maintained through a pattern of deliberately chosen abusive and violent behavior.

But, It Is Not "A Violent Relationship"

When discussing, describing, or defining domestic violence, the specific words used are critical. Language has the power to structure how we view, understand and react to a given situation. In domestic violence, how we react can mean the difference between life and death.

For many years, relationships in which one man was violent with his partner have been erroneously described as "violent relationships," "abusive relationships," and "battering relationships."

This inaccurate language is potentially dangerous to victims. Gay men's domestic violence is not a *relationship* problem, but rather a deliberate, violent criminal act by one man. This is an extremely important distinction: Describing domestic violence as a "battering relationship" inappropriately implies mutuality and *shared* responsibility for abusive and violent behavior, which only encourages the widespread misconception that both men in the relationship are violent. In reality, a victim is not in a "violent relationship," or one half of a "violent couple." He is *in a relationship with a violent man*. He is *coupled with "a violent partner."* In this book the words "violent relationship" are not used to describe a relationship in which one man is abusive or violent, except when other literature is quoted. We ask you, the reader, also to correct your language and not perpetuate this myth of shared responsibility.

RAPED IN SAN DIEGO

Stephen and I have been together about two and one-half years, and we are on a one-week vacation in San Diego. A friend of mine from college has moved here; he is out of town for the week and has invited us to stay in his apartment.

Tonight, Stephen and I are resting on the waterbed in the master bedroom after a long day of being out and about in the sun. We are both exhausted, undressed, and half asleep when Stephen makes it clear that he wants to have sex. He begins to touch and caress me, kissing my neck and shoulders and getting himself really turned on. We embrace and kiss and I say something to the effect of not wanting to have sex and about feeling a little queasy with this waterbed churning underneath us. Stephen is persistent, however, and continues to kiss and grope me, saying "You really want it, Patrick. I know you do." This begins to irritate me, so I try to push him off me, saying, "No! I don't want this, Stephen. So, please get off me."

Stephen grabs the back of my head and pulls me toward him, kissing me very hard. I begin to struggle with him on top of me, shouting, "Get off me, Stephen! I don't want to do this! Leave me alone!" This seems to infuriate him, and he gets even more aggressive. He has me pinned down beneath him, and he is grinding his

*hips into me, roughly, too hard. He is holding my arms down with
his hands and shoving his tongue into my mouth. I am struggling,
angry now, shouting, "Get off me, goddamn you! Get off me!" We
struggle and wrestle on the bed, then roll off onto the hardwood
floor, Stephen on top of me.*

*I am fighting him back with all my might, pushing against him
and inching my way up the floor on my back, shouting, "You're
hurting me! I hate you! Get off me!"*

*Stephen shouts back, "Hold still, Patrick! I'm going to fuck you!
Hold still!" He holds me down with his arm across my chest and
pushes my legs apart with his, positioning himself. I struggle
harder, trying to push him away and trying to slide along the floor.
He gets in. Somehow he gets into me, and with a sudden jab, he is
all the way up inside me. I scream and begin to cry. The pain is
unbearable. My back and head and arms hurt from battling with
him on the floor, and now, he is inside me with no lubrication, no
preparation. I stop struggling and try to brace myself to endure
what he is doing, to somehow lessen the pain.*

*It does not last long. Stephen withdraws after only a minute or
two, without coming. He says, in disgust, "You spoil everything,
Patrick, everything. Why can't we ever do what I want to do?" He
walks out of the room and I remain there on the floor.*

Rape is rape. Whether it is men raping women or men raping
men, it is still rape, a despicable act for which there is no justification.

"Raped in San Diego" is a brutal but, alas, perfect example of
gay men's domestic violence. The action is unwanted, entails physical force and psychological abuse, and is inflicted upon Patrick by
Stephen. In short, it is violence.

This episode teaches important lessons about psychological
abuse, even more than about physical abuse. Though the pain and
the memory of the pain will last for some time, Patrick will probably suffer no long-term physical effects. The psychological effects,
however, are severe. Patrick has been assaulted, blamed, and then
discarded. He has been treated like an object, and he undoubtedly

feels victimized. He has been raped, causing major damage to his self-concept and his self-esteem. Because of this experience he may feel that he is not in control of what happens to his own body.

As pointed out in Chapter IV, a potential victim may be someone who has the tendency to allow others to control him and to blame himself for difficulties. Patrick may inaccurately believe that he was somehow the cause of the rape, and unless he takes action soon to leave Stephen for good, he may have even more difficulty placing responsibility for the rape on Stephen, where it belongs. This experience is seared into Patrick's consciousness, and he will carry it with him for years. This rape will affect, to some degree, how he reacts to future, even loving, sexual encounters.

"Raped" also demonstrates several important points about batterers. Stephen is not drunk. He is not on drugs. He is a conscious, alert person throughout this episode. He chooses to force sex upon Patrick. He decides to violate and harm Patrick. His act is premeditated and fully intentional. He is unable to hear the word, "No!" Stephen must have his way, even if he destroys the person he loves doing so. Part of a batterer's problem, as shown in Chapter III, is a difficulty in dealing with his own reactions to being denied what he wants. Stephen has few skills to respond empathically to Patrick and to see the world from Patrick's perspective at that moment. He has no respect for Patrick's wishes. In the moment of violence, he has taken love out of sex and has taken a big step in permanently destroying their relationship. Stephen is a perfect example of the need all batterers have for psychological help.

This narrative also shows the power, the psychological forcefulness, of a batterer intent on committing violence. Stephen is somewhat smaller than Patrick, but in gay men's domestic violence, size and weight have little to do with who will batter and who will be victimized.

Finally, there are lessons to be learned in this narrative about spousal rape. Rape is a violent crime and should be reported to the police as such. We encourage all gay men who are raped by their lovers or boyfriends immediately to call their local Rape Crisis Hotline for support and then to call the police immediately.

For gay men it is also particularly important to remember what rape is not. Rape is not a crime of passion. It is not something your lover "couldn't stop" because he was so hot for you. Rape is not his way of showing his love or lust for you. Rape is violence, and if your boyfriend or lover has raped you, it is highly likely that more violence will soon follow. Gay men who are raped should immediately break off all contact with the perpetrators.

Chapter II

Why Does It Happen More Than Once?

BATTERED ON NEW YEAR'S EVE

*It is New Year's Eve and Stephen and I are in New Orleans celebrating. We have been partying for several hours, walking around with thousands of other people, reveling in the streets. We enter a bar around 11:45 and people are gearing up for the countdown. I am pretty excited. It's a warm evening. We are in an exciting atmosphere, on vacation. It is all very festive. Stephen and I order drinks and start to dance. I am having fun. All of a sudden he says, "Patrick I've had enough. Let's go back to the hotel." I say, "What?! It's not even midnight yet! Why do you want to go now?" He responds, "Look, I want to leave. I don't like this place. I've had enough. We're going!" He grabs my arm, pulling me off the dance floor. I wrench my arm away, shouting angrily, "Let go of me!" Stephen turns and punches me in the stomach – **WHAM!** I stop, stunned. Heads turn. Then, facing me, **POW,** another punch in the stomach, this one harder. I drop my drink on the floor. More heads turn. Stephen walks out of the bar, leaving me standing there, holding my stomach in pain.*

Now I am fuming, and I storm out of the bar and find him waiting in the street for me. The midnight celebrants jostle us. Horns are honking. People are happy. I grab him by the shirt collar and start shaking him. "You bastard! Fuck you, you bastard!" I rip his shirt open, down the front, and shout, "I never, ever want to see you again!!" I turn around and run through the crowd back to the hotel.

An hour later, Stephen returns, and I'm in bed. Violence occurs almost instantly. He's on top of me, his hands on my neck and throat, shaking me, choking me. He shouts repeatedly, "Are you happy now?!'' I had to walk all the way back to this fucking place without a shirt on! Are you happy now?!'' He's punching me in the head, in the face, in the chest, on the sides, on the head again. I try to defend myself, holding my arms over my head. "Stephen, no! Stop! Leave me alone!'' He stops—but it is too late. The damage is done. I am crying, shaking, hurting. I feel so awful. I am shocked and numb and weak. Stephen is holding me now, as I cry, saying he's sorry, so very sorry, telling me how much he loves me, how beautiful I am. We lie for hours. I am crying, and Stephen is holding me, comforting me.

Domestic violence is versatile and adaptable. This story dramatically shows that domestic violence can happen out in public. It can happen anywhere. Patrick experiences violence in a bar, on a street and in a hotel. Domestic violence is not limited to abuse behind closed doors at home. What is limited, however, may be our understanding of the phenomenon and our ability to label domestic violence when we see it, or when we experience it in public.

"New Year's Eve" also demonstrates that a violent episode need not be preceded by a long period of tension or stress. Patrick and Stephen are on a holiday having fun. Neither had a tough day at the office, lost his wallet, or burned dinner. Stephen became violent after Patrick resisted his demand that they leave the bar.

"New Year's Eve" teaches about victim thinking and about choices. Patrick leaves the bar where he has been punched. On the street more violence occurs and he returns to his hotel where even more violence, it seems, is inevitable. He chose to return to the hotel. He chose to put himself in danger. But, Patrick behaves as if he has no other choices. He is thinking as a victim. Other, more effective choices are available. He could get help, leave town, go to another hotel, get the police, telephone a friend, or go out on his own to another bar. However, Patrick tears Stephen's shirt, demonstrating another choice he makes, his choice to be abusive.

The story also shows an encapsulated version of the "cycle of violence" as described by Lenore Walker in her book, *The Battered Woman*, and summarized in Chapter IV of this book. That same series of events applies to gay men. Violence occurs and immediately following the violence, the "loving" period begins. Stephen becomes a loving man again and the sole source of comfort for Patrick. And Patrick responds. Although this narrative does not describe all the comforting activities, it would not be surprising to learn that Patrick and Stephen engaged in satisfying sex. Sex, as will be explained in a later section, is a major reinforcing agent in causing violence to become accepted by domestic partners, and to be repeated. The most important indication that Patrick has adopted a victim's way of thinking is his willingness to allow his abuser to comfort him.

THE GAY COMMUNITY ALLOWS IT TO HAPPEN

The movement to stop gay men's domestic violence has a ten-year history. But, while we would like to believe that a lot can happen in a decade, little progress has occurred in the movement. First, some facts:

- 1981: The Seattle Counseling Service for Sexual Minorities begins providing services to gay male domestic violence victims and batterers.
- 1986: The New York City Gay and Lesbian Anti-Violence Project begins providing services to both lesbian and gay victims and batterers.
- 1986: The Community United Against Violence in San Francisco opens its Gay Men's Domestic Violence Project, providing services to battered gay men.
- 1986: Men Overcoming Violence in San Francisco expands its services to include counseling for gay men who batter.

These four pioneering projects deserve much praise. They represent virtually all of the services that have been available to gay male victims and batterers in the last decade. They are to be congratulated and supported. And yet, isn't it puzzling that there aren't more of them?

The history of the movement to stop gay men's domestic violence also includes several published articles: "Battered Lovers" was published by the *Advocate* in 1986; "Breaking The Silence: Gay Domestic Violence" by San Francisco *Coming Up!* (now the *Bay Times*) in 1989; "Naming And Confronting Gay Male Battering" by Boston *Gay Community News* in 1989; "The Other Closet," by the *Dallas Observer* in 1990; "Till Death Do Us Part: Domestic Violence Strikes Gay Relationships" by San Francisco *Sentinel*, in 1990; and "Domestic Violence: A Serious Problem Lacking in Resources," by the Washington, D.C. *Blade* in 1990. A few more articles have been published in various papers around the country.

Finally, one small study was completed in 1983. Two social work students at San Francisco State University studied gay men's domestic violence for their master's degree research project and wrote a fifty-seven page report (Moore and Bundy, 1983). And now you know *all* that our community has done to respond to gay men's domestic violence. Five hundred thousand battered gay men per year. Four agencies to provide services, and a handful of articles. What is wrong with this picture? Ten years have come and gone, and as a community we could be much more sophisticated in understanding and addressing this problem. Something is wrong.

In every article that has been written about gay men's domestic violence, one topic invariably comes up: Silence. Sample comments from the above-mentioned articles: "There is definitely a silence in the gay community about domestic violence." "There's a lot of denial." "It's one of the best kept secrets in the gay community." "No one believes what is happening. No one will listen. No one will hear." "There are those who simply deny gay domestic violence exists, and resist the issue coming out in a general discourse." Pierce J. Reed sums it up: "As for violence in the relationships of gay men, there is even greater silence and denial [than there is about lesbian battering]. With the important exception of several programs in San Francisco and New York, the men's community has yet to respond to the problem of gay male battering" (1989).

After two and one-half years of researching and learning about gay men's domestic violence, we have reached the conclusion that as a community we are responding to domestic violence generally the same way a victim responds to domestic violence when it first happens to him.

Our community is minimizing the problem. We choose to believe it is not widespread (false), or that it only affects certain sectors of the community (false), or that the violence itself is not serious (false). Much as a victim does, we downplay the severity of domestic violence in our midst.

Like a victim confronting something as shocking and incomprehensible as domestic violence, we as a community display denial. Too often we say that the problem does not exist or that it will not happen again. We lull ourselves into believing it will stop by itself, or that we don't really need to do anything. We remain, by and large, silent, exactly like the victim who does not talk about the abuse happening to him.

Like the victim, our community hopes for change, despite mounting evidence to the contrary. It is embarrassing, and it makes us look bad in the eyes of others, such as heterosexual America. As a community, we wish it were not happening, and we do not want to have to deal with it. As victims do, we focus our energies on other issues and leave this one alone. We say we are already overwhelmed, or we do not have enough time or enough money to deal with domestic violence. And, it is true: Our community is being stretched to the limit by AIDS, by anti-gay violence, and by political oppression, just to name a few. Yet no matter what we do and no matter how hard we work, when we ignore domestic violence, it continues. And the violence gets more severe and happens more frequently, just as it does to the victim at home.

Finally, as is the case for most victims, we as a community do not understand the phenomenon happening to us. We need knowledge, education, information. We never thought it would happen to us, and so we never educated ourselves. We never thought about it. It shocks us. Just like the victims, we do not yet know how to respond to it.

The time has come for all gay men to stop being victimized by domestic violence. Until the gay community decides that domestic violence must be prevented, not just in New York, Seattle, or San Francisco, but everywhere, hundreds of thousands of gay men every year will be battered by their lovers. And their cries will be ignored.

WHAT IS THEORY?

How can gay men's domestic violence be explained? Is it predictable? How does it start? Why does it continue and why does it happen more than once? Does one act of violence portend another? Do the acts of violence become more and more serious as time passes? More frequent?

These are but a few of scores of questions about gay men's domestic violence for which there are very little data, insufficient research and too few answers. Only when research has been conducted for many years will light be shed on these big questions. But a clear and useful theory of gay men's domestic violence is needed, a theory that will tentatively explain the phenomenon and guide the thinking needed for research to be planned and conducted. By postulating this first theory, we challenge the members of the academic, scientific, and psychological communities in America to get to work on the problem of gay men's domestic violence.

A theory is a coherent group of general propositions used as principles of explanation for a class of phenomena. A theory is also a proposed explanation whose status is still conjectural, in contrast to well-established propositions that are regarded as reporting matters of actual fact. The theory of gravity, for instance, is now accepted as fact, a result of years of research and debate.

Since there is no theory to explain the class of phenomena that comprise gay men's domestic violence, the time has come for the first steps to be taken. Constructing of a theory of gay men's domestic violence consists of analyzing the phenomenon carefully and identifying the elements of behavior, background, personality, and situations that explain how it happens. Research can then determine which of the propositions are true and which are not.

We develop our theory throughout this book, but especially in this chapter and in Chapters III and IV. Many of the elements in the theory that we propose are indeed conjectural and subject to criticism, refutation and rejection. That is fine with us. In fact, most social science theories remain forever conjectural (and controversial) because human beings cannot be experimented upon — in contrast to theory in the physical sciences that can be subjected to rigorous experimental tests.

We welcome the hoped-for debate and political controversy. We want the discussion over our proposed theory to draw attention to the problem of gay men's domestic violence. The more light focused on it, the better. Gay men's domestic violence needs to be brought out into the glare of public scrutiny and into the research departments of America's universities.

Our theory will start that process. We believe it will contribute significantly to the beginnings of research, because, on its face, our theory is conservative. It is believable, rational, and parsimonious. It is also rich in heuristic value — that is, it should serve to stimulate investigations. Thus, it is capable of generating all kinds of extraordinary research: intelligent case study investigations, large and small survey projects, master's and doctoral dissertations, and experimental treatment programs. Once research is under way and theory refined and elaborated on, gay men's domestic violence will be better understood. Then, we can all act responsibly to reduce and eventually eliminate this scourge from our culture.

THE TWELVE UNDERLYING PRINCIPLES

Behind any theory are concepts and principles, a point of view about the nature of the phenomenon that is being explained by the theory. Our theory of gay men's domestic violence has twelve such underlying principles.

1. Domestic violence is unacceptable human behavior. Gay men's domestic violence cannot be tolerated by members of the gay community, and it must be unambiguously condemned by our entire society.
2. Gay men's domestic violence is not difficult to identify. There is a clear, easy-to-remember definition of domestic violence, and the victim is the one who decides if violence is happening or not.

3. Domestic violence is a crime. There are both criminal and civil consequences for assault, battery, rape, and property destruction.

4. Federal, state, and local laws stand properly behind the victims of gay men's domestic violence. The judicial branch of government, law enforcement, and social service institutions of America exist to protect gay men who are victims of domestic violence.

5. Domestic violence is the most primitive method of solving power problems and "getting your way" known to humankind. Resorting to violence is ample evidence of a lack of proper development in the perpetrator and evidence of his lack of adequate methods of reasoning.

6. Batterers choose to be violent, decide to be abusive and premeditatively intend to harm, but they are not insane or crazy. They suffer from a learned, progressive, diagnosable, and curable mental disorder. There is no other way to view these men. No well-functioning, mentally healthy man engages in domestic violence.

7. Nothing justifies gay men's domestic violence. All attempts at rationalizing and justifying it are to be repudiated. (Self-defense is not domestic violence.)

8. The perpetrator is responsible for every act of violence that he commits. No victim is ever the cause of violence done to him nor does he ever deserve it. The perpetrator chooses violence and is accountable for his decision.

9. The victim is responsible for staying in a relationship with a violent partner. It is always up to the victim to exit such a relationship.

10. Domestic violence occurs in the gay community with the same or greater frequency as in the heterosexual community.

11. Violence is learned at home by imitating and modeling significant others, and through many other societal and psychological mechanisms.

12. Violence in the home can be stopped. Violent behavior can be curbed and unlearned by the perpetrators, and rejected by the victims.

BASIC THEORY:
WHY DOES IT HAPPEN MORE THAN ONCE?

The following section outlines, in point form, our proposed theory of gay men's domestic violence. A discussion follows at the end. Here, and at greater length in Chapters III and IV, our purpose is to subdivide the overall theory into very discrete units for ease of research.

1. Gay men's domestic violence exists in three forms: physical, material, and psychological.
   a. Physical violence is assault and battery, any unwanted physical force on the victim—including sexual abuse.
   b. Psychological violence is mental. The perpetrator says or does things that leave the victim intimidated, worried, anxious, threatened, terrorized, or fearful. Many psychologically violent acts can also legally be considered as assaults.
   c. Material violence is done to things. The perpetrator destroys or discards or mutilates objects, materials, property, and possessions of the victim.
2. Domestic violence in all its forms is primarily a power issue.
   a. The perpetrator ordinarily adopts the powerful role.
   b. The victim ordinarily adopts the powerless role.
   c. The proclivity to adopt and perform one or the other role is not necessarily related to gender.
   d. Stereotypical sex roles ordinarily assigned to males and females in American society are not adequate to explain lesbian and gay male domestic violence dynamics.
   e. Both gay males and lesbians are equally capable of adopting either the powerful or powerless roles found in domestic violence.
3. There is an identifiable increase in the strength of force used by a perpetrator that, in time, leads up to a first incident.
   a. Cues abound that, at least in retrospect, portend the occurrence of the first incident.
   b. The first incident does not happen out of the blue.

   c. The cues that precede the first incident will fall into a pattern of perpetrator behavior that almost always escapes the awareness of the eventual victim.
4. There is a single, identifiable, unambiguous first incident of violence.
   a. The incident, in retrospect, can be pinpointed.
   b. The incident falls easily into definitions of domestic violence.
   c. The paths of behavior leading to the incident are identifiable when examined in retrospect.
   d. The victim may or may not be aware, at the moment of the first incident, that a significant event has occurred.
5. There is usually a random, but nonetheless continual, increase in the frequency of violent episodes.
   a. The space of time between incidents will vary, but a second, subsequent incident (and more) will occur.
   b. It is rare that gay men's domestic violence is a once-only phenomenon.
6. There is usually a random, but nonetheless continual, increase in the intensity of the violence.
   a. The strength of force used, including language and manipulative strategies, gradually, or suddenly, increases.
   b. The strength of force used by the perpetrator never decreases.
7. There is usually a random, but nonetheless continual, increase in the severity of the violence.
   a. More and more serious violence occurs. Episodes of violence progress from slapping, for instance, to the use of fists.
   b. It is rare that gay men's domestic violence decreases in severity.
8. There is a spreading effect, a situational and environmental diffusion, that takes place over time.
   a. While at first only one kind of situation or environment preceded (triggered) violence, over time, many different types of environments or situations precede (trigger) the violence.

    b. Eventually, over time, almost anything will precede violence.

    c. Violence is entirely unpredictable.

    d. Over time, any situation or environment, randomly and unpredictably, will precede (trigger) violence of any intensity, severity, or duration.

9. Eventually, there will be a serious incident that will irrevocably change how the victim perceives the perpetrator.

    a. The incident may involve physical violence (including sexual violence), psychological violence or material destruction, or any combination of the three.

    b. The victim will then be aware of a significant problem in both the relationship and the perpetrator.

10. Sex is a primary reinforcer that guarantees the perpetuation of domestic violence.

    a. After violence the abuser is often the sole source of comfort and solace to the victim.

    b. The first time that the couple engages in sex after violence, with both partners as willing participants, that act will be a reinforcement to the perpetuation of violence.

    c. A cycle of violence occurs — tranquility, build-up, violence, cessation, make-up, tranquility — with sex as a major element in "make-up."

11. Violence is a self-reinforcing act for the perpetrator. Its cessation is a release, a satisfier, a reinforcer. In the alternative, violence itself may be a self-reinforcing act for the perpetrator, as a release from the build-up stage.

12. The longer that the individuals are in a relationship, the more likely that violence will eventually occur and that it will be harder for a victim to leave.

13. The victim will make many attempts to stop the perpetrator from committing violent acts, and those attempts will fail.

    a. The victim will employ various strategies of negotiation, apology, denial, placating, new agreements, and submissions.

    b. In so doing, the victim further reinforces his own victimization by accepting the responsibility for stopping the violent behavior of the perpetrator.

14. By use of violence the perpetrator has set a standard for controlling the victim and must maintain it.
    a. The feeling of security in achieving a level of control over the victim is rewarding to the perpetrator and works to reinforce and perpetuate the violence.

15. The victim will make at least one attempt, and often many more, to leave the abusive partner.
    a. The victim will return.
    b. The violence will resume and continue.

16. The victim experiences increased feelings of isolation as the violence continues.
    a. The victim denies that violence exists, or minimizes the violence, and blames himself for it.
    b. The victim adopts a learned helplessness lifestyle.
    c. The victim adopts coping behaviors to survive.
    d. The victim sees no support services available.

17. There is a random, but nonetheless continual, decrease in consideration given to the victim's feelings by the perpetrator.

18. The perpetrator will persistently attempt to persuade the victim that the incidents of violence have been provoked.
    a. The perpetrator will attempt to persuade the victim that the violence is normal.
    b. The perpetrator will attempt to persuade the victim that the victim caused the violence.
    c. The perpetrator will attempt to persuade the victim that the violence was trivial.
    d. The perpetrator will attempt to persuade the victim that the problem lies in the victim.

One of the most challenging theoretical aspects to domestic violence is determining a plausible explanation for why violence would happen more than once.

Domestic violence rarely starts out extremely severe. In a sense, it has a gradual build-up. What once was a gentle tug on the victim's hair becomes a painful yank. Little taps become blows by fists. It makes sense to think about domestic violence as sneaking up on the victim. Thus, many victims, until they think closely about it, cannot quite pinpoint when it all started, and they fail to label it as abuse.

Looking at it from another angle, the victim, when hurt, undoubtedly believes that it was a once-only mistake on the part of the perpetrator. Surely, "He did not mean it." Everyone is entitled to be forgiven for making a mistake, even a violent one. Such thinking can easily be repeated upon the second and third occurrences. The "it-won't-happen-again-I'm-sure" syndrome begins.

Victims do love their men. It is very difficult to think extremely bad things about your lover even when he has just committed a violent act against you. "Love heals all wounds," so the saying goes. It is true, to a point, but it is a way victims go on thinking for too long.

Victims usually believe that they can help their violent mates and stop their violent behavior. They think they can either perform social worker miracles, or else learn how to behave so as to not create the conditions for violence. Victims quickly learn how to "walk on eggs," thinking, falsely, that if they just do everything right, the violence will not occur. Thus, victims take on the responsibility for the violence. Such an approach is bound to fail. But until the victims learn this, they may have been abused another five or one hundred times.

While these explanations are concrete, useful, and cogent, we believe that traditional psychological theory gives better reasons why gay men's domestic violence happens more than once. There are four basic explanations:

1. Mental Disorder. Batterers have a learned, progressive mental disorder and will continue to act out their illness until they obtain help for curing it and follow the treatment prescriptions. They are not insane or psychotic, but they have no incentive to change, and their condition will not fix itself. There is no reason to expect behavior to stop on its own if that behavior is a central feature to a mental disorder. Virtually all batterers do not receive treatment of any kind. Therefore, their mental disorder continues to progress, unchecked.

2. Punishment Theory. Violence is a choice. Batterers actually believe that they will "get their way" if they create an environment and atmosphere of intimidation and terror for their lover. This strongly held belief system operates tenaciously because it works. Many people, including most victims, will naturally give in, fall into line and cooperate with their domestic terrorist, simply to avoid worse consequences. Thus, a victim may behave in a way that appears to be self-defeating as a coping strategy to avoid further abuse or threats to his life. This is a widely accepted law of social learning theory that shows that people will take repeated instances of a lesser punishment to avoid extreme punishment that has been threatened.

3. Positive Reinforcement. Making up, an activity that usually involves sex, is a reinforcement for the violence to repeat. The perpetrator's behavior that precedes the pleasure, or reward, is what always will be repeated, even if it is abusive. This is a law of operant conditioning, a widely accepted principle in the behavioral sciences.

4. Negative Reinforcement. For the perpetrator, once the rage has passed, the cessation of his violence is a reinforcement to the violent act. This principle of operant psychology correctly explains the repetition of many abusive and destructive behaviors. Alternatively, the violence itself may be self-reinforcing to the abuser because it serves as a release from tension.

Chapter III

Who Are the Batterers?

PLEASE DON'T KILL ME!

Stephen and I are having a disagreement while watching TV. I am in bed, and Stephen is on the couch. The disagreement escalates; things are quickly getting heated between us, and I am getting very angry. Before long we are shouting at each other. I get up and leave the room, slamming the door behind me so hard that its glass panes break, and Stephen is after me instantly.

I run into the next room, close the door, and quickly pull a bookcase in front of it to keep Stephen out. Stephen is on the other side of the door pounding, shouting, "Let me in! Patrick, LET ME IN!" I soon realize that a bookcase will not be sufficient, so I pull a bed in front of it, creating a double barricade weighing a ton. I am feeling frightened and desperate, and I'm shouting back, "Leave me alone Stephen! Just leave me alone!!" Soon he is in a rage. He is shouting, "Let me in; I won't hurt you. Patrick, I promise I won't hurt you!"

I begin to panic, knowing—or perhaps more accurately, fearing—what lay ahead. It is late at night, dark and cold outside, and while there are two windows in the room through which I can escape, I am naked. Where am I to go?

Stephen continues pounding on the door with his fists, trying to push his way in. He continues shouting about how he will not hurt me. I am so afraid of him at this moment. He seems out of control, beyond my reach. I feel trapped, and helpless. I am frantically looking around the room for . . . something. What can I do? I cannot go out. I cannot hide. I never once (until writing this) consider the option of just letting him in. Keeping him away from me seems my only option.

In a matter of minutes, I realize that Stephen is breaking the door down. The noise is so loud, this thunderous banging, banging. I can hear the door splintering and chipping, and see the end of the two-by-four he is using to smash his way all the way through.

I hide, crouching down behind the stereo cabinet. Ridiculous, I realize. I do not consider arming myself with . . . whatever I could find to clobber him. I do not yet think in those terms; I am not a violent person. Anyway, he smashes the door apart and storms in.

Once he is in the room I bolt for the door to get out. Stephen grabs me with both hands, and a long struggle follows. We are grappling and struggling with each other, moving all over the room. Finally he throws me down on the bed in a rage. He grabs a brass candlestick holder that weighs about ten pounds and holds it in both hands up over his head—as if to pummel me with it. I am scream-ing, "Stephen, please don't kill me! Please don't kill me!" He throws the candlestick holder to the floor, and he picks up a tennis racket. Again he holds it up over his head, shaking. Again and again I scream, "No, Stephen! No!! Don't kill me! Please don't kill me!!" He runs out of the room. I lie on the bed, shaking, terrified.

The whole room is a mess. The bookcase is knocked over, and books are everywhere. Pieces of the smashed door and chips of white paint cover the floor. The door itself is still on its hinges, but smashed apart, with big splinters of wood sticking out in all directions. The scene in the hallway is the same: broken glass and big splinters of wood and paint chips all over the floor. And Stephen stands in the middle of it, wearing only his pajama bottoms, sobbing.

This story is a rather harrowing demonstration of all three of the powerful and destructive types of domestic violence: physical abuse, psychological abuse, and material or property destruction.

Unlike the psychological abuse, the physical abuse and material abuse in this incident are obvious. Glass panes are broken. A door is smashed with a two-by-four. A bookcase is knocked over. Pa-trick and Stephen have a long, violent struggle, and Patrick is thrown onto the bed.

Everything else that happens here, however, is psychological vi-olence, and it cannot be overlooked or minimized. For example, Patrick's fear of Stephen is so strong that he barricades a door to keep Stephen away. He reports feeling "afraid . . . trapped . . . helpless . . . terrified." He is aware that Stephen can and might possibly kill him; if not today, perhaps tomorrow, or next week.

The toll that psychological abuse takes on its victims is a heavy one. While its damage is not as visible as physical abuse, psychological violence leaves its own scars and bruises on the personalities and mental health of its victims. Fear and intimidation, low self-worth, powerlessness, helplessness, anxiety, nightmares, weight loss, ulcers, headaches, backaches, eating disorders: these all may be traced to psychological abuse in the lives of victims of domestic violence. One need only ask the question: how long will it take Patrick to recover from this incident? Certainly the door will be fixed before he is.

"Please Don't Kill Me!" also teaches an important lesson about victim-thinking. Patrick admits to "knowing — or perhaps more accurately, fearing — what lay ahead," and yet he has taken no precautions to help himself. He has no plan of escape, no safe way out, and nothing to defend himself with. In fact, he locks himself into a room from which there is no escape. These are unfortunately good examples of the victim approach to things: "There is nothing I can do about it." As will be pointed out in Chapter V, "How Do You Get Out?" there is plenty that Patrick can do for himself. The difficulty is in getting him to recognize that fact.

Finally, the mental state of the batterer is made clear in this story. No well-functioning healthy person deliberately plows his way through a door with a two-by-four, threatens the life of his lover, and then later stands in the rubble sobbing.

BATTERERS ARE UNCLEAR
ON THE CONCEPT OF MASCULINITY

All violent men who batter and abuse their partners are obviously confused about the concept of masculinity. There is nothing masculine about battering. For many gay males confusion about masculinity is compounded by the lack of visible gay role models for males growing up gay in America and because being gay is deemed "unmasculine" by the dominant culture. For gays, the result is a complex and often confusing view of masculinity.

Most males learn as they develop that becoming a man is a complicated but thrilling experience. Being male is pretty easy. One just *is* male, and biology more or less takes over, unconsciously. But being masculine, and especially being masculine and nonviolent, is something a male has to think about, learn, practice. Being masculine involves conscious acts. We believe that gay male batterers are amazingly unclear about all of this.

For some men, becoming nonviolently masculine in our society is difficult because in many ways our society links masculinity *with* violence. Hollywood, television, sports, the military, advertising, music, and many visible male heroes and leaders are all guilty of making this unfortunate connection. Most men, however, seem to have overcome these obstacles, because the vast majority of men in America are not violent.

Some workers in the domestic violence field dispute this assertion, claiming that most men are violent, that males are inherently aggressive, and that in 80% of marriages the husbands are abusive toward their wives. We disagree. No body of data supports their contentions. We believe that far too many husbands in America are violent, but that their proportion is closer to 20% than 80% (Gelles and Straus, 1988, p. 104).

Masculinity is an idea about how men should behave. It does not really exist except in people's heads. Masculinity is not mere maleness. Masculinity is a set of attitudes and values. Masculinity is a packet of thinking styles that are acted on in relation to issues such as power and control. Men and women develop ideas about what it means to be masculine, and our society reinforces many of those ideas, both good and bad. There are many common stereotypes in existence, but no agreement in our society about the "ideal masculine man." How does a minority of men get so screwed up about masculinity? Many of the notions about masculinity are destructive and lead those who adopt them to pain, trouble and to the perpetuation of family violence, because some of those notions are equated with the exercise of power and control.

Negative ideas about masculinity popular in America include acting tough at all times, not showing tender feelings at all. The lean, mean, super-cool, stoic cowboy is a perfect example of this (distorted) Hollywood view of masculinity. Another particularly obnoxious interpretation of masculinity teaches men to get their way by flexing muscles, drinking to excess, getting angry, and hitting people. To some men, being masculine means to intimidate, to dominate, and to do what they damn well want to, no matter what the consequences to themselves and to other people. To these men, being masculine is their attempt to control others so that they are sure that no one controls them, because being influenced by others is scarily unmasculine. Far too many men (and women) believe that masculine means to be violent whenever desired, not only in self-defense, but also as an assailant, responding to vague "provocations." To thousands of men, masculine means to take violent action now and to talk later. These are all unacceptable notions of masculinity, but ones that are powerfully endorsed by many influential elements in our culture. Nevertheless, most men reject these ideas of masculinity as patently stupid.

We reject the popular notion that *all* men are invariably socialized in America to fulfill one "idealized masculine role" of physical toughness, fierceness, aggression-as-violence, only to end up as sexist patriarchs, who deny most emotions, are devoid of qualities such as nurturance and cooperation, and who are overintellectualized and competitively detached from their bodies and other people. *Some* men can be characterized as adopting such a malignant masculine ideology, but millions of men cannot be so described. While it is true that America is a violent culture and a patriarchal society at its roots, millions of men who experience all these pervasive forces reject all of them, adopt only some of them, or dramatically neutralize most of them. To relegate the cause of domestic violence to politicized, sex-role socialization notions or to overgeneralized, patriarchal rhetoric is to let individual batterers off the hook too easily. We believe it is the individual violent man who has to accept primary responsibility for all of his conduct, including his maladaptive, unacceptable interpretations of masculinity.

Many gay men who batter their lovers confuse being male with some of these strange ideas about masculinity. Just because one is male does not mean one has to accept Rambo's portrayal of masculinity. While some batterers are indeed hypermasculine or ruthlessly exploitive, the majority, according to Gondolf (1988, p. 4) do "not fit the stereotype supermacho man. Rather they may be typified as 'failed macho complex.'" Gondolf explains that such men see themselves as failing to reach the unachievable and false masculine ideal of "dominance and cool. So they overcompensate by controlling the one they perceive threatens or exposes their insecurities: their wife or lover" (Gondolf, 1988, p. 4). These men attempt to become the ideas of masculinity. They act out the ideas.

Such men are merely following a prescription, a recipe for masculinity that most others have discarded. As real-live puppets, they perform a role, read a script and mechanically act out whatever their ideas are about masculinity. Failure is inevitable. These men, therefore, do not take responsibility for their conduct. They escape accountability for their actions by putting the blame for their conduct onto "society." They further attempt to excuse their violent behavior by claiming that "that is just how males are."

Nonsense. No male has to become a batterer. Most do not. It takes thinking, however, and a lot of it, to be masculine and nonviolent. It takes effort to resist the forces operating in American culture that reinforce violent and disturbed interpretations of masculinity. Nonviolent men know that they have choices other than violence, and they make those choices by evaluating behavioral options against a set of principles and values to which they have personally given considerable thought. Nonviolent masculine men do not act from a script or merely from their primitive emotions. Instead, they act from a foundation of evaluated choices.

Domestic violence is the coward's choice, the consequence of failing to evaluate options, failing to let go of and resist the unacceptable, false masculine scripts offered up by parts of our culture.

The following chart contrasts how nonviolent men and batterers interpret the various components that comprise the concept of masculinity.

THE DIFFERENCE BETWEEN NONVIOLENT MEN AND BATTERERS ON THE COMPONENTS OF MASCULINITY

MASCULINITY COMPONENT	AS INTERPRETED BY A NONVIOLENT MAN	AS INTERPRETED BY A BATTERER
ASSERTIVENESS	Understands difference between assertiveness and aggression.	Confuses assertiveness with aggression. Ignores rights and feelings of others.
STRENGTH	Has endurance and toughness to resist attacks but does not use to intimidate.	Takes license to be violent or threaten violence to create an intimidating atmosphere.

POWER	Accepts personal ability to cause action, to have an effect or influence.	License to terrorize. Confuses with physical power, as if a license to overpower.
FEELINGS	Accepts all feelings in self and others and understands that does not have to act on feelings.	Incorrectly believes that feelings must be acted upon. Feels need to act on all provocative acts.
TENDERNESS	Shows regard, care, and respect for others even during disputes.	Rejects showing regard, care, and respect for the other during disputes.
CONFLICT	Identifies and verbalizes feelings. Nonviolent conflict accepted.	Feelings are repressed. Unable to verbalize. Conflict usually ends up with some form of abuse or violence.
VULNERABILITY	Accepts own vulnerability as normal and inevitable.	Rejects and fears his own vulnerability, and retaliates as if attacked when such feelings occur.
INDEPENDENCE	Sees self as free from control by others without need to control in return.	Rejects influence from others. Impenetrable. Rigid.
CONTROL	Internalized to self. Values self-control.	Externalized to others. Values controlling others and seeks to dominate others.
RESPONSIBILITY	Accountable for all of own behavior. Reliable. Requires others to be accountable as well.	Rejects accountability for self. Blames others for his actions.
MUTUALITY	Freely joins with partner in decisions and actions.	Experiences a loss of self when joining with partner in mutual decision. Must have own way.

WHO ARE THE BATTERERS?

While the focus of this book is not on the gay male batterer, the whole picture of gay men's domestic violence cannot be seen without some examination of who the batterers are, since they alone cause the problem.

What kinds of gay men batter their lovers? Why do they abuse their loved ones? How can their violence be stopped? In this next section the gay male batterer is examined: his origins, his psychology, his deviance, and his need for psychological treatment.

Crazy, Criminal, or Mentally Ill?

Most Batterers Are Probably Not Crazy

This conclusion, however, depends somewhat on your definition of crazy. We contend that no well-functioning gay man commits violence on his boyfriend or lover for any reason except self-defense. Clearly then, abusers do not function in a healthy way in their domestic world with their partners, or they would not batter. By definition, their behavior at home is abnormal. But, are they insane, crazy, psychotic? We think not.

The term crazy, or insane, in our society is reserved for a special, small group of people with severe mental illness, such as psychoses and brain damage. Our society reasons that these crazy people cannot change and probably cannot get well or become "normal." Therefore, the thinking goes, most of these people need to be controlled, corralled (in institutions), treated intensively, kept away from the rest of us, or else, just ignored. The key is: "They cannot change."

The belief that certain people cannot change their mental condition, goes hand in hand with the belief that those people are not really accountable for what they do. If your parents are Irish, you cannot be held accountable for not being Spanish. For crazy people, it is the same idea. It is from this thinking that the "innocent by reason of insanity" concept came. If a person is insane or crazy, they did not know what they were doing when they committed a crime. Therefore, they should be institutionalized for their severe mental condition, but not otherwise held accountable for their actions through punishment, treatment, or some other means of atonement. The insanity defense in our criminal justice system has given rise to a more general attitude in our entire culture that encourages low accountability for *any* negative conduct. We believe that many gay male batterers would take advantage of this apparent societal permissiveness, if confronted about their conduct. They would claim that they are not responsible for their actions because of their interpretation of the "temporary insanity" theory, such as blanking out, being in a dissociative state, losing control, or because of alcohol or drugs or some other form of denial. "It wasn't the real me who hit him," or, "I was completely out of control," is how it would sound.

The fact is that gay male batterers are lawyers, doctors, teachers, policemen, store owners, real estate brokers, bus drivers, writers, salesmen, and hair stylists. At work, and in public generally, they can be successful, competent, sane men. At home they batter their lovers. Our society, and especially the gay community, therefore, must not label the gay male abuser insane, crazy, or psychotic. Such an extreme diagnosis excuses their behavior and does not hold them suitably accountable for their violent actions. While a few batterers probably are truly crazy, we contend that the overwhelming majority of gay male abusers are not.

Are Gay Male Batterers Criminals?

Yes. Domestic violence in most of its forms is a crime. Even so, some gay male batterers may not know that they are committing crimes when they are violent with their lovers — for three main reasons:

First, our society condones and encourages all sorts of violence. Males are *supposed* to threaten violence to intimidate and to get what they want. This socialization process fails to teach some males how to discriminate between which violent acts are crimes and which violent acts are merely crude and primitive behaviors.

Second, domestic violence is usually kept secret. Gay male batterers commit violent acts in the protected environment of the home. For centuries, the home has been a citadel into which authorities or neighbors were not allowed to look, let alone intervene, unless the actions there were "really severe." We all know that parents who kill their children have committed a crime. However, violence that is not "physical" or is "less severe," such as forcing one's mate to have sex or slapping him or her around, has long been considered no one else's business. Most people have by now realized that the privacy of the home should *not* protect violent people from the law. If a criminal threatens the clerk at the corner store with a knife, he knows it is a crime. He now should know that the same violent act committed *at home* is the same crime.

Third, many people may not know which acts of violence really are crimes. Almost all domestic violence involving force and threats, many forms of psychological violence, and most property destruction are criminal acts. Below is a list of violent acts, each of which is a crime in the State of California, with the Sections from the California State Penal Code listed.

Code Section	Description
	Physical Force (Including all sexual violence)
187	Homicide
203	Mayhem
220	Assault with intent to commit mayhem, rape, sodomy, or oral copulation
240	Assault (The threat of violence)
242	Battery (The action of violence)
243.4	Sexual battery
245	Assault with a deadly weapon or with intent to commit great bodily harm
261, 263	Rape
262	Rape of Spouse
266a	Forcible prostitution
266b	Forcible cohabitation
266h,i	Pimping and pandering
273.5	Corporal injury to spouse or cohabitant
286	Forcible sodomy
288a	Forcible oral copulation
289	Penetration with foreign object

| 347 | Poisoning or adulterating food, drink, medicine |
| 415 | Fighting |

Psychological Abuse

220	Assault with intent to commit mayhem, rape, sodomy, or oral copulation
240	Assault
245	Assault with a deadly weapon or with intent to commit great bodily injury
273.6	Violation of court order to prevent domestic violence or disturbance of the peace
417	Drawing, exhibiting or using a firearm or deadly weapon
422.6	Interference with exercise of civil rights
647g,h,i	Disorderly conduct; loitering, prowling, wandering upon the private property of another
650	Letters threatening exposure or accusation of crime
653m	Telephone calls with intent to annoy

Material Destruction

211	Robbery by means of force or fear
240	Assault
422.6	Damaging property
459	Burglary
594	Vandalism
602n	Failure to leave private property
602.5	Unauthorized entry of property
603	Forcible entry; vandalism

Assault is the most commonly misunderstood crime. It occurs on the above list several times. Assault is an apparently violent attempt, or a willful offer, with force or violence, to do hurt to another, *without the actual doing of the threatened hurt*, such as lifting the fist, or an object, in a threatening manner. In "Please Don't Kill Me!" Stephen commits eleven crimes, six of which are assaults.

Many gay male batterers act meekly toward conventional authority, such as the police. We think that if more batterers knew that their actions were crimes, less battering would occur, because the knowledge that they would be held accountable by the law for their behavior would serve as a deterrent to abuse.

Do Gay Male Batterers Have a Mental Disorder?

Yes. We think that batterers are not mentally healthy. Further, we believe that most batterers suffer from some kind of diagnosable, progressive, psychological disorder or mental condition. They are not insane or psychotic, but they have some type of disturbed state of mind. Beyond that, we contend that there may be several diagnostic categories (yet to be devised, perhaps) that describe domestic abusive disorders, because there undoubtedly are many types of batterers. At the very least, we believe that just before, during, and right after a battering incident, batterers are dysfunctional. In those moments, they are completely rational, making conscious decisions about their intentions to inflict harm. Therefore, by definition, abusers are ill men.

Gondolf, in summarizing the research to date on batterers, seems to agree, stating that the findings offer only "generalizations about people we hardly know." He goes on to report that batterers "have several characteristics that distinguish them as 'deviant' individuals," as well as characteristics common to men in general (1985, p. 51).

Dutton, in his exhaustive review of research on wife assaulters, concluded that batterers who were abused as children are "more likely to be personality disordered" than those who learned their violence by observation as children (1988, p. 23-24). Researchers Hamberger and Hastings also cite ample evidence that, contrary to current thinking, a "preponderance of batterers exhibit evidence of personality disorder(s)" (1988, p. 768). In a review of clinical literature on psychological characteristics of male batterers, including studies that use standard psychometric tests, they observe that the data "argue strongly that psychopathology must be considered part of the picture for a majority of identified batterers and, as such, offers clear directions for treatment" (1988, p. 769). Hamberger and Hastings assert that "the psychopathology of abusers can best be viewed as that of a disordered personality—as a deeply ingrained, highly treatment-resistant, and often perplexing set of behaviors" (1988, p. 769).

The Dissenting Point of View

There is considerable disagreement, controversy, and politicizing of this issue in the domestic violence movement and in the mental health field. Some people believe that to shift emphasis for change onto the individual batterers will never really solve the problem. They contend that society has to change, and that battering will stop only when that happens.

Some believe that to label gay or lesbian batterers with a psychodiagnostic category is to play back into the bigoted hands of those who still believe that being gay or lesbian is itself a psychological disorder. Others say any labeling is stigmatizing. Still others point to the criminal laws against sodomy still on the books in many states and see further legal dangers for gay men and lesbians in those states if psychodiagnostic categories are used to describe gay and lesbian batterers. Some professionals, who provide treatment to batterers or victims in mental health centers, contend that battering is not a mental health issue! Others are fearful that the labelling process does further damage to the already dysfunctional batterer.

Grass roots workers fear a take-over of the domestic violence field (as many claim may have happened in the alcohol treatment field) by professionals if the batterer is "pathologized" by psychodiagnostic categories. They believe that therapists untrained in domestic violence will then provide services in and dominate a field in which they have little experience. Some community service workers fear that "their field" will be overtaken by professionals providing services that no one can afford. Some women fear that the use of mental disorder categories by therapists treating lesbian batterers will lead to further victimization of women, a group already damaged by incompetent, sexist, or homophobic therapists and institutions for hundreds of years. They also fear a similar fate for gay men. Strong concern comes from certain mental health workers who think that labeling a batterer with a mental disorder will work as a disincentive for the batterer, who will feel less accountable for his behavior and have less motivation for working at changing it.

We reject all of these positions, although most have some merit and can be argued with vigor. Most of the above dissenting positions are too narrow in view; some are motivated merely by sexual politics; and all may actually serve as a hindrance to progress in the domestic violence field. We do not suggest that any existing treatment or theoretical approach should be eliminated. Rather, we want to increase and improve the availability of psychological help for batterers that can only come from proper use of psychodiagnostic categories by treatment providers. We want to stop the violence, now, and if labeling the batterer as mentally disturbed will help to stop the violence, as we believe it will, then it should be done now.

Accountability

Our intention is not to be harsh or punitive in our labeling of gay male batterers as mentally disturbed. We want to be realistic. In our society there are lots of mentally ill people, and we as a society willingly label them as such. Few people would criticize labeling as obsessive individuals who wash their hands every three minutes. No one thinks that arsonists or serial killers are mentally healthy. No one thinks it is wrong to label someone who cannot go to work because of imagined fears as having an anxiety disorder. There are at least a dozen alcohol-identified mental disorders that label otherwise "normal" people to assist those individuals with alcohol-related problems. Being labeled as mentally ill does not have to be a death sentence or stigmatizing. On the contrary, it can be an incentive for the afflicted one to change, to get well. Many disturbed people are relieved when they finally learn what is wrong with them. When proper psychodiagnostic categorizing of gay male batterers is done it will place responsibility squarely on only the individual batterer to change, and it will force batterers to acknowledge that they are choosing to be violent and must make other choices. People who are ill get well. Thus, abusers must be generally thought of as individuals with a curable mental disorder. We know that abuser behavior is a learned condition, and since it is learned, it is treatable, and the dysfunctional individual can overcome the disorder to become a healthy, nonviolent gay man.

Failure by the psychological community to classify batterers in proper psychodiagnostic language can be interpreted as aiding and abetting the batterers to avoid their sole accountability for their conduct. Perpetrators exhibit conduct that is unacceptable, illegal, and demanding of change, but apparently 99.9% of batterers do not accept these facts. One factor contributing to batterer defiance of society is that their conduct has not been properly labeled. Batterers batter, in part, because society, including the mental health profession, tolerates their conduct.

Criminal Conduct

Gay bashing, hate crimes, murder, and knifings are all considered crimes by our society, and the people who commit them are considered deviant. Beating your lover over the head with a baseball bat, burning his clothing, and threatening to tell his homophobic landlord that he is gay are also crimes. Domestic violence is learned criminal behavior. Such acts committed in our society, and in the gay community, need to be labeled as disordered.

Mental Health

Batterers, especially when judged by lay people in general and victims of abuse in particular, do not fit accepted definitions of good mental health. In San Jose, California, a support group of seven battered wives and another of 18 male batterers each went on record with a newspaper reporter hoping that the public will "see domestic violence as an illness not unlike alcoholism and other addictions" (Gathright, 1990). The commission of violent, criminal acts in the home is all the evidence needed to conclude a lack of psychological well-being in the perpetrator and an unsatisfactory adjustment to society and the ordinary demands of living. Normalcy (sound mental health) is defined, in part, as the absence of certain dysfunctional signs and symptoms. Breaking the arms of your spouse on purpose is certainly a sign of dysfunction. Such conduct must, therefore, be viewed as symptomatic of a mental disorder. Consider a visitor from outer space asking you how it could become a mentally healthy, normal member of our society. Would you tell this alien that it must learn how to be violent, that it must acquire the "skills of battering," that it must learn to control its mate by creating an atmosphere of intimidation and fear at home in order to be thought of as normal? Of course not. You would do no such thing, even though you might admit that our culture is violent. Domestic violence is commonplace, but it is not normal. Mental health workers tell batterers that they are responsible and accountable for their conduct, but there are no teeth in such comments. Until we confront batterers with the criminality and abnormality of their conduct, they will continue to deny its severity and will be insufficiently motivated to own up to their problems, to seek treatment, and to stop the battering.

Individual Causation

As mentioned earlier, some domestic violence workers claim that the roots of batterer conduct are solely in the socialization processes of our culture. These people believe that all young males are literally trained to be violent by virtue of growing up in America. Those who hold such positions, however, inadvertently take responsibility off the batterer and place it on society. It is just as wrong to blame society for one man's acts of violence against his mate, as it is to blame his victim. It is the batterer's mental condition and his own internalized set of standards that determine his conduct. Sane, but mentally disturbed, people exist in our society, and their behavior must be examined within the sociological milieu. But it is a sociological myth, a grievous deception, to believe that society causes individual acts of domestic violence. Individual abusers commit violence.

The social learning theories and the sociopolitical theories, which purport to explain the development of male perpetrators in our society, are unable to account for the development of violent women who batter their husbands, violent women who abuse their children and elderly parents, and violent lesbians who batter their lovers. Further, these theories are unable to account for the fact that the vast majority of men and women are not batterers. How do nonviolent people emerge from the same society as the violent ones? From the same family as a batterer? It is a minority of *individuals* who become domestic abusers in our society. Not only is abuser conduct deviant, therefore, but its causation is within the individual. Consequently, a loud, unambiguous, noncontradictory message needs to be sent to batterers, to victims and to society at large: The precise cause of the problem of domestic violence is located in large numbers of individuals (both men and women) who have a disturbance. Domestic violence, by definition, is a mental health issue.

Insult to Victims

It is an insult to the millions of victims of domestic violence all over the country not to assert that batterer behavior is abnormal. Victims from one end of the nation to the other must by now be tired of hearing (even from some batterer treatment providers) that batterers are merely "normal people in pain whose perspective on the world is a little off." That sounds dangerously paternalistic to us. Resolving the mental disorder issue is a constructive way our entire society can become accountable and make amends to victims by properly labeling perpetrator conduct for what it is.

Double Message

Good batterer treatment programs already directly focus their basic intervention strategies with batterers on the unacceptable, illegal, and deviant aspects of battering, and not on its sociological or sociopolitical foundations. The first priority in treating a batterer is to get him or her to cease battering and to adopt alternate, normal, nonviolent behavior with his or her mate. Even some good treatment programs deliver a double message, however. Message One: "We are first going to work with you as an individual batterer so you fix your terribly messed-up psychology and change your extraordinarily deviant conduct, but we will never tell you that you are messed up and deviant." Message Two: "We are going to tell you that your violence is unacceptable and that you are responsible and accountable for it, but we will also tell you that you are normal and it is our screwed-up society that causes you to behave the way you do." Such double messages are dishonest and an obvious disincentive to a batterer to change or own his or her abusive behavior.

Only when everyone in our society recognizes, through the proper naming of batterer conduct, that abusers are ill people in dire need of extensive attention and treatment, will we mobilize our communities to provide that treatment so that batterers can overcome their affliction and become well-functioning members of a household.

HOW DO BATTERERS DEVELOP?

If we are to understand batterers, before we can investigate their characteristics, it is important to examine how they come to be batterers in the first place and to review the streams of influence that contribute to theory about their development.

Social Learning Theory

As individuals grow up, they are exposed daily to the culture, the group in which they live. This socializing process is important because it is a strong force in eventually shaping how people think, how they act, and what values they adopt. A society forms its people. The attitudes gay men have toward other men, for instance, are in part the result of this process of group socialization. Attitudes toward violence result from living every day in a society, a family, and a neighborhood. One learns to behave as the society teaches.

In the case of gay male batterers, these men have picked up from our society some of the worst it has to offer. They have imitated the violence they have seen at home, on television, and in the streets. Children pick up these ineffective ways of dealing with disputes through imitation learning and modeling, the same way people learn how to talk and how to drive. Gay male batterers learned how to be abusive by watching, listening to, and then imitating their models. They learned how to control, dominate, and manipulate the same way.

This kind of learning does not happen in a very formal way. Children just watch abusive parents (or are abused by their parents) and then, without a word being exchanged, years later they imitate exactly what their parents did. Socialization is extremely powerful. Social learning theory explains how males and females learn sex roles. A man's view of himself, his ideas on masculinity, and his ways of treating other people are acquired largely by this method of learning. People end up with attitudes and behaviors without knowing where they came from. By these specific learning mechanisms, the social group, family, and society at large teach future abusers how to control, manipulate, dominate, and batter others.

Developmental Theory

Many gay men who batter have probably experienced some kind of developmental impairment. This means that for one reason or another they did not learn well the positive "how to" lessons that were being taught at home, in church, by relatives, by friends, in books, on TV, in sports—everywhere. As every person develops, certain developmental tasks must be learned. At about nine months of age, a baby begins to learn how to walk. That is a developmental task. Many developmental tasks are physical: riding a bicycle, holding a pencil, eating with a knife and fork. Others are mental: adding and subtracting numbers, forming sentences, thinking abstractly. Others are communicative: listening to others, talking about feelings, saying what you mean.

These developmental tasks are deliberately taught in our society. School, parents, and the media are intent on teaching certain developmental lessons so that when children grow up, they have at their command all of the skills that they need in order to live effective lives. If a young boy was not paying attention when certain lessons were taught, or, if these lessons were not taught to him, he grows up without knowing how to act in certain circumstances. These skills are extremely important, especially the people-skills. One of the essential skills in adulthood is knowing how to deal with a conflict situation that makes you angry. Gay men who batter, we contend, learned how to decide to be violent toward someone who does not want to do what they want, but did not learn how to decide to be nonviolent. We believe that when batterers were children, they acquired a cognitive, developmental flaw, through parental neglect, inappropriate modeling and inept teaching by the adults around them, resulting in an inability to make decisions to be nonviolent in a negatively charged situation. However, millions of other men as children early in life learned these thinking and decision-making skills. Some even learned these skills later in life, if they missed them when they were children. Gay men who batter did not learn these skills at all.

Communication Theory

One of the most difficult skills of living that people must learn while growing up is that of communicating effectively with others. Communication theory suggests that men who abuse their lovers have failed to acquire adequate skills of communication. Among these skills is the ability to verbalize anger without resorting to violence. A big problem for gay male batterers is that they think that when they feel anger, they must express it physically, when in fact the mark of a mature gay man is that he is able to tolerate his feelings, talk about them, and describe them verbally, but does not feel compelled to act upon them. Anger is the most dangerous emotion, and gay men who physically express their anger are abusive men.

Communication skills are among the most difficult skills of all to learn and master. Good models and good examples are scarce. Good teachers of effective communication are even rarer. Parents especially are not very good teachers of how to handle disputes and disagreements. Many parents have not the slightest idea how to teach (or set an example for) their sons and daughters to talk about feelings and settle disputes without hitting people or being otherwise abusive.

Personality Theory

Personality theory suggests that people have various enduring traits which find patterned expression in their daily lives. Some people are humorous. Others are fastidious. Some are jealous and others competitive.

No one knows exactly how personality traits are acquired. They may be inherited in part or they may be learned. Parenting is an important factor in the development of personality. Children are reinforced and rewarded for certain expressive tendencies when very small. Parents laugh (thus reinforcing the behavior) when the child does something funny. Young people watch and imitate others. Some researchers believe that because males in our society are raised primarily by mothers, female school teachers, and female day care workers, they have to overexaggerate their masculinity to validate being male against the femininity surrounding them. Further, some psychoanalysts think that some men channel resentment for overmothering onto their wives. Misogyny can develop in similar fashion, as can the hatred of men by women in reaction to their fathers. Thus, the behavior of the mother (or her surrogates) is conceivably as big a factor in the development of a male batterer, as the example of an abusive or overaggressive father.

But there is also self-choice. A person can simply decide he is going to have a certain characteristic and set about acquiring it, much like one learns an athletic skill. We propose that batterers may have certain personality traits in common, even though existing personality tests may not be able to differentiate between groups of batterers and groups of nonbatterers. The ineffectiveness of tests to differentiate groups is not a new problem. The Minnesota Multiphasic Personality Inventory, one of the most respected diagnostic tools available, was not designed to—and cannot—differentiate well between batterers and normals, nor can it differentiate rapists and many other criminal categories of people from normals. But this does not mean that batterers are not different from normal men.

Sociopolitical Theory

This theory postulates that American society is patriarchal, or male dominated. A patriarchal structure subjugates women into subordinate roles through discrimination and through an ideology that presupposes that women are innately inferior. Women are systematically excluded from business, legal, political, and religious leadership. Men, the theory contends, believe they have the right to keep women subordinate in the family, through historically exercised power and privilege. This theory is the origin of the concept that domestic violence is fundamentally both a gender issue and a power issue, as the male uses domination, authority, control, and intimidation at home just as he does in the greater society. Society sanctions the man's violence, and, by systematically neglecting the woman victim—through lack of resources, meager institutional response, antagonistic public action, inadequate laws, and an unfathomable judicial system — society condemns the battered woman to perpetual victim status. Thus, violence against women finds its roots in the patriarchal society, and as males develop, they literally have no other choice than to maintain the patriarchy.

It is not difficult to ascribe to gay men who batter all of the values and characteristics of heterosexual male batterers who develop in a patriarchal culture. Controlling one's spouse need not be viewed as gender-specific.

All of the above theoretical streams contribute in some way to understanding how gay men who bash their lovers develop. All are important influences. Socialization theory (some men pick up the worst that society offers); developmental theory (some men fail to acquire necessary skills needed to live nonviolently); communication theory (some gay men have not learned how to communicate effectively about their feelings and thoughts); personality theory (some gay men have developed an unfortunate, maladaptive set of personality characteristics); and sociopolitical theory (gay men can embody the outcomes of a patriarchal society as readily as heterosexual men) suggest that a combination of all of these forces operate in the development of abusive gay men. None of these forces, however, *causes* an individual gay man to commit specific acts of domestic violence. Gay male batterers have ample opportunity every day to escape the bonds of their proclivity to violence. What they once learned they can and must unlearn. Domestic violence is always a choice.

THE MENTAL DISORDERS OF BATTERING

The American Psychiatric Association publishes one of the most important books used by mental health professionals, the *Diagnostic and Statistical Manual of Mental Disorders*, Third Edition — Revised, 1987 (*DSM-III-R*).

This book, the *DSM-III-R*, is a kind of Bible/catalogue for psychologists, psychiatrists, social workers, other providers of psychological services, and mental health agencies. These professionals and their agencies use this manual to classify the disorder of which a client or patient has symptoms and for which treatment is requested or needed. In the manual are suggested criteria to guide mental health professionals in making the correct diagnosis and proper classification of the presenting problem. *DSM-III-R* is 567 pages long and contains 313 separate, numbered and titled mental diagnoses, ranging from (292.11) Cocaine Delusional Disorder, to (301.84) Passive Aggressive Personality Disorder, to (303.90) Alcohol Dependence, to the 29 separate classifications for various types of Schizophrenia. Every known mental condition on which there is agreement and data in the psychiatric-psychological community is listed in this manual.

A name is given to each disorder and it has an accompanying unique classification number. When the client or patient is covered by an insurance plan, in turn, health insurance providers reimburse the mental health provider for treatment fees based on these classifications. Often, no reimbursement is made in health plans without these exact, by-the-number, *DSM-III-R* classifications.

DSM-III-R grows and changes, begrudgingly at times, as a result of new discoveries and increased research, clinical data, and arm-twisting. There was a time when homosexuality itself was considered a mental disorder by the APA. The APA deleted the "disorder" of homosexuality when the gay civil rights movement brought gay men out of the closet and they confronted anti-gay bigotry in the APA. This political victory is still challenged by homophobic and homohating professionals around the nation. Many women, feminists in particular, are critical of the APA and its *DSM-III-R*, wary of the oppressive and arbitrary tendency to mislabel and subjugate women. Gays are similarly suspicious.

In the area of domestic violence, we feel that the APA and *DSM* editions are dangerously out of touch with reality. Domestic violence affects between 15 million and 25 million people in America annually. Yet, nothing remotely resembling psychodiagnostic categories expressly for this widespread aberration is present in *DSM*. Drug, alcohol, and even reading disorders have merited abundant exposure, however.

We sincerely hope that sets of Battering Disorder classifications will soon appear in the pages of *DSM*. We recognize that men who batter, especially gay men who batter, are a very difficult group to study, a point validated by Gondolf (1988, p. 8), who calls batterers an "elusive population." These men remain hidden, despite their large numbers, and do not readily present themselves to psychiatrists or to mental health clinics. Thus, it is hard to obtain data on them. Most of what is known about men who batter comes from their victims. This is true both for straight and gay abusers. We realize that before domestic battering can be included as a set of disorders in *DSM*, sufficient numbers of gay and straight male batterers need to be studied both in research projects and in clinics delivering treatment. In the last ten years, some research on heterosexual batterers has emerged. We hope that the motivation to do much more research will be furthered by our advocating *DSM* status for abuse disorders.

The Need for Psychodiagnostic Categories for Abuse

With so many people affected by the phenomenon of domestic violence, something needs to be done immediately to lessen the problem, provide services for abusers, and protect victims.

DSM's definition of a mental disorder. The *DSM-III-R* definition of a mental disorder should require that battering in its various forms be so classified. According to *DSM-III-R* , a mental disorder is:

> A clinically significant, behavioral, psychological, or physical syndrome or pattern, that is associated with a present distress (a painful symptom), or a disability (impairment in one or more important areas of functioning), or a significantly increased risk of death, pain, disability or important loss of freedom. . . . it must currently be considered a manifestation of a behavioral, psychological or physical dysfunction in the person. (APA, 1987, p. xxii)

Most batterer conduct just before, right after, and during violence would easily be deemed as fitting precisely into that definition. We cannot think of one other mental health problem in America that cries out more obviously for recognition and inclusion in the one volume that might help most in its eradication.

Current methods are failures. The current approach used to stop domestic violence is clearly not working. Conservatively speaking there are at least 7 million batterers in the United States, straight and gay, men and women. How many are receiving treatment? At best, 10,000 batterers per year (approximately 0.1 percent) have contact with some kind of treatment program. A one-thousand-fold increase is needed in the amount of batterer treatment, a result not likely to occur with our present methods.

Clearly, the present "system" does not work, in part because there is no real acknowledgment in the legislatures of our state governments and in the psychological, medical, mental health, and law enforcement communities that the problem is real. The position, fashionable in some mental health circles, that battering is not a mental illness may be little more than societal denial of a serious mental health problem.

Professional entrepreneurism. The biggest reason to include Abuse Disorders in future editions of *DSM* is to increase the availability of treatment for batterers. We propose that some of the treatment ought to be turned over to the professional, treatment-providing entrepreneurs. Professional treatment providers ought to be reimbursed for the treatment of batterers who claim the expense on their health insurance plans. Proper *DSM* Abuse or Domestic Violence Batterer Disorder categories are needed for that to happen. It is no accident that so many drug abuse and alcohol abuse categories are included in *DSM-III-R*. They exist so that therapists and other treatment providers can get paid for doing treatment. Using mental disorder classifications has become a common and perfectly acceptable method for dealing with psychosocial problems in America.

Research. *DSM* categories of mental disorders stimulate important research. In the first seven years following the publication of *DSM-III*, over 2,000 articles that directly addressed some aspect of it appeared in the scientific literature. Research in domestic violence will become a more fully legitimate enterprise after Batterer Disorders are added to *DSM*.

Naming the violence. It is vital that domestic violence as a problem should be named for what it is: criminal and abnormal conduct. Powerful clinical and political volumes (such as *DSM*) are important formal mechanisms to name this problem. The experience of Mothers Against Drunk Driving (MADD) provides an excellent example of the proper naming of a problem. MADD dramatically changed the public's attitudes about drunk driving, has caused increased criminal penalties to be enacted, and has stimulated creative approaches to solving the problems caused by drunk drivers. We think that the exact same thing needs to happen with domestic violence.

CURRENT PSYCHODIAGNOSTIC CATEGORIES

Until such time as Domestic Battering becomes a *DSM* category, there are six existing *DSM-III-R* categories for mental health workers to use in diagnosing batterers, five which are applicable and acceptable only to a small proportion of batterers and one that seems very applicable to greater numbers. However, the most acceptable category, the Sadistic Personality Disorder, has three serious defects and remains today only in a "proposed" status. It can be found in Appendix A of *DSM-III-R* (APA, 1987, p. 369).

1. Organic Personality Syndrome (310.10). This classification requires confirmation of specific damage to the brain, and as such it would not include the overwhelming majority of male batterers who have absolutely no organic flaw. We would not expect this classification to apply realistically to any more than one percent of the male batterers (APA, 1987, pp. 114-116).
2. Conduct Disorder, Solitary Aggressive Type (312.00). Conduct disorder is useful because it has roots in early development, but, therefore, it is used mainly to diagnose children and adolescents. Its essential feature is the predominance of aggressive physical behavior. Interestingly, Conduct Disorder is very prevalent, existing in an estimated nine percent of American males under the age of 18, or 5.5 million individuals. Criteria (only three of which need to be present for diagnosis) include: theft; lying; destroying others' property; forcing someone to have sex; using a weapon in a fight; initiating fights; and being physically cruel to people. This would be the easiest disorder on which to classify a batterer, especially a young abuser. We think that no more than five to ten percent of batterers would best be classified with this disorder,

because, in part, of its age-specific orientation (APA, 1987, pp. 53-56).

3. Intermittent Explosive Disorder (312.34). As the name suggests, this is an impulse control disorder and therefore carries characteristics similar to Pathological Gambling, Pyromania, and Kleptomania. In this category, the individual experiences episodes of loss of control of aggressive impulses which end up in serious assaultive acts and/or destruction of property. While on the surface, these descriptors sound like behaviors of a male batterer, and indeed they are, the diagnostic criteria for this disorder are much too general to account for what we believe is the more specific and more patterned personality profile of batterers. Since most clinicians do not think that impulse control is a problem for most batterers (batterers are rational and know what they are doing at all times), we would not expect this classification to apply realistically to any more than five percent of the male batterers (APA, 1987, pp. 321-322).

4. Borderline Personality Disorder (301.83) The essential feature of this disorder is a pervasive instability of self-image, interpersonal relationships, and mood. As such, it speaks only tangentially to typical batterer conduct, specifically: impulsiveness in at least two areas that are potentially self-damaging (such as shoplifting); inappropriate, intense anger or lack of control of anger (frequent displays of temper, constant anger, recurrent physical fights); recurrent suicidal threats, gestures or behavior; and frantic efforts to avoid real or imagined abandonment. We think that only two to five percent of gay male batterers would meet the required five of eight diagnostic criteria in this disorder (APA, 1987, pp. 346-347).

5. Antisocial Personality Disorder (301.70). This category comes close, at times, to describing the condition of battering, except that it is too closely tied to a pre-existing adolescent conduct disorder and it contains too many specific criteria which may not apply to large numbers of batterers. However, this classification specifically mentions aggression and spouse-beating as criteria. The definition suggests that this disorder is prevalent in about three percent of the males in

America (2.5 million men), but it also is likely to be a young man's disorder, diminishing after age 30. Domestic violence knows no such age limitation. All in all, we would expect this classification to apply realistically to no more than five percent of the male batterers, and possibly even fewer gay male batterers (APA, 1987, pp. 342-346).

6. Sadistic Personality Disorder (301.90). The diagnostic criteria for Sadistic Personality Disorder are reprinted from *DSM-III-R* by permission of the APA (APA, 1987, p. 371).

The major feature of this disorder is the pattern of cruel aggressive behavior toward others with the goal of establishing dominance. In over half of gay male battering cases, we hypothesize that five of the eight listed criteria shown will be present. (Only four of the criteria are required to be present for a proper diagnosis of this condition.) Most gay male abusers (1) use physical cruelty or violence; (2) humiliate or demean their victims in the presence of oth-

---

Diagnostic criteria for Sadistic Personality Disorder

A. A pervasive pattern of cruel, demeaning, and aggressive behavior, beginning by early adulthood, as indicated by the repeated occurrence of at least four of the following.

(1) has used physical cruelty or violence for the purpose of establishing dominance in a relationship (not merely to achieve some noninterpersonal goal, such as striking someone in order to rob him or her)

(2) humiliates or demeans people in the presence of others

(3) has treated or disciplined someone under his or her control unusually harshly, *e.g.*, a child, student, prisoner, or patient

(4) is amused by, or takes pleasure in, the psychological or physical suffering of others (including animals)

(5) has lied for the purpose of harming or inflicting pain on others (not merely to achieve some other goal)

(6) gets other people to do what he or she wants by frightening them (through intimidation or even terror)

(7) restricts the autonomy of people with whom he or she has a close relationship, *e.g.*, will not let spouse leave the house unaccompanied or permit teen-age daughter to attend social functions

(8) is fascinated by violence, weapons, martial arts, injury, or torture

B. The behavior in A has not been directed toward only one person (*e.g.*, spouse, one child) and has not been solely for the purpose of sexual arousal (as in Sexual Sadism).

Note: For coding purposes, record: 301.90 Personality Disorder NOS (Sadistic Personality Disorder).

ers; (3) lie; (4) intimidate and terrorize their victims; and (5) restrict the autonomy of those with whom they are in close relationship. Especially noteworthy in the diagnostic criteria are the mention of "establishing dominance," and getting "other people to do what he or she wants by frightening them (through intimidation or even terror)." These criteria describe accurately the ongoing atmosphere of fear and intimidation created by a batterer, an environment that needs only occasional violence, or threat of violence, to be maintained.

In the discussion in *DSM-III-R*, it is pointed out that the sadistic behavior is often directed toward family members but seldom displayed in contacts with those in higher authority, an observation in which we concur regarding the gay male batterer. The discussion goes on to describe a person with Sadistic Personality Disorder as incapable of showing respect or empathy for others: again, a correct description of gay male abusers, but only toward their partners, especially during abusive incidents, and even more readily apparent as the frequency and severity of violence increases over time (APA, 1987, pp. 369-371).

Three Problems

The category of Sadistic Personality Disorder has three flaws. First is the title. It is not clear why the word Sadistic is in the title. As the disorder is described in Part A, sadism is not a central feature (if sadistic means to "gain cruel pleasure"), or even a theme in the totality of all the criteria. Particularly in gay men's domestic violence, there is no sadistic (or masochistic) element. If this category becomes a standard for domestic violence disorders, we suggest that the word Abusive or the word Battering replace the word Sadistic in the title and that Criterion #4 be eliminated.

The second flaw is the unfortunate, restrictive first part of Part B. We see no defendable reason why abuse directed toward "only one person" would rule out a diagnosis. The occurrence of numerous violent incidents, over time, even if "only" directed toward a mate, seems to us to qualify a perpetrator amply for diagnosis with this disorder. A violent person should not be kept from proper diagnosis and treatment because he has been abusive to only one partner at a time! At any rate, a clinician using the current disorder could easily circumvent this unfortunate restriction in most cases by identifying prior battering of another person on the part of the perpetrator.

The third flaw is the exclusion of important criteria. For new abuse or battering disorders, we would add at least four additional criteria: (1) frantic efforts to avoid real or imagined abandonment; (2) use of unwanted physical force, or unwanted sexual behavior, or various forms of psychological abuse, or unwanted destruction of material property; (3) persistent blaming of the victim for having "provoked" the violence; and, (4) shows progression of violent conduct over time from less to more severe.

It is our hope that until special classifications for domestic battering are created, the necessary systematic research and clinical study will be pursued with vigor on Sadistic Personality Disorder so that it will be elevated out of its current proposed status into the main body of the manual for the next edition of *DSM*, with our suggested changes. Because this is the disorder that, we expect, at least 50 percent of male batterers suffer from, it can and should be used now.

THE PROGRESSIVE DISORDER OF BATTERING: DIAGNOSIS, NOT ACCUSATION

The following section is a proposed theory of perpetrator behavior. This theory makes no assumption about the origin and causes of perpetrator behavior and violence. Causation could be from an organic disorder, from a developmental failure, from a personality defect, or from any other of a number of societal and individual factors or combination of factors. Our purpose is to outline parsimoniously the elements of the theory in very discrete units for ease of research. A discussion follows at the end.

1. There is a pre-existing tendency in the abuser to desire and attempt to manipulate, control, and dominate others, especially the partner — and to succeed.
   a. The batterer tends to control and dominate the behavior, speech, decisions, thoughts, general activities, circle of

friends, spending patterns, clothing choices, reading material, and eating habits of the victim.

b. Over time, the perpetrator increases his efforts to widen the circle of control to include more and more of the victim's life.

c. Attempts by the victim to resist the control and domination are met with anger, criticism, accusations about how argumentative and defensive the victim is, and, possibly, more violence.

d. The abuser shows an overall pattern of lack of respect for—and, over time, an increasing inability to empathize with—the victim.

2. There is a pattern for the violence and abuse to become progressively more serious.

a. The perpetrator's violent behavior will become progressively more intense, frequent and severe, regardless of the level at which the violence began.

b. If untreated, the violence may progress such that the perpetrator may permanently injure or kill his partner.

c. Perpetrators are incapable of halting the progression toward more severe violence without outside intervention and assistance.

3. The abuser usually shows a pronounced difficulty managing his own frustration, anger, patience, and impulses toward the victim.

4. The abuser has a specific tendency to restrict the autonomy of people with whom he has a close relationship, especially the partner.

a. The abuser will interrogate the partner about his activities, both before they occur and after.

b. The abuser will actively discourage victim freedom and independence, especially the formation of independent friendships and relationships.

5. There is a pattern in the batterer to use cruel, demeaning, and aggressive behavior toward and actual violence against the partner. The violence will take the form of any one or any combination of the three types of domestic violence.

a. The abuser will use unwanted physical force on the partner, including unwanted sexual behavior.

b. The perpetrator will employ various forms of psychological abuse, including many forms of intimidation and terror, such that he creates a pervasive atmosphere of intimidation and fear for the victim.

c. The abuser will destroy, damage, or discard the material property of the victim.

6. Before violence, there is a discernible decision-making pattern in the perpetrator (Sinclair, 1990), which reveals a premeditated intent to commit violence.

a. The perpetrator decides to objectify his lover with demeaning, depersonalizing names prior to violence.

b. The perpetrator decides to pursue (chase) his lover, physically or verbally or both.

c. The perpetrator decides to inflict physical (including sexual), psychological, or material abuse.

d. The time required for the decision-making cycle is unrelated to the seriousness of the abuse and to when the abuse occurs.

7. The batterer has a pressing need to keep secret the fact and extent of the violence. The perpetrator cajoles the victim or threatens more violence if the victim expresses interest in revealing information about the violence to outsiders.

8. The batterer shows a strong pattern of always justifying his violence by blaming the victim for having provoked it.

9. The batterer usually shows a certain personality profile, including, but not limited to, a tendency toward:

a. Low self-esteem;

b. Self-hatred, perhaps with internalized homophobia;

c. Depression, perhaps chronic depression;

d. Minimizing and trivializing his own violent actions;

e. An ability to deny responsibility for his own violent actions;

f. Holding exceedingly high expectations for self, partner, and relationships;

g. Suspiciousness;

h. Jealousy, perhaps pathological jealousy;

i. Extreme criticism and judgment of others;

j. Extreme insecurity and inability to trust others;

k. Lying;

l. A fascination with violence of all kinds, weapons, martial arts, injury, and torture;

m. A "Jekyll-and-Hyde" type of personality;

n. Strong feelings of guilt and failure.

10. There is a pattern of extreme emotional dependency by the perpetrator on the victim.

   a. The perpetrator perceives the victim as the sole provider for his emotional needs including sexual, conversational, intellectual, companionship and even financial.

   b. The perpetrator's reliance on the victim for emotional support can be so complete that he will engage in violence and abuse (including murder) to keep the victim captive.

11. The perpetrator has a strong tendency to obsess about the victim such that over time a significant proportion of the perpetrator's thinking is consumed with thoughts about the victim.

   a. Such obsession is exacerbated when the victim either threatens leaving or succeeds in leaving.

   b. When the victim leaves, the perpetrator's frantic and dogged pursuit of and attempts to contact the victim are driven in part by the obsession.

12. The abuser has an identifiable life history, a history that fits some or all of the elements in the pattern below. The most important elements — those expected to be the most powerful predictors of future violent behavior — are listed first. The batterer, most likely:

   a. Has a history of prior battering and has engaged in prior abuse in his relationships;

   b. Was abused routinely as a child, by an adult, probably a parent;

   c. Was abused on occasion as a child by a parent;

   d. Witnessed routine physical and psychological abuse as a child;

   e. Had a father who abused the child's mother or siblings;

   f. Had a father who abused non-family members;

    g. Has a history of being cruel, demeaning, or violent with others;

    h. Was abused by his mother;

    i. Was neglected as a child and may have "hunger attachment" syndrome;

    j. Is (or was) alienated from father and/or mother;

    k. Has a history of alcohol abuse.

13. The abuser may show a pattern of some or frequent life disappointment or perceived failure in relationships, school, occupation, finance, love, family, and the general circumstance of living.

14. There is a pattern of poor communication skills, especially in relation to feelings and conflict resolution.

15. There is a specific tendency in the batterer to have unusually rigid and unachievable, stereotyped concepts of masculinity and sex-roles.

16. The batterer has some mental disorder, state or condition, from many possible causes or origins, as indicated by episodes of domestic violence of which he is the perpetrator.

    a. This condition is diagnosable under the current accepted standard of practice and the state of knowledge in the mental health professions.

    b. This condition may be, in its least dysfunctional form, a decision-making impairment in emotionally-loaded situations.

17. There is a strong tendency in the abuser not to display violence or his violent tendencies toward people in positions of authority or higher status.

    a. The abuser may have a tendency to choose partners whom he thinks he can control and intimidate.

18. The batterer has a strong resistance to receiving or seeking help from outside sources and instead evidences a need for, and over-reliance on help and support from the victim.

The theory outlined above describes the pattern of behavior, background, personality, and tendencies in gay men who abuse their lovers. The theory is designed to stimulate research on the topic so that a body of data can be created to understand gay men who batter. Except for our position on the mental disorder of the batterer, these 18 propositions represent a compilation of the best and most reliable information about batterer profiles available. We predict that when carefully applied, the elements in the theory will accurately describe the vast majority of gay men who batter their mates.

What is described in the theory, however, is the disorder, not so much the people. We also understand that it is individual men who have the disorder of battering, not groups. As such, each person will have his own profile of background, behavior, and deviance. Some, for instance, will show a greater proclivity for dominance and control, others less. We would expect very few to exhibit all elements of the model. Some batterers will not have had any history of prior violence, but most will.

This theory is a working model to be used and investigated until a better, more refined one is developed. We welcome suggestions for its improvement. We particularly look forward to the day when a great body of reliable data has been generated from the study of gay male batterers, so that the progressive disorder of battering can be said to rest upon a solid base of research data and clinical experience.

TREATMENT PROGRAMS

The purposes of this book do not specifically include a detailed discussion of treatment programs for gay male batterers. We are deeply concerned about the issue, however. The legal approach our society takes toward batterers, and the treatment it prescribes, are vital issues, and we want to influence both.

No one really seems to know quite what to do with batterers in treatment. Three organizations in the United States (in New York City, San Francisco, and Seattle) provide treatment for gay male batterers, and these programs are embryonic. They have provided services to fewer than 500 gay men. They are valued pioneers but their programs are not necessarily models.

In the more established area of straight batterer treatment, points of view, treatment strategies, and intervention philosophies change rapidly. Therapy, treatment, imprisonment, education, counseling—what should the approach be? Our position is that everything is needed. Batterers are people in serious psychological, legal, and interpersonal trouble, and a limited approach is not going to meet with success. With awareness and education, some batterers will alter their behavior. Many will require jail time. All need to make amends to their victims. Still others will need to be sued in civil court by their ex-victims to recover monetary damages for injury and destruction of property. Some will need intensive individual or group therapy. Most will require treatment in groups to re-socialize them so that they stop their abusive conduct. Sex-role and masculinity concept restructuring will need to occur. All batterers need to learn, probably for the first time, how to make decisions to be non-violent in emotionally-charged situations. Re-education is necessary. Communication skills need to be acquired, as all batterers need to learn better ways to resolve conflict with their next mates.

How long does this take? Phyllis Frank, at the Volunteer Counseling Services of Rockland County, Incorporated, in New City, New York, after years of experience in treating batterers now believes that batterers need a minimum of one to two *years* in treatment (Frank and Engleken, 1990).

William Gondolf, in the most comprehensive and current review of research on batterers in the United States, writes, "We have to proceed as if batterer programs [for straight men] were still very much laboratories" (1988, p. 11). He further declares that the main problems in all batterer programs are "low recruitment and high dropout rates" (1988, p. 8). And, of those in treatment, recidivism is more common than not. The Seattle Counseling Center for Sexual Minorities dispassionately looked at its data on treatment of batterers and found an 85 percent recidivism rate (Farley, 1990). Gondolf confirms that little impact is achieved on batterers with the current approaches (1988, pp. 8-9).

Batterer treatment programs are in total disarray. Of the 150 treatment programs in the country, 59 percent used multiple counseling formats with 17 different treatment approaches. Gondolf concludes that "our research has been limited by small samples, questionable assessment instruments, unstated biases or the absence of fundamental theory" (1988, p. 3).

In other words, a batterer treatment program in Florida will not look anything like one in Los Angeles. Even within a facility, there is apparently little agreement on how best to help batterers stop their violence. The theories that translate into useful stop-violence programs are often characterized by political rhetoric. As a result, today there is almost no widely accepted base of knowledge about batterers on which to construct effective stop-battering treatment programs. Treatment programs do not reach any significant number of batterers, and there is real doubt that treatment works anyway, especially since dropouts are the norm.

A FINAL WORD ON ACCOUNTABILITY

Important work has begun in Minneapolis to conceptualize behavioral outcome measures which gauge the effectiveness of treatment for lesbian batterers. Beth Zemsky and Luan Gilbert, who work in the Lesbian and Gay Counseling Program at the Family and Children's Service of Minneapolis, have postulated an accountability matrix that specifies unambiguous measures which show how accountability has been accomplished by the batterer and by the gay community. Their fundamental assumption is that batterers must accept responsibility for their actions and the consequences of their actions. These two mental health workers also contend that the gay community is accountable to us all, especially for its silence and complicity in minimization and denial of the problem.

Their work is noteworthy for its unwavering allegiance to the principle that all perpetrators choose violence (Zemsky and Gilbert, 1990).

Zemsky and Gilbert state that all lesbian batterers are accountable to the survivor [victim] to:

1. Talk about the abusive behaviors without denying or minimizing the extent, frequency, or severity of the abuse that occurred.
2. Acknowledge that we alone are responsible for choosing our abusive behaviors.
3. Acknowledge that there are consequences to the relationship with the survivor because of the abuse (i.e., that the survivor's

fear and lack of trust are legitimate consequences stemming from the abuse).

4. Make amends to the survivor. This includes, but is not limited to, direct apologies and financial reimbursement for costs directly or indirectly related to the abuse.
5. Respect the boundaries or limits set by the survivor. Take the survivor's probable emotional reactions (e.g., fear) into account when making decisions about activities.
6. Acknowledge that the desire or promise to change is not enough and that it is improbable that lasting change will take place without assistance from others. Make a commitment to learn and practice new skills to manage our abuse and interact non-abusively.

They further specify that batterers are accountable to the (gay) community to:

1. Take responsibility for telling others about the abuse we have perpetrated without denying or minimizing.
2. Take full responsibility for having been abusive and acknowledge that the choice to be abusive is our choice alone and had nothing to do with our partner or "relationship dynamics."
3. Make amends to any secondary victims and the affected community. This includes direct apologies and financial reimbursement when appropriate.
4. Acknowledge that there are consequences to friendship networks due to the abusive behavior.
5. Ask for help to change from professionals and friends and make a commitment to integrate new behaviors into all our interactions. (Zemsky and Gilbert, 1990, p. 1, cited here by permission of authors)

Zemsky and Gilbert's radical accountability scheme gets to many of the roots of the problem. Violence is a choice that all batterers make. It is unacceptable and must end. Batterers must stop denying and trivializing their actions, and acknowledge that their actions alone cause tremendous relationship consequences. Of special interest is the correct requirement that the abusive partner make amends to the victim. We believe it is time that responsible people in this country require of those who destroy that they replace, fix, or reimburse the damage and apologize to those they have injured.

We are concerned that no mention is made of the criminal aspects of battering in this accountability matrix. Accountability must include acceptance by the batterer of all criminal consequences. These might include, at a minimum, acceptance of arrest, jail time, restraining order restrictions, and a public admission by the batterer that he or she understands and admits to the illegality of his or her conduct. We are also concerned that little acknowledgment is present in this accountability matrix for the obvious mentally unhealthy behavior of the batterer.

With the inclusion of criminal conduct accountability and recognition of the mental health component, we urge all interventionists who treat batterers to adopt the no-nonsense approach postulated by Zemsky and Gilbert. Battering will cease only when abusers learn that their unhealthy and unacceptable behavior will not be condoned and that the responsible people in our society require them to fix the damage they caused, take the consequences for their conduct, and learn more appropriate behavior.

Chapter IV

Who Are the Victims?

I STRIKE FIRST

*The first time I hit Stephen **first** in an argument is in April, 1987, about a year and a half after the abuse has started. We are arguing about I-don't-remember-what while in the apartment of our friends, Timothy and Alexandra, and I can feel the tension escalating. We are pacing around, shouting back and forth, getting louder and angrier. Stephen assumes what I later come to recognize as his "violent stance": he stands about five feet away, facing me, his feet spread apart about shoulder width, his arms at his sides, not limp, but slightly forward, and his fists clenched. But this time as he comes toward me he is saying, "C'mon Patrick, hit me! Just hit me! Go on – hit me!" He is shouting this, standing right up against me, shouting, shouting. This continues, and I begin to panic, as I know what Stephen is capable of. I am pacing around, feeling extremely angry and anxious; Stephen is really pushing me to hit him.*

Part of me wants so badly to hit him, to hit him so hard, and yet I am afraid to meet his challenge. I know he is manipulating me. He persists, "C'mon, Patrick! You know you want to hit me! Why don't you just hit me? Go on. Hit me. HIT ME!" Finally I hit him. Again and again and again. I feel completely out of control. He puts his arms up to protect his head, and I hit him in the head, in the face, on his sides, on his back. I pound on his back. Stephen runs out of the apartment onto the landing, and I follow and continue to hit him, pounding and pounding.

And then I stop. The anger and rage passes, and it is over. Stephen is sullen and numb; he walks back into the apartment, in silence, puts his coat on and leaves. I stand on the landing, dazed, exhausted. Hitting Stephen is almost as bad as being hit myself. I feel guilty and ashamed. I know how awful it is to be hit, and now I have done that to someone. It is worse being the abuser (for me), because I have to accept responsibility for my actions, and I find my actions to be despicable.

Worse yet, a barrier has been broken in me: I have struck first.

One of the main points of "I Strike First" is that the use of violence is always a choice. Patrick must accept responsibility for his violent behavior. Despite Stephen's baiting and harassments, Patrick cannot claim that he has been provoked into violence or that Stephen causes him to be violent. The barrier that Patrick breaks here is in choosing to be violent.

A second, and perhaps more subtle, phenomenon addressed in this incident is the apparent but not actual exchange of roles between victim and batterer. Patrick has abused Stephen. So, are both men batterers? Are both men victims? The answer to both questions is "No." One battering incident does not make a batterer out of a victim. Here is a victim who has chosen to be violent, and a batterer who has been abused. Their roles, however, do not change, because their roles are not determined by who hits whom. Rather, it is the significant imbalance of power in a relationship that ultimately determines which person is the victim and which is the batterer.

This victim-batterer dichotomy is somehow easier for us to recognize and understand when the two people involved are not of the same sex. For example, a battered heterosexual woman who, after 18 months of abuse, attacks her husband/batterer as Patrick did is still considered a battered woman, a victim of domestic violence. One violent incident cannot shift the power imbalance in the relationship such that roles change. This woman does not suddenly become the all-powerful batterer, nor is her husband suddenly rendered helpless and powerless.

With two men in a relationship, however, the roles of victim and batterer may appear blurry to an outsider. This apparent blurriness can make it difficult for counselors, therapists, medical personnel, police, or friends of the couple to determine which man is the victim and which the batterer. Again, the issue is power. The batterer is not necessarily the person doing the hitting, but he is always the person with the power in the relationship. The victim/batterer power imbalance is still present and unchanged even when a victim behaves violently.

In this incident then, Stephen, despite being attacked, is still very much a batterer. In fact, it is highly likely that he will use this incident to "justify" more frequent or more severe violence against Patrick in the future.

VICTIMS ARE UNCLEAR ON THE CONCEPT OF RESPONSIBILITY

Victims of domestic violence, contrary to popular belief, are often strong and powerful people who are in control of every aspect of their lives, except that they are in a relationship with an abusive partner. How is it then, that intelligent, influential, powerful men can become victims of domestic violence? A central theme in the answers to this question is that victims are unclear on the concept of responsibility.

Victims of gay men's domestic violence may demonstrate a strong and potentially harmful tendency toward over-responsibility. They may accept and live under the burden of a responsibility for conditions in their lives that are actually far beyond their control. Over-responsibility is most clearly seen in victims' accepting blame for the violence perpetrated by their partners. This belief, of course, only contributes further to their victimization, and is followed, naturally, by the belief that the cessation of violence also rests on their shoulders. Over-responsibility saddles the victim with the psychological strain of both self-blame and of "walking on eggs" to prevent more violence.

Many victims of domestic violence also believe that they are responsible for their batterer's feelings or state of mind. For example, if the batterer is relaxed, the victim believes he is the cause. If the batterer is depressed or angry, the victim believes he is the cause. As a result, victims may exert a tremendous amount of energy trying to "make" a depressed lover happy, or an angry lover calm.

Victims may also accept sole responsibility for making their relationship a success. If they experience problems with their batterer (a given), they may think it is up to them to resolve the difficulties and get things back to a steady and pleasant state. Since the batterer has made his violent method of problem-solving all too clear, any nonviolent conflict resolutions are, the victim assumes, his own responsibility.

Finally, many gay males may, for a variety of rational and healthy reasons, accept financial responsibility for their lover-batterer. In certain circumstances, however, financial responsibility for the couple may be used to restrict and victimize the wage-earner.

Thus, here is the gay male victim, behaving responsibly, at least in his own eyes. He takes on the responsibility both for being battered and for preventing further battery. He feels responsible for how his lover feels and behaves. He believes it is up to him to make the relationship work and perhaps even to earn enough money to support both of them. No man, of course, can be expected to handle this. With the pressure of all this responsibility, something, as the saying goes, has got to give. What victims of gay men's domestic violence give, or more accurately "give up," are their responsibilities to themselves.

Many victims, while overresponsible for their batterers and for events beyond their control, demonstrate an underresponsibility in looking after themselves. They may neglect their own safety, mental health, or the fulfillment of their own needs, desires, and life-ambitions. For example, a gay male victim may quit school and work two jobs to put his lover/batterer through college. The victim thwarts his own plans for higher education to meet the batterer's needs. In their efforts to fix their failing relationships, victims may zealously try to "change" or "improve" themselves in the eyes of their batterers, expending the time and energy they could spend on pursuing their own goals.

It would be unfair and inaccurate, however, to say that all victims neglect their safety needs by staying with their violent partners. On the contrary, for many victims, staying with their abusive partners and struggling to control the violence *is* their strategy for survival. In many cases, leaving or attempting to leave is truly more dangerous than staying. Although we understand and acknowledge the seemingly insurmountable difficulties victims face in leaving their partners, we contend, nonetheless, that the ultimate responsibility for leaving their partners and living an abuse-free life is the victim's. Until victims of gay men's domestic violence accept this responsibility as their own, they will never leave their partners.

Furthermore, victims must accept responsibility for deciding *when* to leave their partners. Difficult and dangerous as leaving may be, victims must acknowledge that the longer they stay in relationships with violent partners, the harder it will be to get away. Unless a victim is saving money, plotting, planning, or in some other way actively working on a way to get out, he is failing to accept the responsibility to leave. Victims choose not only *to* leave their partners, but also *when* to leave.

Finally, victims must take responsibility for any illusions they maintain in order to stay in the relationship. The notions that the violence will stop, or that the batterer will change, or that further violence can be prevented, are all illusions. Reality demonstrates that, while involved with their victims, batterers do not change; violence continues with increasing frequency and severity, and victims remain powerless to stop it. Victims must accept their false hopes as such, and in so doing, acknowledge that leaving the relationship is their only real hope of ending the violence in their lives.

Victims of gay men's domestic violence clearly exhibit a skewed sense of responsibility. On the one hand, they accept responsibility for many of the aspects of their lives that they cannot control. On the other hand, they neglect their responsibilities to themselves and deny the control they exercise over their own fates. The victim alone creates the opportunity for an exit. Unless he makes the effort to get out, again and again if necessary, he will never escape. Ultimately, the key to escaping from an abusive partner and never returning may be in the victim's shifting his sense of responsibility from his batterer to himself.

WHO ARE THE VICTIMS?

What kinds of men are victims of gay men's domestic violence? Do they have common personality traits? Can they be spotted before they become victims? Are victims as troubled as their battering mates are — merely the other half of a well-matched, deviant pair? Are victims predisposed to a life of victimization through some quirk of fate or a childhood tragedy? What can be said about them and what kinds of research can be conducted so that they can understand themselves better and so that they can receive effective, short-term treatment from domestic violence mental health professionals when they finally leave their abusive lovers?

We assert that victims of gay men's domestic violence, by and large, are not preprogrammed or predisposed to become victims. They do not suffer from any mental disorder, except as a result of being coupled with abusive partners. Gay men who become victims of domestic violence generally are normal, healthy men. They indeed experience serious problems as a consequence of being battered, one of which is their apparent inability to leave their violent partners.

Most victims of gay men's domestic violence, then, are neither predisposed to become victims nor are they mentally ill prior to abuse. Of course, among any large group of people there will be those who suffer from one kind of mental disorder or other. There will be those few victims who unwittingly seek out batterers, so that they continue a lifetime of preprogrammed misery and victimization. These few men are undoubtedly suffering from a type of mental disorder, but we would expect that they constitute no more than one or two percent of the total victim population of gay men's domestic violence. Many members of both the gay and straight community would like to believe that victims choose a life of victimization, that victims seek batterers, and that victims and batterers magically find themselves and deserve what they get. Such thinking is depraved and is fed by a total misunderstanding of the phenomenon of domestic violence. Victims do not choose violence. Abusers do.

HOW ARE VICTIMS CREATED?

Abuse creates victims. Batterers create victims. Victims simply would not exist were it not for batterers. Domestic violence perpetrated by the abuser creates the conditions for victimization. Batterers have a proclivity to violence. Victims do not have a proclivity to victimization. Victimization does not happen to the victims all by itself.

Because of the proclivity to violence in the batterer, we assert that it is far easier for a victim to become an ex-victim (and, thus, never experience abuse again in his life) than it is for an abuser to become an ex-abuser. The reader must not make the mistake of thinking of victims and batterers together in the same psychological package. They are not men coupled helplessly together as if according to some conjoint theory of domestic violence psychology. There is not a tight, symbiotic psychological explanation for their behavior.

At this point in the development of victim theory, it is much better to view the victim as having an entirely separate psychology from the batterer, and we discourage attempts to link up the victim's psychology with that of the batterer. The victim is coping in order to survive, and that makes all the difference. (See Chapter IX for elaboration on this point.)

The following list suggests the proper point of view for understanding how victims are created.

Situations That Create Victims
- Airplane crashes create victims
- Robberies create victims
- Concentration camps create victims
- War creates victims
- Earthquakes create victims
- Congenital defects create victims
- Institutionalized discrimination policies create victims
- Racism and homophobia create victims

In none of the above situations would any clear-thinking person claim that the victim caused the problem that created his being a victim. No one would suggest that the victim had some psychological condition that lent itself to his becoming a victim. Obviously, no one would look at the victim of an earthquake and say, "What did you do to cause this earthquake?"

The next list identifies people who create victims, a second necessary step to develop the proper point of view to understand how victims are created.

People Who Create Victims
- Terrorists create victims
- Kidnappers create victims
- Murderers create victims
- Rapists create victims
- Nazis created victims

- Gay bashers create victims
- Thieves create victims
- Criminals create victims
- Batterers create victims
- Violent gay men who abuse their lovers create victims

By definition, victims do not create themselves. Victims of gay men's domestic violence are exactly like other victims caused by the violent action of people. Their victimization resulted from the actions of others, not from action or inaction on their part. None of the victims listed above invited the violence, deserved the violence or was psychologically predisposed to having it happen to him. No innocent gay man walking home at night can be accused of desiring violence done to him by a gay basher. None of the above had a personality defect, a character flaw, or a life pattern that doomed him to victimization. Were it not for the behavior of violent gay men, there would be no victims of gay men's domestic violence.

WHY DO THEY STAY?

For many people, perhaps the most incomprehensible aspect of domestic violence, straight or gay, is why the victim stays with an abusive partner. Why does the victim remain, tolerating what seems to be a never-ending rainstorm of physical and psychological abuse? Why not just pack up and leave? Why not just walk out the door the first time it happens?

In attempting to answer these questions, several of the myths surrounding domestic violence come into play. For example, the myth that victims enjoy the violence they experience provides one answer: "He stays because he likes it." The myth that victims provoke abuse provides another answer: "He stays because he provokes his lover into beating him, and he gets what he deserves." These "answers," grossly inaccurate as they of course are, provide insight into the utter lack of awareness and understanding in our society of the phenomenon of domestic violence, particularly of the predicament victims face in attempting to escape their abusive partners.

The fact is, nobody knows for sure why battered gay men stay with their abusive partner. Each gay male victim, of course, has his own set of reasons for staying with his batterer, and unfortunately, no research, statistics, or literature exists to help answer the question. What is helpful, however, is an understanding of the dynamics involved in domestic violence.

An examination of the considerable literature on battered women provides a sturdy foundation on which theories about battered gay men can be built. Four pioneers in the field of domestic violence, Lenore E. Walker, Del Martin, Ginny NiCarthy, and Angela Browne, have addressed in their research and writing the issue of why battered women stay with their abusive partners.

The Cycle of Violence

In her book, *The Battered Woman*, Lenore Walker details a cycle of violence theory that we believe applies not only to heterosexual couples, but also to lesbian and gay male couples. According to this theory, derived from interviews with hundreds of battered women and the people who work with them, domestic violence operates in a three-phase cycle: the tension-building phase; the explosion or acute battering incident; and the calm, loving respite. In summary, minor battering incidents and escalating tension in phase one lead to a serious explosive violent episode in phase two. This acute battering incident is followed by the "make-up," or honeymoon period, phase three. In phase three, the loving, caring, attentive man resurfaces, begs forgiveness, showers his victim with flowers, cards and gifts, and promises never to batter again. Thus, unlike what many people believe, victims of domestic violence are not continually abused. Rather, they experience periods of abuse followed by periods of intense affection and love with their partners.

It is, understandably, after a phase two violent episode that most people think a battered woman should pack up and go. However, according to Angela Browne, author of *When Battered Women Kill*, leaving after a violent episode is, for the battered woman, "precisely when she is least able to plan such a move. Frightened, in shock, and often physically injured, all she wants to do is survive" (Browne, 1987, p. 111). In addition, Lenore Walker points out that the battered woman wants to believe "that the (loving) behavior she sees during phase three signifies what her man is really like . . . "

(Walker, 1979, p. 68). She "wants to believe that she will no longer have to suffer abuse . . . she convinces herself that he can do what he says he wants to do (stop the violence)" (Walker, 1979, p. 68). Adds Ginny Nicarthy, in *Getting Free*, the batterer's humble and loving behavior in phase three triggers love and guilt in the battered woman. Her decision to stay is influenced by "her concern for him, her feelings that she's responsible for his life and feelings, her hopefulness, her idea that she should be a trusting, nurturing, forgiving woman" (NiCarthy, 1987, p. 11). She loves him. She believes him. She hopes for change. "She unpacks her bags. The cycle begins again" (NiCarthy, 1987, p. 11).

Learned Helplessness

Here, then, is the battered woman who decides to stay, and before long (and without a trace), the loving phase three period ends and the minor battering incidents of phase one begin again. Why doesn't she leave now? Del Martin, in her book, *Battered Wives*, explains that "many women, along with many professional theorists and therapists, are brainwashed into believing that male aggression is innate and therefore, inevitable" (Martin, 1976, p. 80). These women may operate under the widely held notion that "you just have to take it" (Martin, 1976, p. 80).

In addition, Walker adds that many women "were socialized to believe that they must be doing something wrong if their men were constantly beating them" (Walker, 1979, p. 13). Thus, "they may even believe they deserve their beatings. Attempting to improve, but failing to end the beatings, they sink further and further into despair and misery" (Martin, 1976, p. 83). This self-blame, crippling as it is by itself, is often reinforced by outside help. Battered women who seek help from counselors, therapists, friends, family members, police, attorneys, and the clergy are often encouraged to return home and to stop "provoking" the violence. At this point, learned helplessness begins to play its central and devastating role in keeping battered women in their relationships. "When they seek help, and, as is usually the case, do not receive it, their circumstances begin to seem utterly hopeless. They feel trapped and regard attempts at freeing themselves as futile" (Martin, 1976, p. 84).

Believing she has no way out, the battered woman instead concentrates on improving her relationship and goes to great lengths to please and appease the batterer so as to avoid "causing" further violence. Here the steady decline of self-esteem and feelings of self-worth become obvious. Not only are they "beaten and then blamed for not ending the beatings" (Walker, 1979, p. 115), but, as women in our culture, they may "believe that the failure of marriage represents their failure as women" (Martin, 1976, p. 82). The vicious spiral downward continues: self-blame for the violence; failure to stop violence from occurring; self-esteem erosion; belief that escape is hopeless; and failure as a woman, as a partner, as a wife. Still the violence continues, escalating both in frequency and in severity.

Fear

In addition to helplessness and hopelessness, battered women report a third and perhaps even more powerful feeling that keeps them in their relationships with violent partners: fear.

Angela Browne explains that the women she studied stayed because "they had tried to escape and had been beaten for it, or because they believed their partner would retaliate against an attempt to leave him with further violence" (Browne, 1987, p. 113). For many battered women leaving is not even a safe topic of conversation, as "even attempts to discuss a separation can set off a violent attack" (Browne, 1987, p. 116).

Their fears are justified. "Some men would rather kill 'their' women than see them make a new life" (Martin, 1976, p. 78). Chilling, and unfortunately true. However, let us say for the sake of discussion, that despite perceived helplessness and fear of retribution, a battered woman manages to escape from her attacking husband by fleeing in the middle of an argument. Is she safe now that she has left her home? Absolutely not. In fact, "separation is one of the most dangerous times for partners in a violent relationship . . . evidence suggests that, in many cases, the man's violence continues to escalate after a separation" (Brown, 1987, p. 115). Says Del Martin, "If the wife does manage to escape, her husband often stalks her like a hunted animal . . . [and] unless she can afford to leave town and effectively disappear, a woman is never quite safe from a stalking husband. Sometimes the harassment, the threats, and the beatings continue for years after a wife has left" (Martin, 1976, p. 78). More than anyone else, battered women understand that leaving, attempting to leave, or even discussing leaving their partners may mean risking serious injury or death. "Fear immobilizes them, ruling their actions, their decisions, their very lives" (Martin, 1976, p. 77).

Nowhere to Go

Let us say that the battered woman manages to escape. Where is she to go? Her husband will certainly scour the neighborhood, contact all the neighbors, friends, family, and even distant relatives. Keep in mind that "the threat of abandonment is so devastating to some men, that they would rather kill the woman than see her go" (Browne, 1987, p. 117). Her husband will search every place where she is likely to seek shelter and protection. *Every* friend will be called. *Every* family member harassed. He may show up at her workplace (if she takes the risk of even going to work). He may follow her back and forth to work, or to school, or to friends' homes. He may follow her, as batterers have in the past, to another town, another city, another state. The reader who finds this unpleasant and difficult to believe is encouraged, right now, to imagine how the battered, hunted woman feels. She must maintain a constant and exhausting vigil against further attack, as the batterer may be around any corner, only waiting for a chance to grab her, beat her, kill her. "Will he be outside work today?" she wonders. "Will he wait outside the grocery store? Will he carry out his threats to kill my mother? Will he be waiting outside my front door when I get home? Is that he, down the street, looking this way? Is that he behind me? Is that his car outside my house? Is that he calling me all night . . . those calls I never answer? Will I be safe tomorrow? And the day after?" Angela Browne points out, sadly, that "for many battered women, leaving their mates and living in constant fear of reprisal or death seems more intolerable than remaining, despite their fears of further harm" (Browne, 1987, p. 115).

No Money to Get There

What about finances? Since "violent husbands generally handle all the money . . . even if she has a place to go, she may not have the money to get there" (Martin, 1976, p. 84). She must find somewhere safe to live, hide from a pathologically violent man who is hunting her down, keep a job (if she is lucky enough to have one), pursue legal help, initiate divorce proceedings, and, of course, eat and take care of herself. All this, with only the clothes she is wearing when she fled her home, and no money in her pocket. And we have not even mentioned the children. Let us say she managed to escape with them. Now she needs shelter for a family of, say, four. For how long? Even she does not know. She must bring her children to and from school (does she have a car?), but by doing so she is providing the angry batterer with ample opportunity to get at her and the children. And, of course, she has four mouths to feed.

1,000 Reasons

Remember, she may have no money. She hides from her stalking husband. Friends and family are urging her to "stop running away from her responsibilities"; to "stop breaking up her family"; to "go back where she belongs, with her husband"; to "try harder to make it work, and to stop provoking him." All of her clothes, and her children's, toys, beds, all of her things are "at home." She has nowhere to go. And always, always, the relentless fear of an attack, the fear of more violence. Her self-esteem is at an all-time low. She may be ill or injured from recent violence. She may believe, like many battered women do, that the law cannot help her. She may be afraid of the threats the batterer made to kill himself, her parents, or someone else were she to leave him. She must also go to work everyday, because if she is going to stay away, she will need that income more than ever. Dazed, confused, depleted, overwhelmed—she returns.

Does this sound like a worst-case scenario? It is, and it is exactly what many battered women face as they try to escape from their violent partners. The question that needs to be asked is not, "Why does she stay?" Rather, it is, "How will she ever get out?"

WHAT ABOUT LESBIANS?

Similar to heterosexual battered women, battered lesbians also face seemingly insurmountable difficulties in their attempts to leave abusive partners. As victims of domestic violence, gay or straight, these women must overcome many of the same problems. The cycle of violence theory and the learned helplessness theory seem as applicable to lesbian battering as they are to heterosexual battering. Lesbians, too, are subject to the gradual, yet powerful and debilitating, domestic violence trap. Like straight battered women, battered lesbians also report feelings of helplessness, futility, and fear when attempting to escape a battering lover. In addition, however, battered lesbians face their own set of particular problems both as members of the gay and lesbian community, and as members of a society that so vehemently hates homosexuals.

To many lesbians, the idea that a gay woman may batter her lover is absurd. Much of the lesbian community, in fact, may still cling to the widely held myth that women are not violent. Pervading the lesbian community for years, this myth has contributed significantly to the wall of silence surrounding lesbian battering, adding the "burden of proof," so to speak, to battered lesbians. Nobody has trouble believing that it is possible for a man to be violent, cruel or abusive to his wife. We may wish it were not so, and admit that it is unpleasant, but we never doubt the possibility of its happening. This is not true for lesbian battering. Many people, and particularly lesbians (among whom will be, most likely, the first people a battered lesbian turns to), deny that it is even possible for a woman to be physically and psychologically abusive and violent. Even more "impossible," so goes the myth, is that a woman would behave abusively to another woman. Finally, the idea that a *gay* woman might batter—a politically correct, socially conscious, intelligent, lesbian feminist raise her fist to another gay woman—impossible! Right? No, dead wrong. Yet the myth persists, and battered lesbians continue to suffer, as a community denies that the problem even exists.

It would be unfair and inaccurate, however, to say that the entire lesbian community has maintained a wall of silence around lesbian battering. Thanks to many courageous lesbians, there is now a National Coalition Against Domestic Violence Lesbian Task Force; and an invaluable book, *Naming The Violence*, published in 1986, directly addresses lesbian battering. At least two dozen articles have been written on the subject, and there are lesbians all over the country working hard to stop lesbian battering, providing services to both lesbian batterers and victims. Despite this progress, for battered lesbians the domestic violence trap is as real and lethal as ever.

Homophobia and the hatred of homosexuals in America also contribute to the difficulties of battered lesbians. Many gay men and lesbians are cut off from the usual support systems in our society: their families, who cannot or do not want to accept homosexuality; the church, which almost universally condemns homosexuality; and, in many cases, the medical and mental health professions, which have a history of labeling lesbians and gays as sick or mentally ill. Thus, several powerful forces are at work keeping lesbians in their relationships with violent women. First, the lesbian and gay community's reluctance to acknowledge domestic violence within its ranks. Second, the compounding effects of a society that is profoundly homophobic on one hand and heterosexist on the other. Reports one victim of lesbian battering, "None of us ever sought professional counseling out of fear that our lifestyle would be revealed, and that any therapist would view homosexuality as 'the problem'" (Lobel, 1986, p. 52). In addition, "many lesbians would be horrified at the thought of calling the police for protection, or arrest of their partner, an option increasingly more available to white heterosexual women" (Lobel, 1986, p. 196). Even if police are called, they may label what they see as "two dykes fighting," rather than domestic violence where one woman is clearly a victim.

Counselors and the law may be off limits, or at least perceived as off limits to battered lesbians, due to homohatred. Battered women's shelters are no better: So homophobic are many shelters that "lesbians who are battered have pretended they were involved with a man, and found welcome sanctuary in shelters, but the deception has certainly taken a toll" (NiCarthy, 1987, p. 282). Obviously, this does not describe a loving, accepting, safe space where the battered lesbian can deal with the confusion, fear, and emotional turmoil, characteristic of battered women after an escape from a violent partner.

What about their families? "Lesbians are less likely than heterosexual women to turn to family members for emotional support in the aftermath of violence. Those who are not out (of the closet) would have a hard time talking around the issue. Those who are out may fear reinforcing stereotypes of the 'sickness' of lesbian relationships" (Lobel, 1986, p. 196). The idea of confiding in a family member becomes unthinkable. As one battered lesbian points out, "What would they think after all the years spent trying to educate them about your lifestyle?" (Lobel, 1986, p. 37).

For many lesbians and gay men, the fear of bad press about the lesbian and gay community adds to the silence around lesbian battering. "We fear fueling society's hatred and myths by speaking openly about lesbian battering. We fear hostile responses from police, courts, shelters or therapists. Consequently, we are hesitant to call the police, seek counseling, or write articles. Speaking about violence or seeking help is an especially terrifying prospect for lesbians who need to remain closeted" (Lobel, 1986, p. 200). The battered lesbian speaks out in her community and is silenced. She neither tells her family nor talks to a therapist. She does not consider calling the police and dreads the homophobia of a battered women's shelter. She stops speaking out. She stays with her partner, and the violence continues. The downward spiral goes on and further and further she sinks, unable to get out.

GAY MALE VICTIMS

Clearly, victims of domestic violence are up against incredible odds as they attempt to escape their batterers. From straight women being told by the local priest to go back and stop "provoking" further violence, to lesbians, cut off from families and legal support, being told by militant feminists that women do not batter, the picture is worse than gloomy. For many battered women, it seems hopeless. When addressing the issue of gay men's domestic violence, we see a somewhat different yet nonetheless grim picture.

Like all other victims of domestic violence, battered gay men are susceptible to the deceptive cycle of violence and to learned helplessness. They, too, have every reason to fear retaliation for trying to leave, and they, too, are hunted, followed, and attacked by (ex-) lovers. Homophobia, heterosexism, and plain old ignorance about the phenomenon are at work against them, as they contend with a gay community that is just beginning to learn about domestic violence, and a dominant culture that does not want to know anything about homosexuality. Unlike their battered gay and straight female counterparts, however, gay male victims of domestic violence confront several other forces that may keep them with their violent partners.

Men Are Not Victims

Given our socialization in American culture, it is expected, even "natural," to see women as victims. Our sexist culture prescribes for women characteristics such as frailty, dependence, weakness, emotionality, and need of protection. The bridge between these traits and our notion of what a "victim" is, is easily crossed. Men, however, according to our culture, are not victims, but victimizers: strong, tough, powerful, decision-making, self-reliant, and controlling. Men may be victimizers — rapists, gay bashers, muggers, child molesters, but not victims.

In the context of this socialization theory, gay men who have experienced violence at the hands of their lovers may be unable to see themselves as victims, simply because they are men. To them, battering is something that happens only to women. They do not think of their own relationship in the context of domestic violence. As a result, gay men may choose to stay with violent partners until such time that the cycles of violence are in motion and they find themselves unable to get out. Their inability to recognize their own victimization early in the relationship may perpetuate their victimization.

The culturally-based view of men as victimizers, but never victims, affects more than just gay men. Virtually everyone — friends, family, therapists, nurses, doctors, and even emergency room personnel — who comes into contact with a battered gay man may fail to recognize the problem of domestic violence, simply because the injured party they see is male. Nobody recognizes the violence as "spouse abuse." Instead, the "problem" is viewed as "two guys fighting," and responsibility for the violence is inappropriately attributed to both men. And the victim stays, because he too does not see himself as a victim. It is "our problem." The violence continues, every incident more severe than the last.

"Innate" Male Violence

Many gay men may also adhere to the false notion that male aggression and violence are natural and innate, all a part of what it is to be male. As a result, these men may allow themselves to stay with an abusive partner and tolerate what would certainly be labeled "domestic violence" in a heterosexual relationship, but is labeled by the gay male victim as a natural part of gay relationships. Combine the misconception that men are "violent by nature" with the absence for many gay men of healthy nonviolent relationship models, and the stage has been set for victims who, at least at first, do not try to leave their abusive partners. Rather, the gay male victim is apt to believe that with two men in an intimate sexual relationship, "enough stress, enough complicating factors, enough 'provocation,' and violence is bound to occur" (Lobel, 1986, p. 28). So, the "inevitable" violence occurs, and devastating as it may be, the victim views it as par for gay relationships, because "that's the way men are." He stays, believing that it will probably happen again, but, "Really," he tells himself, "it's not so bad." He blames himself for the incident, and the erosion of his self-esteem begins. Another violent incident occurs, perhaps weeks or months later. Still he does not see himself as a victim. He stays. The cycles are in motion. Leaving becomes more and more difficult, and the violence continues, unabated.

What about those men who do leave? Let us say we have a battered gay male, subject to the immobilizing learned helplessness and the cycle of violence. Out of guilt, shame, and self-blame he keeps the violence a secret. One day, however, his lover attacks and injures him, and he escapes. What does he do now? There are no shelters to call or go to, and only four agencies in the entire country to provide services. So, he turns to his friends and his community for help. After hearing his story, his friends tell him he is a fool for "allowing" the violence to happen. Or, he is told to stop running away, because there is nowhere to run to, and besides, "What are you, afraid of him or something?" He is told to go back and "take it like a man." And, "if he hits you again," say his friends, "well, hit him back, harder." Because that's what men do. They fight; they stand their ground; they never let someone else push them around or victimize them. Few people, if any, are likely to believe that he was a victim. He will be seen as a culprit, and reminded that "it takes two to tango." The violence will be trivialized or dismissed: "How could he hurt you? You're a big guy!" Or, he will be blamed or ridiculed: "You let him hurt you? I'd never let anyone hit me." "So what does it feel like to be a battered woman?"

Since few people in the general public are aware enough to accept the gravity of a victim's situation, many battered gay men leave with little or no support. Very few men utilize the police and/or legal system, due to their perception of, and the harsh reality of, institutionalized homophobia. The police are not called. The batterer is not arrested. The mental health profession is just beginning to learn about and provide services to battered gay men, but no outreach is done. Like battered lesbians, they may rarely turn to their families for fear of even harsher and nonsupportive judgments.

Nowhere to run, nobody who understands or takes him seriously or offers help. Stalked and hunted by his batterer. No less than a battered lesbian or heterosexual woman, the gay male victim is exhausted, confused, overwhelmed. He returns. The honeymoon lasts for days or even weeks or months. The violence continues.

THE VICTIM THEORY

Can a victim theory be postulated? Yes, it can. What you see when you examine victims, however, is dependent upon when, and over how long a period, the analysis takes place.

We believe that there are four appropriate time periods to consider in the study of victims (or potential victims) of gay men's domestic violence:

- Before abuse—These men are prospective victims of gay men's domestic violence.
- During abuse—These men are currently experiencing domestic violence and they have not left their partners.
- After abuse—These men are ex-victims who have left their abusive partners for good.
- After recovery—These men have fully recovered from the effects of the abuse and from the effects of leaving the relationship.

The rest of this chapter will describe a theory of victim behavior and victim psychology at each of these four points in time.

Prospective Victims

When examining victims of gay men's domestic violence, can we say, with hindsight, whether or not there are any predisposing factors that might cause them to become victims?

We contend that prospective victims, those men who eventually become victims, are fundamentally normal, and that they come from any and all psychological, sociological, biological and demographic backgrounds—truly a random sample of gay men. They will show no greater incidence of mental disorders, character flaws, organic dysfunction, or personality deviance than any other group of males. However, they may have tendencies or leanings and combinations of factors which may show some inclination toward victimization. This following section outlines a proposed theory of prospective victim behavior—again in point form for ease of research. A discussion follows at the end. We propose that the prospective victim:

1. Will tend to have relatively sound mental health, to lead relatively normal lives and not to evidence any diagnosable personality disorder, organic dysfunction, developmental gaps, character disorders, or other problems in functioning in frequencies greater than those found in any random group of males.

2. Will not necessarily have had a prior history of, or contact with, abuse of any kind.
3. Has a history of handling life problems in a reasonably confident and effective manner. He, therefore, overestimates his capability of handling, understanding, solving, and eliminating most future life problems, including interpersonal difficulties, and has little or no insight into his limitations.
4. May tend to blame himself for most interpersonal problems with others and to absolve others.
5. May tend to want to be pleasing to others and, at times, to submit to control and influence by others.
6. May tend to mistrust his own judgment about people.
7. May tend to have an unease with disagreement, to be conciliatory, though argumentative, in response to interpersonal disagreements.
8. May tend toward:
   a. Taking responsibility for others;
   b. A strong sense of independence;
   c. Low self-worth or easily deflated self-esteem;
   d. A fatalistic world-view;
   e. Tapping easily a considerable reservoir of guilt;
   f. Liking people;
   g. Trust and lack of suspicion;
   h. Insecurity, such as a need or desire to trust in the "comfort of control" by others;
   i. High ego strength;
   j. Trivializing or denying the negative or unpleasant.

This profile seems normal, especially when the elements are examined one at a time. Almost all people exhibit some of these characteristics. The possibility exists, however, that these elements, when the conditions are right, could set up a prospective victim to become an actual victim. A man who believes himself to be at blame for all of the problems he experiences with others, for instance, will tend to work too hard at trying to please a partner, whose conduct others would label as offensive, to resolve the problems by changing his own behavior. The man will look at the problem as his own, rather than his mate's. With his strong sense of independence, history of solving problems, and his need to be conciliatory and pleasing this person could find himself in a situation of considerable abuse before he is able to place responsibility for the abuse properly on the shoulders of the abuser.

Thus, while the above theoretical description of the prospective victim shows him to be normal indeed, the possibility is there for later denial, trivialization, and self-blame for violence or abuse that clearly is the responsibility of another.

But, now, the test. If it were possible to mix 1,000 prospective victims together with 1,000 other gay males who never became victims, would it be possible to pick out, better than chance, those who would become victims? We think not. However, it might be possible to identify those future repeated victims who do not receive treatment after the first victimization.

Current Victims

Current victims are those men who are in a relationship with a violent man and to whom violence is happening. The essential feature of their profile is coping behavior. They are struggling to understand the violence, prevent it from happening, heal from episodes of abuse, and deal with the myriad of problems created by their lover's abusive conduct.

The following tersely worded section, as all theory sections of the book, is a proposed theory of current victim behavior. Our purpose, again, is to outline parsimoniously the elements of the theory in very discrete units for ease of research. A discussion follows at the end.

1. A current victim is presently experiencing cruel, demeaning, and aggressive behavior and actual violence from his battering lover. The violence will take any one or any combination of three forms.
   a. Unwanted physical force, including unwanted sexual behavior.
   b. Psychological abuse, including many forms of intimidation and terror, exploitation or neglect, creating a pervasive atmosphere of intimidation and fear.

     c. Property and possessions destroyed, damaged, discarded, or mutilated by the partner.

2. The victim may or may not perceive that he is being controlled, manipulated and dominated by his abusive partner.

3. Because gay male relationships involve two males and set out to be more egalitarian than heterosexual relationships, the current victim may tend to believe that even violence perpetrated entirely by the partner is a shared responsibility of the two partners.

     a. The victim will feel a male-male, same gender parity, which is obviously not present in heterosexual relationships.

     b. The victim may, therefore, inappropriately feel accountable for the violence.

     c. The victim's perception of his accountability is fed and nourished by the batterer who blames him for the violence and tries to persuade him that the battering is a shared problem.

     d. The victim will consequently show a tendency to tolerate more than one instance of violence and a hesitation to leave the relationship when repeated instances of violence occur.

4. The current victim increasingly believes that he, himself, causes the violence.

     a. The longer the victim stays, the more susceptible he may become to persuasion by the batterer of his complicity.

     b. The longer the victim stays, the less he sees an alternative to believing that he is the cause of the violence.

5. The victim will make at least one, and possibly many, attempts to leave the relationship, will fail, and will return.

6. Once the victim makes a decision to leave the relationship, he may find himself unable to do so.

7. The victim tends increasingly to relinquish control and to submit to manipulation and domination by the partner.

     a. The victim will be increasingly unable to see options for his own behavior.

     b. The victim will increasingly believe that there is nothing he can do to stop the batterer's violence or change the batterer.

8. The victim tends to deny that he is increasingly controlled and dominated by the abuser.

9. There is a strong tendency in the current victim toward "learned helplessness," a cognitive syndrome that takes over his thinking style. The victim increasingly:

   a. Thinks that he is trapped and sees no way out of the relationship.

   b. Sees fewer and fewer behavioral options to prevent further violence.

   c. Believes he must simply endure the violence.

   d. Becomes vulnerable to the abuser running his life.

10. There is a strong tendency in the victim to deny and minimize the violence that is occurring. The victim will:

    a. Act to cover up the violence, not disclose it to friends and relatives, for fear of further abuse and because of shame.

    b. Attempt to live as normal a life as possible with as few signs of violence showing as possible.

    c. Gradually become resigned to the abuser's assertions that the violence is not that bad, is normal and is inconsequential.

11. There is a strong tendency in the current victim to move from *perceived* helplessness to actually behaving in a helpless manner.

12. There is a pronounced tendency in the current victim to be in a chronic state of mild to severe anxiety.

13. There is a pronounced tendency for the current victim to develop, adopt and employ numerous coping strategies in his attempts to avoid or control the violence. The victim will:

    a. Go to great lengths to appease the abuser, to agree with the abuser, to make or not make changes and decisions according to what the abuser desires, regardless of the real wishes of the victim.

    b. Avoid arguments, because he knows that arguments may lead to violence.

    c. Tolerate minor instances of battery, psychological abuse,

and property destruction so as to avoid major violent episodes.

   d. Play counselor, nurse and "overindulgent mother" to the
abuser, behaving in an unconditionally supportive manner
so as to "prevent" further violence.

   e. Keep silent on matters on which he knows that if he voiced
his opinion or took action, there will be threats of or actual
violence thereafter.

   f. Uses a conciliatory tone to the abuser in most matters.

   g. Tends to isolate himself from other relationships because
he perceives that the batterer's pathological jealousy will
be triggered into harassment or violence by the threat of
other relationships.

   h. Learn to "walk on eggs" at all times so as not to do anything, say anything, or demonstrate anything that might
trigger the abuser's premeditated and unpredictable violence (and the justification thereof).

14. The current victim will make one or more attempts to seek
help for himself and possibly also the abuser, and the abuser
will ridicule and reject these attempts.

   a. The victim may experience increased violence when such
attempts are made.

   b. Such failed attempts will reinforce the victim's learned
helplessness.

15. The victim tends to become a living example of punishment
theory in operation, because he believes that by staying in the
relationship, he has some hope of controlling the violence.

   a. The victim believes that worse violence may occur if he
leaves.

16. The victim tends to negatively reinforce his own staying in
the relationship (making it harder to leave) by not thinking
about, talking about or attempting leaving, since such
thoughts, conversation, and actions are fear-arousing.

17. Fear tends to fill up the victim's thoughts, thus rendering him
unable to develop plans and strategies for getting out.

This theory helps to distinguish and make clear the various behaviors that gay male victims of domestic violence may manifest

while in relationships with violent partners. Two central points about this theory need attention. First, the theory as a whole cannot describe all gay male victims. We are confident that most victims will manifest most of the behaviors cited, and some may manifest them all. The theory is intended not to describe individual victims, but instead, to describe the psychosocial condition of victims. Second, as described below, the postulates of this theory are cyclical and help to describe the cycle of victimization that renders so many gay male victims powerless to change their situations.

The first 12 postulates of the theory describe behaviors that contribute to the victimization of the battered gay male. For example, the tendency to tolerate more than one instance of violence (#3), and the failure to escape the batterer (#6) certainly play a role in victimizing the gay male. It is shown that forces within the man, in addition to those outside him and even those outside the relationship, work together in the victimization process.

Postulate 13 describes the "coping strategies" that a victim may employ in order to survive chronic abuse. These behaviors may appear to be passive, codependent, masochistic, or self-defeating. They are not any of those. Instead, they are, more accurately, the victim's attempts to avoid more violence, given the two false beliefs that he may have adopted: (1) he causes the violence, and (2) he cannot escape from the relationship. Coping strategies among victims vary greatly, but all share the common characteristic, in the eyes of the victim, of being violence-prevention behaviors.

The last four postulates of the theory detail how the accumulated effects of fear, learned helplessness, and the inability to escape immobilize the victim. The end of one victimization cycle marks the beginning of another. More specifically, fear of more violence and increased learned helplessness further victimize the battered man. Further victimization then leads to both more desperate and varying coping strategies and to diminished hope of escape. These in turn increase the fear and immobilization of the victim, and so the cycle continues and feeds on itself.

This cycle of victimization may span a long period of time, anywhere from several weeks or months to years or even decades, and is thus, understandably, extremely difficult for battered gay men to break out of.

Ex-Victims

Ex-victims are those battered men who have just left their abusive lovers *permanently*. These are men who have experienced at least two, and more likely, numerous episodes of domestic violence, have recognized that they need to exit the relationship and have done so. For them, the act of leaving their lover and the relationship is traumatic. What has been weeks, months, or even years of periodic to frequent abuse has finally been rejected by the victim. The victim has taken decisive action and has embarked on a new life course, by himself. The violence was expected. The victim at one time had believed he even could control or stop the violence. The abuser was there where he could watch him, and the victim adjusted his own behavior to the abuser's moods. Though violent and repulsive, it was a known world. Though filled with anxiety, it was an existence that the victim had grown accustomed to, and, therefore, to some extent, it was a life of some "predictability." The moment the victim leaves, however, all of that is changed. Nothing is "known." The abuser is nowhere to be seen; his actions and his plotting are unobservable to the victim. Everything is new and dangerous. Though he is out, he may be alone and unprotected. Clearly the new situation is traumatic. Thus, we believe that victims, immediately upon leaving their abusive lovers, suffer from a diagnosable, temporary mental condition, the Post-Traumatic Stress Disorder.

In the previous chapter we explained what the *DSM-III-R* was and how it serves the psychological and psychiatric communities. Post-Traumatic Stress Disorder (309.89) comes relatively close to capturing the mental condition of the victim upon leaving a batterer. Intense fear, terror, and feelings of helplessness are characteristically evident, as well as understandable swings back and forth between reliving the traumas of violence on the one hand and wanting to avoid all stimuli that remind the victim of the past on the other. In the discussion about this disorder, the manual suggests that such a diagnosis is not made unless the "disturbance" lasts at least one month (APA, 1987, p. 247). Victims of domestic violence and therapists alike can be well-assured that the disturbance will last more than one month! We believe that one year, or more, is a more likely duration of this disorder for victims of gay men's domestic violence.

Of particular importance in Post-Traumatic Stress Disorder are the symptoms of hypervigilance and an exaggerated startle response. In other words, as applied to domestic violence, the victim is constantly on the lookout for the abuser and his attacks and will, upon hearing unusual sounds such as a loud noise, a door opening or trees brushing against a window in the middle of the night, overreact with a much more exaggerated response than a person who has nothing to worry about. The victims are highly anxious, somewhat numbed emotionally and yet subject to wide swings of emotion, from fits of rage and anger to morose depression and lengthy bouts of crying. The diagnostic criteria for Post-Traumatic Stress Disorder are reprinted on the next page with permission from *The American Psychiatric Association* (APA, 1987, pp. 250-251). While by no means a perfect summary of the condition that a victim suffers from upon leaving an abusive lover, it is nonetheless close enough and captures significant features of the distress experienced by victims. Absent from the criteria are specific references to heightened anxiety and worry and the taxing consequences of having to deal with so many survival activities at once (job, security, finances, transportation, restraining orders, police, judges, lawyers, agencies, therapists, new living quarters, new friends, loss of old friends, daily confrontations, relatives).

What is especially heartening to victims who may be reading this with some dismay so far, is that in the discussion about this disorder in *DSM-III-R* it is forthrightly stated (and we agree) that the disorder can develop in people without any preexisting conditions when the stressor (violence and the departure from a significant relationship) is extreme (APA, 1987, p. 249). In other words, perfectly normal people, without any prior history of mental instability, can and do suffer from Post-Traumatic Stress Disorder, and, of course, they recover to lead their normal lives again.

On the following pages is our tersely worded theory of the ex-victim of gay men's domestic violence — as in prior sections outlined point by point for ease of research. A discussion follows. The ex-victim suffers:

Diagnostic criteria for 309.89 Post-traumatic Stress Disorder*

A. The person has experienced an event that is outside the range of usual human experience and that would be markedly distressing to almost anyone, *e.g.*, serious threat to one's life or physical integrity; serious threat or harm to one's children, spouse, or other close relatives and friends; sudden destruction of one's home or community; or seeing another person who has recently been, or is being, seriously injured or killed as the result of an accident or physical violence.

B. The traumatic event is persistently re-experienced in at least on of the following ways:
   (1) recurrent and intrusive distressing recollections of the event (in young children, repetitive play in which themes or aspects of the trauma are expressed)
   (2) recurrent distressing dreams of the event
   (3) sudden acting or feeling as if the traumatic event were recurring (includes a sense of reliving the experience, illusions, hallucinations, and dissociative [flashback] episodes, even those that occur upon awakening or when intoxicated)
   (4) intense psychological distress at exposure to events that symbolize or resemble an aspect of the traumatic event, including anniversaries of the trauma

C. Persistent avoidance of stimuli associated with the trauma or numbing of general responsiveness (not present before the trauma), as indicated by at least three of the following:
   (1) efforts to avoid thoughts of feelings associated with the trauma
   (2) efforts to avoid activities or situations that arouse recollections of the trauma
   (3) inability to recall an important aspect of the trauma (psychogenic amnesia)
   (4) markedly diminished interest in significant activities (in young children, loss of recently acquired developmental skill such as toilet training or language skills)
   (5) feeling of detachment or estrangement from others
   (6) restricted range of affect, *e.g.*, unable to have loving feelings
   (7) sense of a foreshortened future, *e.g.*, does not expect to have a career, marriage, or children, or long life

D. Persistent symptoms of increased arousal (not present before the trauma), as indicated by at least two of the following:
   (1) difficulty falling or staying asleep
   (2) irritability or outbursts of anger
   (3) difficulty concentrating
   (4) hypervigilance
   (5) exaggerated startle response
   (6) physiologic reactivity upon exposure to events that symbolize or resemble an aspect of the traumatic event (*e.g.*, a woman who was raped in an elevator breaks out in a sweat when entering any elevator)

E. Duration of the disturbance (symptoms in B, C, and D) of at least one month.

Specify **delayed onset** if the onset of symptoms was at least six months after the trauma.

---

1. Trauma. The victim has experienced not only episodes of domestic violence against his person, but also the trauma of leaving his home and relationship—a combination of experiences that is outside the usual range of human experience and is markedly distressing to anyone.

2. Anxiety and worry. These feelings increase dramatically.
3. Life complication. There is a dramatic increase in the complexity of the victim's life and the need for him to handle many unfamiliar and further-anxiety-producing new activities.
4. Fear. There is a dramatic increase in the victim's feelings of fear and terror, a constant worry that, instead of being safe, he might be found, pursued, attacked, humiliated, injured, or killed.
5. Vigilance. There is a dramatic increase in the victim's need for vigilance, a constant watchful awareness for the presence of and the attacks of the ex-abuser.
6. Depression and grief. There are increased and sustained instances of depression and crying.
7. Detachment. There are increased feelings of detachment and estrangement from others, perhaps all others.
8. Dampened affect. The victim's emotional range may become somewhat restricted, and he may show an inability to demonstrate feelings of affection and love.
9. Decreased trust. The victim's ability to trust people with whom he has contact, including therapists and other helpers, is diminished.
10. Vacillation. The victim tends to miss and feel the loss of the abuser, alternating with rage toward and rejection of him.
11. Sleep disturbances. The victim tends to have difficulty falling asleep and/or staying asleep.
12. Re-experiencing. There is a profound tendency in the victim to re-experience and relive both the episodes of violence from the old relationship and the traumatic experiences of leaving and coping with leaving the relationship.
13. Doubt. There is a pronounced reaction in the victim to his having, in one moment, stopped and terminated a love relationship, resulting in feelings of doubt, discouragement, second-guessing, regret, sadness, and loss.
14. Dual feelings for the abuser. The victim desires on one hand not to hurt the ex-abuser; to act fairly and reasonably, and even, on occasion, to protect and want to comfort the abuser from his loss and pain. On the other hand, there is an equally

pronounced reaction of hatred toward the abuser with accompanied feelings of revenge.

15. Generalized dismal outlook. The victim tends periodically to evidence a dismal outlook toward the rest of his life, feeling that he will never find another love relationship, never be happy again, never be able to put aside the trauma, vigilance and fear, that his ex-lover will always pursue him, and that he will never be able to trust anyone again.

16. Anti-violence militancy. The victim tends toward outbursts of rage and uncontrolled verbal denunciation of those who engage in violence of any kind.

17. Concentration disturbances. There is a pronounced tendency in the victim to experience difficulty concentrating, especially in early weeks and months, and especially on those activities that require mental discipline, such as reading, writing, listening intently to others, and those activities involving high levels of technical and professional skills.

18. Physiological reactions. The victim to experience a physiologic reaction to stimuli that remind him of either the abuse or the experience of leaving the relationship, with symptoms such as increased heartbeat, sweating, nervousness, or shortness of breath.

19. Avoidance of certain stimuli. There is a pronounced increase in the victim's avoidance of any thoughts, feelings, or situations that remind him of the episodes of violence or the act of leaving. He may avoid activities (such as going to a violent movie) that could lead to such memories, and may even be unable to recall certain aspects of his past traumatic events.

20. Clear recall of violence. There is, at the same time, an uncanny ability in the victim of gay men's domestic violence to be able to recall, verbatim, the verbal exchanges between the abuser and himself during violence as well as the physical, psychological, and emotional reactions and memories of those events.

21. Terrifying dreams. The victim experiences a pronounced increase in terrifying dreams, related or unrelated to exact instances of his traumatic events; he may wake with a startle on occasion and feel significant distress.

22. Distress with associated stimuli. There is a pronounced increase in the victim's feelings of intense psychological distress upon exposure to events or thoughts or stimuli of any kind that resemble any aspect of the traumatic events, including anniversaries of those events.

The key traumatic event that triggers the acute reaction in the victim is his leaving the relationship. Immediately his entire life is in a brand new turmoil. Anxiety skyrockets. He is in constant fear for his life. He imagines that his abusive ex-lover is furious, angry enough to stalk him and injure him. He has nightmares, jumps at the sound of loud noises and believes his batterer is peering in on him from a distance. He is alone and must accomplish by himself many difficult actions, such as going to court.

Upon leaving a lover of several years, a man will also become melancholy, missing his lover. Too many observers do not understand that most domestic violence is periodic, not constant, and that the two men really did love each other. Thus, the departing victim will achingly yearn for the love, comfort, and other satisfying aspects of the old relationship. But, he has severed the cord and understands, sadly, that he will never again be in contact with the man he once loved. This emotional ordeal is massively taxing on the victim, and he will succumb to instances of depression and crying as he tries to manage his loss.

The combinations of anxiety and loss, rage and depression, emotional detachment and need for support devastates the victim and renders him a candidate for delicate and thoughtful professional help.

Not all victims will conform to all of the elements of the theory, of course. Some ex-victims will sail through the process of leaving their abusive ex-lover as if energized by the activity. Others will yield fully to the pressures and depths of depression. Many will evidence mild symptoms in all areas. None will be unaffected, and all are in need of uncritical support, strong encouragement that they are doing the right thing by leaving, and significant contact with responsible gay men who are trustworthy and sane.

Recovered Ex-Victims

Recovered ex-victims are those men who have fully recovered from their Post-Traumatic Stress Disorder and from the abuse they endured at the hands of their abusive ex-lover. Full recovery can take two or three years. These men may have undergone therapy for months, may have enacted a comprehensive self-help program to change their lives and outlook, and may have received massive assistance from public agencies, friends, and relatives. They may have moved to another state and started over. These ex-victims of gay men's domestic violence are testimony to the assertion made earlier in this chapter that there is no predisposing disorder for victims. Domestic violence can happen to anyone, and when the victim takes responsibility for his own recovery, he then becomes an ex-victim. He resumes normalcy.

Ex-victims who have received treatment and recovered from the trauma of gay men's domestic violence and its aftermath are a most interesting group of healthy men. These men stand significantly less chance of ever being victimized again than men who have never experienced domestic violence. The lessons learned, the iron-willed resolve never to let it repeat, and the internalized vigilance for signs of abuser behavior combine to form a new non-victim, a gay man attuned to the deviance of batterers. The recovered ex-victims realize that they are responsible for only their own behavior, that they and they alone make decisions about whether they stay in or leave any relationship, that they will condemn, reject, and not tolerate any instance of domestic violence. These men are confident, trusting in themselves, and are capable of discussing their limits with potential lovers. No batterer will be capable of victimizing any gay man with such experience behind him because the recovered ex-victim will have the knowledge, skills, and attitude to leave at the first indication of abusiveness.

The following section is a proposed theory of the ex-victim, the recovered victim. We believe that this section of the theory is useful in creating outcome measures for treatment and therapy of victims of gay men's domestic violence. A discussion follows at the end.

1. No PTSD symptoms. The recovered ex-victim does not show symptoms required for diagnosis of Post-Traumatic Stress Disorder.

   a. The traumatic events of abuse and of exiting the relationship are not persistently re-experienced, through recollections, dreams, sudden actions, and feelings approximating the experiences, or psychological distress at exposure to symbolically similar events and experiences.

   b. There is no persistent avoidance of stimuli associated with the trauma of abuse and of exiting the relationship, nor is there a numbing of general responsiveness. The recovered ex-victim may not, however, find himself particularly interested in approaching the previously avoided stimuli.

   c. There are no persistent symptoms of increased arousal (those that began with the trauma of abuse and exiting), such as difficulty sleeping, irritability, difficulty concentrating, hypervigilance, exaggerated startle response, or physiologic reactivity. The recovered ex-victim will, however, have incorporated and internalized a more realistic level of vigilance for signs of abusive tendencies in any new potential lovers or men he is dating.

   d. Sufficient time has elapsed for the recovered ex-victim to have successfully overcome all of the above, and any other, symptoms of Post-Traumatic Stress Disorder.

2. No self-blame for violence. The recovered ex-victim does not blame himself for any interpersonal difficulties he experiences, other than the ones he himself may cause.

   a. He is able to place responsibility properly on the party who creates difficulty, especially in matters of domestic violence.

   b. He does not feel responsible for the behavior of others.

3. Behavior is a choice. The recovered ex-victim understands that all behavior is a choice, that it is learned (and can be unlearned) and that each person's behavior is his or her own responsibility.

4. Termination of old relationship. The recovered ex-victim de-

sires no contact, has had no contact and will have no future contact with the abusive ex-lover.

  a. At least six months has passed since the last and final contact.
  b. The recovered ex-victim repels and rejects all attempts of contact by the abusive ex-lover.

5. Rejects provocation attempts. The recovered ex-victim evidences clear understanding that he never did and never can provoke another to violence, and that controlling abusive behavior is the responsibility of the abusive person.

6. No new love relationship. The recovered ex-victim has not yet entered a new, primary, permanent love relationship.

7. Less other-centered. The recovered ex-victim evidences a manner, approach and attitude toward others that is:
  a. less conciliatory in style;
  b. less focused on pleasing the other;
  c. absent of a desire for the "comfort" of the control by others;

8. More self-valuing. The recovered ex-victim evidences in his personality:
  a. trust in his own judgment;
  b. knowledge of what he wants and believes;
  c. increased feelings of self-worth;
  d. a less easily deflated state of self-esteem;
  e. increased independence.

9. No minimization. The recovered ex-victim does not trivialize or deny the unpleasant or the negative, especially in others' behavior toward him.

10. Can change only self. The recovered ex-victim no longer believes that he can change other people.

11. Intolerant of domestic violence. The recovered ex-victim is intolerant of all three forms of gay men's domestic violence, condemns every instance of it, and would exit any relationship in which it surfaced.

12. Rejection of control. The recovered ex-victim rejects and condemns any and all attempts by others to manipulate, control, and dominate him.

The key physical element in the ex-victim's full and speedy recovery is a total and absolute severance of all contact, forever, with his battering ex-lover. Even periodic conversation or superficial (pleasant) contact on the street will hamper recovery. The ex-victim owes no duty whatsoever to the man who once was violent with him. Thus, a measure of the ex-victim's total recovery is his unwavering repudiation of the batterer.

The first key intellectual component in the ex-victim's recovery is learning that all behavior is a choice, and that batterers choose and decide to be violent and victims choose to stay in (or get out of) relationships with violent men. The sooner that the ex-victim learns these principles, the more rapid is his recovery.

The second crucial intellectual concept that an ex-victim learns is that victims do not provoke violence. (See Chapter IX for a detailed analysis of provocation.)

The essential emotional component of recovery is an increased valuing of the victim's own valid perceptions of his experiences and his resolve not to allow anyone to manipulate, control, or dominate him. The ex-victim and the ex-victim alone is the judge of what is best for him.

Such a renewed man may at times appear evangelical in his condemnation of and repugnance toward domestic violence. His internalized vigilance for signs of abusive behavior in others may stifle some new friendships from time to time. But, he is rightfully resolved never to be victimized again. And he will not be.

A recovered ex-victim may not show evidence of growth or change in all aspects of the theoretical model. But, key changes will be evident, among them the absence of symptoms and signs of Post-Traumatic Stress Disorder. Anxiety will be lowered. Rage will have subsided, and the frenetic reliving of abusive experiences will have faded. Since all ex-victims do not have the same personality profile or history of abuse, their final recovery status will be different as well.

An important sign of recovery is when the ex-victim finally becomes merely annoyed with the abusive ex-lover who may still be wretchedly violating a restraining order for the 20th time. Any harassment by the abuser will now seem to the ex-victim simply an irritant. Make no mistake, however. The recovered ex-victim will nonetheless take seriously every continuing affront by the perpetrator, deal effectively with it, and then retire the incident to oblivion. His recovery is then complete. The abuser is out of his life and the ex-victim has grown beyond him. Such growth and new confidence are the essence of the recovered ex-victim.

Chapter V

How Do You Get Out?

THE ESCAPE

*I escape from Stephen on September 8, 1987. That day I leave
and break out of the whole cycle of abuse. The story actually begins
the evening before, at about 7:15 p.m. I am on the telephone with
my Aunt Clare who is telling me that she recently learned I was gay,
that she is happy about it, and that she wants me to feel included in
the family. She wants to assure me that I don't need to keep away
from Connecticut, where the whole family lives. Clare says that her
son Christopher is getting married, and she wants to fly me back to
the East Coast for the wedding. I am thrilled with all of the news.*

*But while I'm on the phone, Stephen is getting more and more
agitated by the conversation. Stephen, our friend Joe, and I are
preparing to go out to the movies, and I know we have plenty of
time. Stephen is shouting at me while I am on the phone, saying
"Who is she?! What does she want?! Patrick, hurry up! We have to
get ready."*

*By the time I hang up the phone, Stephen is raging. "I hate your
family. I hate your family. I HATE THEM. I HATE THEM! They
always want to interfere!" Then he begins berating me for what he
calls "giving them information about" him and me when I talked to
Clare about being gay and my relationship with him. Tension begins to build up in the apartment, even with Joe there.*

*I try to put the issue aside and say, "Stephen, it's really no big
deal. Why do you always say this about my family? It was a very
nice phone call and everything is fine. Let's just go to the movies."
But for some reason, he can't let it go. I walk into the bathroom to
brush my teeth. The atmosphere is tense. The three of us walk*

around the apartment in silence, putting our coats on and getting ready to go. I feel uneasy, slightly nervous.

We finally get outside into the fresh air, and as we walk down the street Stephen says he wants to hold my hand. He grabs it and squeezes, holding it really tight. I don't like it, of course, so I try to pull my hand away. He holds on, and finally I yank my hand away saying, "You're hurting me. I don't want to hold your hand. Leave me alone." Stephen retorts, "Patrick, why are you being like this? Why are you being so difficult? Why don't you just hold my hand? Why are you always like this? Well?!" He is getting nastier, and the tension escalates.

We get on the subway and ride downtown in silence. As Joe and I walk up the stairs of the subway station, we look back and notice Stephen standing at the foot of the stairs, sort of whimpering in a characteristic way of his. These sounds, and a face he is making, are cues for me to come down and hug him and be really nice to him. Instead I say, "Hurry up, you old dog." There is an obvious strain of bitterness in my remark, and it is not the "right thing" to say. Stephen's reaction is to turn around, mutter something under his breath, and walk back into the station.

Joe and I keep climbing the stairs and wait at the top for a few minutes. Stephen is nowhere to be seen. I walk back down into the station and find him on a platform waiting for a train. I hand him the keys to the apartment and say, "You'll need these if you're going home." Stephen takes the keys and says nothing. "Okay, Stephen," I say, "do whatever you want to do." I turn and walk away and Stephen follows. As we turn to go up the escalator he mutters something about my "spoiling every evening," and I explode. I grab him by the shirt collar and shake him, furious. I shout, "If it's so bad then get the hell out of my life! Get out and leave me alone." I pull him up onto my step of the escalator and continue shouting, making a scene. People are watching. Then Stephen grabs my hair, twists me around, and starts punching me. He hits me in the head, in the chest, anywhere he can. I hit back the same way. We are riding up the escalator battling with each other.

Before we reach the top, I shove him away from me, hop over the escalator onto the stairs, and run back down into the station. Joe is there looking for us. I rush up to him and exclaim, "Joe it's really bad, fists flew. I don't know what we're going to do." Joe looks rather alarmed and says, "Don't look now, but here comes Stephen." As I turn around I see Stephen, coming at me full steam ahead. I split. I run out of the station onto the street, hop on a bus and go home.

That night I sleep in the bedroom and Stephen sleeps in the living room, the first time that has ever happened in that apartment. The next day I get up early and go out, leaving him asleep. We don't see each other all day until I come home, about six o'clock in the evening. I come in and see Stephen sitting in the chair by the window. I take off my things, put my bag and coat down in the kitchen, and sit at the kitchen table. Stephen asks, "Where have you been all day?" I say that I have been out walking around. "Well, what have you been doing?" "Oh, nothing," I say, "just walking around." I can see that he is getting angry.

Then a predictable interaction begins. He begins a game he often plays that is designed to make me feel guilty for having been violent with him. It usually works, as I like to see myself as a nonviolent person. Stephen says, "I bet you feel real good about the argument we had last night, don't you Patrick?" I respond, "No, no I don't Stephen." Then he continues, "So you feel really rotten then?" I can tell that he is trying to provoke me now, trying to push me to get angry with him and make another scene. I say, clearly and directly, "Stephen, I have absolutely no regrets about last night's argument. None." This infuriates him, and as he gets up he shouts, "Oh! So that's how you feel is it?" In an instant he is standing on the opposite side of the kitchen table. He reaches down under the front of the table and flips it over into my face. This was not the first time he had done that. (When I think about it now I am appalled, and I cannot believe this sort of thing was part of my life.)

As he flips the table over on me he shouts, "I'm going to sort you out once and for all." It is a real threat, and I know it. I immediately put on my coat and grab my backpack, and Stephen roars, "You're not going anywhere!" What Stephen does not know, however, is that I have spent the morning at the Community United Against Violence (CUAV), talking to a counselor in their Gay Men's Domestic Violence Project. I am ready for this. My bag is already packed and I have a planned escape route out of the apart-

ment. Stephen runs and locks the front door just like I thought he would. With my coat on and my backpack over one shoulder, I walk toward the front door and say, "Look Stephen, get out of the way. I'm not staying here." Again he roars, "You're not going anywhere! I'm going to sort you out once and for all!" I back up from the front door toward the big front window that opens onto the second-floor fire escape. As Stephen approaches me I say, "Stephen the minute you leave the front door unguarded, I'm out of here." Just as I hope, he backs up quickly to block the front door. As he does that, I turn to the window and unlatch it. It swings open easily with one little handle. In three seconds I am out of the apartment and going down the fire escape as fast as I can. I hear the front door open, and I know he is after me. I dash down the fire escape, jumping down onto the street from the first floor level. I run for blocks and blocks, turning down obscure side streets to lose him. All of a sudden I'm on Market Street, a main thoroughfare, and I think, "OK, here I am again. Now what?"

After a minute or two I have an idea. I know I can call David, with whom I have spoken just this afternoon. He is someone I think I can trust, someone to talk to, someone to listen to me. I know that I have to get off the street, and fast, too, because if Stephen finds me there is sure to be more violence. I run to a telephone booth and call David. I tell him there has been some violence between Stephen and me, and that I need a place to sit and collect my thoughts. He says he will come right away.

I go into the Metro Bar entry and hide under the stairs. I wait, shaking, hoping that Stephen will not appear. I'm terrified. Stephen has always said, "Wherever you go, I'll find you," when I threatened to leave him. All I can think is that I heard him open the front door and run down the front stairs. I know he is out looking for me. I know that if he sees me he will run up and grab me. Frantically, I look out from time to time to see if David's Bronco is in sight. It's a tense five minutes: hiding, waiting, looking for David's truck, scanning the area for Stephen. I am afraid, confused, and don't know what in hell is going to happen next.

David drives up. I look around for Stephen, and, not seeing him, run and jump into David's truck. We drive quickly to his house. I duck down out of sight the whole way.

This narrative clearly illustrates the obsessive-jealous quality many batterers demonstrate. Stephen is incapable of responding positively to a loving phone call Patrick receives. He is threatened by Patrick's family, and by anyone else who "interferes" with Patrick. This pathological jealousy of batterers contributes to the isolation of many victims of domestic violence. For many victims, maintaining relationships with friends and family can become phenomenally difficult, because the price victims often pay for these ties is both physical and psychological abuse.

This narrative also demonstrates the benefit of preparation for victims who are trying to leave their abusive partners. Patrick manages to escape from Stephen (and more violence) and to get out of their locked apartment because he is prepared. He has discussed with a counselor at CUAV how to get out of his apartment without being battered, should Stephen become violent and, in characteristic fashion, lock the front door. Patrick has devised a "mental map" of escape, and has discussed and rehearsed it with a counselor. Fortunately, the plan goes without a hitch and, though frightened, he is able to escape before Stephen seriously harms him.

In addition to his "mental map" out of the apartment, Patrick has a backpack ready with a few basic necessities so that once out, he can begin the long and difficult process of staying out. The goal for victims of domestic violence who leave their partners is to stay out of those relationships. As this often entails staying away from their own homes, having a few basic amenities can help make the first 24 hours or so a little easier for the victim. Simply having a bag packed can be enormously empowering for many victims, as they take those first steps in regaining control of their lives.

HOW DO YOU GET OUT?

For most victims of gay men's domestic violence, leaving their abusive, violent partners is not easy. As pointed out in Chapter IV, for many victims of domestic violence it may be harder to leave the relationship than it is to stay. Threats of more violence, feelings of isolation and powerlessness, criticism and blame (including self-blame) for being abused, and societal homophobia all combine to form powerful forces that make leaving relationships with violent and abusive partners incredibly difficult for many victims. In short, getting out is much more difficult than most people realize, and the advice to "just leave" that most victims receive fails to take into account these difficulties.

We contend, nonetheless, that while the batterer is solely responsible for his violent behavior, it is the responsibility of the *victim* to get out of the relationship. Difficult and dangerous as it may be, victims, it is up to you to leave.

What follows in this section, then, are tips on how to get out of a relationship with a violent man. Given that you are about to leave your batterer, or want to leave but do not know how, or do not believe that you will be able to do so, these tips will help prepare you for what lies ahead. Preparation here may save you time, money, emotional hardship, and a lot of aggravation. Preparation may be what helps you stay away, this time for good. And, finally, preparation may save your life.

The tips that follow are but five of a number of actions you can take to get away from your violent partner. These items provide you with practical information about how you can help yourself. They are designed to empower you, to demonstrate that seemingly insurmountable obstacles can be overcome, one step at a time. Perhaps most importantly, they are designed to start you thinking about your own situation, and how you can get out. The short list presented here is based on Patrick's experience (white, middle class, living in San Francisco), and as such it is limited. What you do in preparing to leave your violent partner will depend on a variety of factors: your income level; your access to help and resources; the gay community you live in; and the part of the country you live in. Always remember, however, no matter where you are, no matter what your situation, there are things you can do.

The tips covered in this section are listed here as a quick check list or reference.

1. Admit That You Are Being Abused
2. Start Telling People About the Violence
3. Find a Safe-Space
4. Develop a "Mental Map"
5. Pack a Bag

6. Get a Post Office Box
7. Open Your Own Bank Account
8. Leave, Leave, Leave

An important point needs to be made here, however. A victim does not absolutely *need* to do anything as a prerequisite to leaving a relationship with an abusive partner. If he believes that he can get up and walk out now, never to return, then he should do it! For many victims however, leaving seems the impossible task. And when undertaking something that feels so difficult, preparation can work wonders. (*This I learned in retrospect.*)

1. Admit That You Are Being Abused

The first thing you need to do is admit that you, a man, are a victim of domestic violence. As gay men you probably do not think in terms of "batterer" and "victim," nor do the words "domestic violence" come to mind when thinking about your own relationships. Instead you may say, "he hits me sometimes," or, "we have really nasty fights." You are encouraged here to start thinking in terms of domestic violence, and if you are a victim, to admit it to yourself.

How do I know if I'm being abused? If he just hits me occasionally, am I a victim? He doesn't actually hit me, but I'm scared to death of him when he gets angry . . . am I a victim? The answer to these questions lies in the definition of gay men's domestic violence presented earlier: any unwanted physical force, psychological abuse, or material destruction inflicted on one man by another. Does his behavior hurt or bother you? Do you want him to stop? Does he know you want him to stop, and yet persist? If so, his behavior is abusive. If so, you are being abused, and your lover is also your batterer.

Please do not play a semantics game with the definition of domestic violence, or with the questions asked here. Do not kid yourself. Armed with a little understanding of the phenomenon, gay men's domestic violence is easily identified. Ask yourself the simple question: am I being abused? The hard part may be in admitting that you ("I'd never let that happen to me") are a victim.

Perhaps it is hard for you to see yourself as a victim of domestic violence because of stereotypes you may have about what victims look like. You may picture battered gay men as frail, timid little men with gaunt faces and perhaps a black eye or cut lip. While some victims of domestic violence may fit this description, most do not. You may also picture battered gay men as part of the leather, or bar, or S&M scene. Men with leather vests, chaps, chains, and the whole gamut of sadomasochist paraphernalia. Remember, S&M and domestic violence are totally different.

Victims of gay men's domestic violence are as diverse a group as gay men are. (And we know how diverse a group that is!) So if you have an image in your head of what a gay male victim might look like, remove it. Chances are it is wrong. There is a chance, however, that someone you know is a victim of gay men's domestic violence, because many men are.

Admitting that you are a victim of domestic violence may also be difficult in that it entails facing up to the violence that has occurred in your life without trivialization or denial. Stop saying to yourself, "Well, he didn't hit me that hard," when the truth is "he hit me." Do not say "he kicked me in the shins, but it really wasn't that bad," when the truth is "he kicked me." Admit it! Tell yourself the truth, and stop covering for him. If it's true, say it: "He has hurt me. I'm afraid of him. I'm afraid of what he'll do to me."

Victims may also have to put to rest other myths they may be clinging to in order to understand or explain the violence. Admitting that you are a victim means holding your lover fully accountable for his violent behavior. You can no longer rely on the myth that it is because your lover drinks or uses other drugs that he is violent. Facing your victimization means admitting that as a batterer, your lover is choosing to use violence. Your choice, and it is a choice, is staying in the relationship.

Admitting that you are being abused also means admitting that the man you love, and the man who says he loves you, has been violent and abusive with you. We have a tendency to view our batterers as Dr. Jeckylls and Mr. Hydes, almost as if they are two different people. One is the loving, caring, witty, intelligent man, a good cook and a wonderful sex partner, while the other is violent, cruel, mean, intimidating, harsh and abusive.

In fact, they are the same person: he is the same man. Admitting that you are a victim means putting an end to the duality with which you view your lover. Face it: domestic violence does occur in gay relationships. If it is occurring in yours, the man who loves you also batters you.

By May of 1987 violence in my relationship with Stephen was occurring on a regular basis. What used to happen only once every several months had increased dramatically to once a month, then to twice a month, then there were violent incidents every week, sometimes several times a week. By this time I was truly bewildered about what to do. In retrospect, I can see that I had all the manifestations typical of a chronically battered person: I was almost completely isolated from my friends and family; my self-esteem was at an all-time low; my body was in poor shape; I was nervous and jumpy, on edge constantly; I lived to some extent in fear of, and desperate to prevent, Stephen's next outburst; and perhaps most significantly, I was succumbing to the belief that I was causing the violence. I believed, reluctantly, that if only I could be a better cook, or develop a nicer body, or be smarter, or wear nicer clothing, or make more money, or not say such "stupid" things, or not be "so clumsy," that somehow the violence would stop. I also falsely believed that there was no way possible for me to end my relationship with Stephen, as he had promised and threatened for years that he was never going to let me "get away," because he loved me "too much." Stephen would also threaten, "If you ever try to leave me, wherever you go I will find *you, and when I find you . . . !" So I lived for several months, afraid to leave, and trying desperately to figure out how to "fix" things between Stephen and me.*

A major turning point came one day when I was walking down a street in one of the gay neighborhoods in San Francisco. I saw a small pink flyer stapled to a telephone pole and something on it about "male violence" caught my eye. The flyer turned out to be an advertisement for the Gay Men's Domestic Violence Project of Community United Against Violence. It began with the question, "Does the hand that holds you in public strike you in private?" I was awe-struck and could not believe what I was reading. They were talking about me! And . . . this was happening to someone else? There were others besides me? On this flyer I saw for the first time the words "Gay Domestic Violence." Quite suddenly my life became a lot clearer. The pieces of my bewildering relationship began to fit together and all of a sudden so much made sense. I thought, "It's not my fault! It happens to other people, too! It's a widespread social problem and there are people who know about it!" I was not a worthless man who drove his lover to beat him. I was a victim of domestic violence. My view of my whole relationship immediately changed: I was a victim, Stephen was a batterer. It was not, as Stephen always claimed, a normal part of all relationships. Right then, I stopped thinking about how I could change myself to make our relationship better and thus stop the violence (something that had never worked anyway). Instead, I began thinking about leaving Stephen, about somehow escaping from him and his abuse. I began thinking, planning, plotting . . . there had to be some way to get away. Four months later I succeeded.

2. Start Telling People About the Violence

Since many victims of domestic violence feel responsible for the violence — that, somehow, they provoke it and deserve it — it is very common for them to keep the abuse a secret. The only way to break the silence that surrounds domestic violence is to start telling people about it. Telling people will help end the isolation that the abuse in your life has created. Also, people cannot help you unless they know what is happening. Do not be surprised if even your closest friends have no idea that you are being abused. Tell people, and begin to get empowered and supported by those who love you.

You may have to be careful, at first, about whom you tell. Use your own good judgment, keeping in mind the risks involved. Your lover may have threatened you into silence. Tell someone who will not repeat what you say to your lover. Do you have a close friend with whom you share intimate parts of your life?

If you are so isolated that there seems to be nobody at all to tell, you can get the support and empowerment you need over the telephone. Call a local lesbian and gay switchboard or anti-violence project. A battered women's shelter is also likely to have people on staff who can understand your situation. You can also call a 24-hour crisis or suicide prevention service. It is not important that you give people your name and address (unless you feel the need to do so). What is important is that you tell someone. You will be pleasantly surprised and immensely relieved to find there are people who will not blame or ridicule you, but instead will simply listen and support you. Telling people about the violence may be your first important step toward empowering yourself and eventually leaving your violent partner.

This lesson I learned in retrospect. I made the mistake of not telling anyone that my lover was abusing me. To those few people who asked questions, I trivialized the marks and bruises, or the noise from a fight. I wore turtlenecks or buttoned my shirts all the way up. When I left Stephen and began to tell people about the violence, I was shocked to find so few people who believed me. So well had I kept the violence a secret that friends assumed that since they did not know about it, it could not have happened. People found it difficult to believe that Stephen had hit me even once, never mind on and off for two years. Rather than believe me, friends accused me of making the whole thing up, of exaggerating, or of being "typically dramatic" about my relationship. I eventually concluded that I had inadvertently contributed to people's inability and unwillingness to believe what they were told about the violence by keeping it a secret for so long. Do not make this same mistake. If your lover is abusing you, do not keep it a secret. Start telling people about the violence.

3. Find a Safe-Space

Many victims of domestic violence stay with their abusive partners because there seems to be nowhere else to go. In reality though, there *is* somewhere to go, and if you want to get out and stay out, you may have to figure out where that place is before another major battering incident occurs. Do not wait until your lover is attacking you to figure out where to run to. Generally that does not work, or, at the very least it certainly makes staying out more difficult. Think now about where you will run to. Is there a friend you can stay with where your lover will not find you or call you? Is there a relative in a nearby town, city, or even state that your batterer does not know about? You will need a safe house for a while, ideally where he cannot find you, harass you, or further brutalize you. Think of everyone you know, and especially about people you know that he does not know. When your escape occurs, it will be much easier if you have a place to run to, rather than just one to run away from.

Perhaps you are so isolated that there are no friends or relatives to go to. Or perhaps you are in a new city and do not yet know people. Find out about local hotels or bed and breakfasts that you can afford. Find out about shelters for homeless men, which virtually every city has. Perhaps you can stay in one for a day or two or three. Call the local gay anti-violence project and find out if they have suggestions for housing or homes of people you can contact. Call the local battered women's shelter and ask them for suggestions and about emergency housing. Try everything and utilize every resource. It may be difficult and even painful, but try not to get discouraged.

Once you have found a "safe space" to go to, rehearse how you will get there. Can you get there safely and quickly on foot? Can you drive there? Find out exactly where this hotel, home, or apartment is located, and then learn the fastest way to get there. Take a practice drive, or walk there from your house. Remember, when the time comes to escape and get to your safe house, you may be extremely anxious, frightened, and possibly injured. Your lover may be following or chasing you. Be prepared. Learn how to get there. The more prepared you are, the easier your escape will be, and the better your chances will be of getting out and staying out.

I was lucky. Even though I had not yet figured out where to go to by the time my escape occurred, I knew someone to call and his house became my shelter for four months. Victims who have tried to escape but have gone back may know how crucial it is to have a safe place to go where your batterer cannot harass or seduce you into returning. You need a place to live, to hide, and to let down your guard, even if just a little. For extremely isolated victims cut off from all family or friends, consider hotels or hostels. As battered gay men you face a particularly difficult situation as there are no shelters to provide you with temporary housing. If you are having trouble finding somewhere to go, plan every other detail of your escape, prepare as best you can, and keep searching. Keep your safety as a priority. Like me, you may end up leaving before all your plans are ready. That's okay. It's sure better than more violence.

4. Develop a "Mental Map"

An additional and equally helpful step in planning how to get out of your relationship with a violent man involves developing a mental map of escape routes out of your apartment. These are alternative ways to get out if and when violence occurs. Remember, you want to get out before your batterer harms you again. After the violence you may be dazed and weak and hurt, and your lover will probably be loving and comforting. This is an extremely tough time for you to get away.

Plan to escape before the battering. Is there a back door out of your apartment? Is there a stairway to the side yard that leads to a street? You may have tried to get away before, during an episode of violence, and it did not work. Don't let that discourage you. Think about it: How many ways are there out of your apartment? What are they? Develop a plan of escape in your mind, and rehearse it; and, perhaps when your batterer is not at home, go through it step by step to make sure there are no hitches, such as a window that sticks or a door that is locked from the other side. Your mental map is your path to safety, and the next violent incident may be the time he seriously injures or kills you. Don't let him. Use your mental map and get out.

Having a mental map was the key to my escape. As some of the narratives in this book demonstrate, my reaction to most of the violence was to flee the apartment, or at least try to. Stephen caught on to this, however, and began to lock me in. My mental map empowered me. There was a way out. I think for all victims, no matter how hopeless it looks, there is a way out. You just have to believe that there is, figure it out, and use it.

5. Pack a Bag

You may know the experience of "leaving him," fleeing the apartment once the violence starts, and finding yourself on the street without your wallet, without enough money even to last you through the next day, and with only the clothes on your back. While some victims have escaped this way, never to return, it generally does not work. Having a bag packed is one preparation that may prove invaluable in helping you survive those first few days. Include things such as a spare set of keys, your address book, a change of clothes, and perhaps a towel and toothbrush. The idea is to have things with you so that you will not feel the need to return, and you will at least be able to stay away long enough to sit and think clearly about what you are doing.

You can also include in your bag important documents such as your copy of the lease or mortgage, any legal or medical documents you value, and your passport. And, since we are talking about practicalities, can you keep the bag at a friend's house? If not, it should be small enough to carry with you, so that when violence erupts and the need to escape arises, you can grab it and flee.

I learned from a long, cold night sleeping on the steps of a junior high school about two blocks from my apartment that if I was ever going to truly escape and stay away, I had to plan better. I started keeping necessities in my backpack the last month or so that I was with Stephen. Violence was happening fairly regularly, but I still had nowhere to go. It was not until I sat down with a counselor at Community United Against Violence, the first person to really take my situation seriously, that I considered "packing" my bag. My goal then was to get out before more violence occurred and be able to stay out for at least a day or so. It worked.

6. Get a Post Office Box

This time you are leaving your abusive partner forever, an action that necessarily precludes the luxury of stopping by your apartment to pick up your mail. One of the first steps we encourage you to take, even before you leave, is to get a post office box as soon as possible. Post office boxes are wonderful inventions that will serve you in several ways. First, only *you* pick up your mail, so it cannot fall into your ex-lover's hands. You thereby cut off one of the many avenues your ex-lover will typically use to get at you. Do not underestimate the tenacity of your abusive partner to get at you or retaliate. He will try everything. The idea of a post office box is to keep your important papers out of his hands and to cut off one avenue of access to you. Having a post office box is a simple and practical step you can take now that will make your life easier in the difficult period after you leave.

One word of caution: Be sure to check out the procedure your local post office uses to rent boxes. Sometimes the process entails sending documentation to your current address, which may be very risky for you. Always make your safety your highest priority.

One additional note about post office boxes. They are also useful because you can get your mail without anyone knowing where you actually live. Your ex-lover cannot get your new residential address from some neutral source, or from a friend who does not get the picture and is "trying to be helpful" to him. Save yourself the whole mess and get a post office box.

7. Open Your Own Bank Account

It will be helpful, and perhaps even critical, during the initial stages of your life as an ex-victim of domestic violence to have your own bank account. Perhaps your lover, like many batterers, controls all of your joint finances. Perhaps your savings and checking are in a joint account, or, an account in his name. Whatever the case, do not leave yourself financially high and dry, dependent on your lover for survival. If depositing a lot of money in your new account seems impossible, at the very least open an account with a minimum deposit, so that you will not have to completely reorganize your finances when you leave. If your lover controls your finances, it may be too late to take control of your money when you leave, and you may end up penniless for a while, feeling sorely tempted to return to him as a result.

I left my lover on a Tuesday and spent Wednesday morning opening a new bank account and transferring all my money into it. I was uptight and emotionally wrecked, fearing my ex-lover had already gone to the bank and drained "our" account. I did not have the proper documentation with me, and at first the accounts person said it would take two or three days to transfer my money. With no other option, I explained my circumstances, and I think I looked frazzled enough to be believed. A new account was opened, and I moved my money out of our joint account before Stephen got to it. I was lucky. Very lucky.

8. Leave, Leave, Leave

Now the hard part, leaving. Hopefully by now you have come to realize several facts about domestic violence that make your leaving a necessity.

First, despite what you might like to believe, the violence will not stop. Your lover may be the most wonderful man in the world to you, but the fact is if he has abused you once he will abuse again. Chances are the next time it will be worse too, as domestic violence tends to increase in severity over time. It will happen more often, too.

Second, there is nothing *you* can do to stop the violence. Making more money, preparing better meals, getting in better shape, becoming (somehow) smarter, more attractive, or more interesting will not help. All your attempts to change yourself, or your living environment, or the way you relate to your batterer will fail. Violence will occur again, and no amount of your "prevention" will be able to stop it.

Third, you are not responsible for the violence. Nothing you do or say or think or feel or want or like or dislike justifies violence. You do not provoke, incite, cause, trigger, or deserve violence. Ever.

Ask yourself some questions. Do you want the violence to stop? Do you want a life free of harassment? Do you want to get out of this relationship with a violent man? If the answer is, "Yes," *you must leave.*

What Else Can I Do?

As mentioned earlier, what you do to prepare to leave your violent partner will depend on what resources you have, and on what you think you need to do. You know best, so think about what you may need to do to make your life easier and safer right after you leave. For example:

- Make a list of important telephone numbers and keep it in your wallet.
- Save whatever money you can, and keep fifty dollars (or thirty, or twenty, or as much as you can) hidden in your wallet for emergencies, such as getting into a taxi when he is chasing you, or spending one night in a hostel.
- Photocopy all important documents (lease, insurance, car registration, contracts) and keep them at a friend's house.
- Have copies of all necessary keys made, and keep these, too, at a friend's house.
- Don't tell anyone that you have done these things.

Remember, you do not want him to have access to you. The goal is to get out and not to need to go back for any reason.

GOING BACK WITH THE POLICE

The day after I escape from our apartment, and from yet another violent episode with Stephen, I have to return and collect some of my things. I have with me only the clothes I am wearing, and the few things I have in my backpack. I need clothes for work, and some other basics. I know, however, that I cannot go back to the apartment alone; in fact, the idea of going anywhere near the apartment with Stephen there terrifies me. I imagine him to be infuriated that I stayed away, and certainly capable of more violence.

I spend the morning at Community United Against Violence, talking with the director of the Gay Men's Domestic Violence Project. I learn from her that I can get the police to stand by in my apartment to protect me from Stephen. This seems a perfect solution.

Upon hearing the plan, David agrees to go with me, without hesitation. He will pose as a "social worker" and be there to help me out and offer support. This is a tremendous relief, because even after preparing a list of things I want to get, thinking through exactly where each item is in the apartment, and rehearsing what I will say to Stephen, I am petrified. This trip means going back to that small, confined space, where so much violence has occurred, and possibly confronting Stephen: looking at his face, hearing his voice. And the fear that he will somehow get at me persists.

In addition to the fear that Stephen will attack me again, I am afraid that he will be able to reach me emotionally. I have left Stephen many times before this, and always I have gone back. I have always listened to his soothing words, his declarations of love, his (spoken) determination to change, his assurances that he would never be violent again. And I have always believed that perhaps things would change. I thought about the love we shared, and about our commitment to each other. In the past Stephen has put pressure on me emotionally, and it has always worked. I am now afraid to go back to the apartment because there is a chance that I will cave in. I do not want to see a sad or lonely or needy look on his face. I am afraid that if Stephen starts to cry, or beg, or apologize, that I will go back. I think about the difficulty I have always had staying away from him, despite the abuse. I love him and I do not want to leave him. I do not want the relationship to end. I want the violence to stop. But I know that for my own sake and sanity, I must get away from him.

I call the police, and make arrangements to meet them at a corner, about half a block from my apartment. Over the phone, the police are cooperative, and while I have not told them that Stephen is my lover, they do not question my needing a standby. In a matter of minutes all arrangements are made, and David and I head off for my neighborhood to wait for the police.

Unfortunately there is some mix-up in communication, and the police are late. David and I sit in his Bronco waiting and waiting and waiting. It is grueling, as we are parked about fifty yards from my apartment waiting for this horrendous confrontation to finally begin. I have knots in my stomach.

After about half an hour I get out of the truck and run up the street to call the police again. They say a cruiser has been sent already, and somehow we have missed it; another will arrive in about ten minutes. Shortly thereafter a cruiser arrives and parks near the apartment, and we are ready. I explain to the officer that I need his help because I want to get into my apartment to get some of my things, but because there has been violence with "my roommate" I do not feel safe coming here alone. He asks "Who is this man? Who is your roommate?" and I tell him that Stephen is my lover. "OK, fine," he says, and we go upstairs to the apartment.

I unlock the door with my keys, and, as I expected, Stephen is there, sitting on the living room couch. Standing across the room from him, with David on one side of me and the policeman on the other, I say my well-rehearsed lines: "Hello, Stephen. I'm here to get some of my things, and I did not feel safe coming into this apartment by myself, so I brought a policeman," and I gesture toward him, "and a social worker," and I gesture toward David. That is all. I say my piece, turn around and walk into the bedroom to pack, leaving David and the policeman in the living room with Stephen.

At this point I am shaking: fear, anxiety, tension. I do not like being in that apartment with Stephen, especially now. I know he is fuming. I remain relatively calm, however, and quickly pack everything on my list. David comes into the bedroom after a few minutes to make sure I am getting the things I need. "You've got time Patrick. Check your list. You're doing great, Patrick, just great."

I hear Stephen get up in the next room and say something about wanting to speak to me. I also hear the policeman loud and clear say back to him, "You just sit down! If you want to talk to him, you telephone him."

I move quickly and pack everything I need from the bedroom in about seven or eight minutes. The last thing I have to do before we leave is to get some things out of the kitchen, which means walking very close to where Stephen is sitting. We do not make eye contact. The policeman is in the room. I feel pretty safe. Three or four minutes later I am ready to go. Again the three of us stand by the door, me in the center, this time with two packed suitcases. I say "Goodbye, Stephen," and there is no reaction. I say it again. Stephen and I make eye contact, and I turn and leave the apartment.

As we leave the apartment building, I feel absolutely amazed that it has gone so smoothly. It was just like David and I had rehearsed, and everything worked without a hitch. Or so I think at the time. Unfortunately, it is not over.

David and I get into his truck, parked down the street a bit, and the policeman walks in the opposite direction toward his car. Within seconds Stephen is outside the apartment building and has run up in front of the truck and is now shouting at me. "Patrick! What are you doing?! Where are you going?!" He is panicking, shouting loudly. David and I quickly lock the doors, and David starts the engine. Stephen continues yelling and screaming, and now is pounding on the hood of the truck with his fists. "Patrick! What are you doing?!! Don't do this!" David then starts the truck moving slowly forward, and Stephen dives down in front of it, out of sight. I am terrified we will run him over.

It is a nightmare. Everything has gone so smoothly, and now this. Stephen is acting like a madman, and it is getting worse. He jumps up again, and bangs on the hood, screaming, "Don't leave! Don't leave!" And then he begins pulling his own hair. He stands in front of the truck, his head turned up toward the sky, his hands pulling at his hair. He is screaming and screaming.

By now David is leaning on the horn, and slowly creeping the truck forward. Stephen is still screaming, and now running around in circles in front of the truck. The horn is blasting and the truck is inching ahead. I sit pasted to the passenger seat, aghast. Finally, the policeman realizes something is happening and comes running down the street toward the truck. He grabs Stephen by the arm, pulls him away from the front of the truck, and David and I drive off down the street. By the time we reach the next stop sign we are both crying.

The planning, the rehearsing, the waiting, the fear and tension in the apartment, and now this dreadful scene in the street: We are dazed and completely shaken by it. At the stop sign we hug and cry, and David shakes his head in disbelief, tears running down his cheek saying, "He is a sick man, Patrick. He's a very sick man."

"Going Back" is a narrative about empowerment and about victims taking control of their own lives. In this incident the benefits of planning and rehearsing are obvious. Patrick is able to return to the place where he experienced considerable violence, and to confront Stephen face to face, because he is prepared. He has protection, a source of support, rehearsed lines, and a list to follow. The message here is loud and clear: Victims of domestic violence *can* prepare for the unpredictable. Victims *are* in control of their lives. Victims *have* power. Learning to recognize and use that power is the challenge that victims face, but it is, and always has been, at their disposal.

This narrative also sheds light on the difficult plight victims of domestic violence face when leaving their abusive partners: In order to stop the violence they must, paradoxically, leave their own homes, and leave the person that they love. This fact is often realized slowly, as victims first try everything they can think of to stop the violence. For many victims of domestic violence, leaving their partners is a last resort, following months or even years of trying to "fix" the relationship. Thus, while Patrick wants the violence to stop, he loves, cares about, and wants to stay with Stephen. More importantly, however, he understands that he cannot do both. This story, then, touches on the emotional turmoil victims face when leaving their (abusive) loved ones.

A third, and probably for many people, surprising point this incident illustrates, is the role the police can play in gay men's domestic violence. As made clear in the section on Myths in Chapter I, the police can, and will, help victims of gay men's domestic violence. Clearly, the training and education of the San Francisco Police Department is paying off.

"Going Back" also provides insight into the complex psychology of domestic violence from both a victim and a batterer perspective. While Patrick struggles with fear, apprehension, and dread, Stephen is devastated by the loss of his partner. For victims, leaving can be painfully difficult and confusing. For most, if not all batterers, losing their partners is so overwhelming that they would rather kill them than let them go.

Thus, this incident, like every other one in this book, allows the mental disorder of batterers to show itself. One need only read the narrative to understand this point.

Chapter VI

How Do You Stay Out?

CHASED DOWN CASTRO STREET

Six weeks after I leave my abusive lover, never to return, our paths cross during rush hour on Castro Street one afternoon. I have been to court three weeks earlier and have been granted a restraining order prohibiting Stephen from coming within 150 feet of me. Having a copy of that restraining order with me, I feel "safe." (As safe as I am able to feel at the time.) On this day, Stephen violates the restraining order for the first time.

It is about five o'clock in the afternoon and I am walking down Castro Street with an acquaintance, George, when I hear someone call out "Patrick! Patrick!" from behind. I stop and turn around (George keeps walking), and there stands Stephen about three feet away. "Just say 'Hi'" he insists. "Why can't you just say 'Hi'?" Crisis rules flash through my head, well rehearsed rules: avoid eye contact, don't speak to him. At first fear prevails – but after standing frozen for a moment, I turn and cross Castro Street, not looking back. When Stephen yells, "Don't run away from me!" a second later, I know he is after me and I begin to run. I run up Castro toward Market Street, pushing through the crowds exiting the subway station and waiting for buses. I run around Harvey Milk Plaza, and up Market to Collingwood Street, a block away. Not seeing Stephen anymore, I stop running and begin to walk. Five seconds later I hear footsteps and Stephen is right behind me again, angry. He shouts, "Why did you run? Can't you just say 'Hi'?! Don't run away!!" This time I run like the wind, and I can hear Stephen shouting behind me, "Patrick, I'm sorry!! I'm sorry! I'm sorry!" I do not look back. I run in terror back onto Castro, and go into

Crown Books and . . . well, "hide." After three or four minutes I go to the doorway and, looking down the street, I see Stephen standing in the street at the corner of 18th and Castro, scanning the crowds looking for me. I duck back into the bookstore for a minute or so, then see that Stephen is gone. I leave Crown Books and run all the way back to David's.

Fifteen minutes later David and I are on our way to the police station.

"Chased Down Castro" addresses four important points about gay men's domestic violence. First, it illustrates the concept of "batterer tenacity," the frantic and relentless pursuit of the victim by the batterer. Patrick wrongly believes that a restraining order will sufficiently deter Stephen from harassing him. He has made the potentially grave error of underestimating Stephen's determination to get at him.

Second, the incident demonstrates the need for victims of domestic violence to be prepared for chance encounters with their batterers. Worst-case scenarios need to be thought out in advance. Victims need to establish, rehearse, and abide by a set of "crisis rules." These are behavioral guidelines for victims to follow when confronted with a potentially dangerous situation. For example, Patrick's "rules" included avoiding eye contact with Stephen and *not ever* speaking to him. At the moment of crisis, instead of panicking, Patrick operates from his rules: He averts his eyes and says nothing.

Third, a point about victim safety also made clear in this incident is the need for victims, when in danger, to run toward people and toward help. Running down deserted streets or into empty parks can be a fatal mistake. In this instance Patrick runs toward a crowd of commuters and later into a busy bookstore. He is safer in these places than in those where Stephen can get at him alone.

Finally, this incident introduces the importance of having restraining orders and of making police reports on all restraining order violations. As will be explained later in the chapter, in order to get the wheels of justice turning for victims of domestic violence, victims need to possess restraining orders.

HOW DO YOU STAY OUT?

"Why not just leave?" "You guys don't have kids or anything, so why don't you just walk out the door?" "I'd leave the first time it happened. Why did you put up with it?"

These are some of the most common remarks made to victims of domestic violence. Nobody seems to understand why victims stay with the men who batter them. While this issue of staying was addressed fully in Chapter IV, a short list of ten common reasons for staying is also helpful here.

1. The victims love their batterers.
2. Victims do not want to leave the men they love; they only want the violence to stop.
3. Victims hope and believe, often for a long time, that the violence will stop.
4. The violence is periodic, and the loving periods between violent episodes entice victims to stay.
5. Victims may believe they provoke or cause or deserve the violence.
6. Victims are often told by others that they provoke or cause or deserve the violence.
7. They may have left before but were encouraged by friends, family, therapists, the clergy, or the police to "go home" where they belong.
8. Victims may have tried to leave and been beaten for it.
9. Learned helplessness sets in, and victims no longer believe they can escape.
10. Victims are threatened with more violence, or even death, if they try to leave, and, with good reason, they believe these threats.

This list could actually be a lot longer, and pages of "reasons to stay" could be written. The focus of this section, however, is on how to help victims stay out once they leave their partners. We fully acknowledge that victims of domestic violence are up against walls of opposition and unimaginable difficulties as they try to stay away from their (stalking) abusive partners. As many victims may know, leaving is one thing, but staying away is completely different. Staying away is at first a full-time, 24-hour-a-day job. It is also very difficult to do alone. What follows here are five tips that are instrumental in helping victims stay out of their relationships with violent men. Since we know that victims are bombarded with confusion and difficulties during their first few weeks and months after escaping, we do not list 75 more things for them to remember. We hope and believe that if the five tips presented here are followed, staying out may not only be possible, it may be a lot easier.

The following five tips will be covered in more detail in this section, and they are listed here as a quick checklist or reference point.

1. Find a Lay Helper
2. Contact Support
3. Get a Restraining Order
4. Develop Crisis Rules
5. Stay Focused

As in the previous section, these tips are not applicable to all gay male victims. How you manage to get support and stay out of your relationship with a violent man will depend, in part, on where you live, how much money you have, what resources you have access to, and many other factors. Remember, wherever you are, whatever your situation, it is possible to get out and stay out.

1. Find a Lay Helper

After you leave your battering lover, you may be in for a very rough time. You will face painfully difficult decisions, perhaps experience a complete lack of support, and have to deal with financial hardship and emotional turmoil like never before. To make this period less treacherous, and to help you to stay out, it will be helpful for you to have someone you can call on 24 hours a day. In addition to seeking both individual and group therapy, if possible, we encourage you to find a lay helper.

A lay helper is ideally a friend or acquaintance, a man or woman, whom your lover does not know. He is someone who will support your decision to leave 100 percent and who can be there for you when you need him. He is someone who you have access to at all hours of the day and night. Maybe what you need is a safe way to get to work in the morning. Or, someone to help you fill out restraining order forms. Perhaps you need help finding a new apartment for yourself. Or, you may need someone to help keep track of all the things that are happening, as the list of things to do may seem endless. In addition, you are also probably more familiar with feelings of helplessness when overwhelmed than you are with organization, planning, and action. Your lay helper can help you with any or all of these things and more. She is someone who commits time and energy to you as you escape from your battering lover and set up a new life for yourself.

A few words about what a lay helper is *not*. He is not someone to make decisions for you. Instead, he is there to help you decide what you want and to figure out with you how to go about getting it. She is not someone to step in and run your life for you. She is someone to follow your instruction and to help you learn how to run your own life. It is crucial that you keep your relationship with him clear and honest, with no strings attached. You have just left a very tangled and confusing relationship, and the best thing for you now is independence, self-reliance, and the building of your self-esteem. Working with a lay helper can help you build the sturdy foundations of independence that are necessary for your new life as an ex-victim of gay men's domestic violence.

2. Contact Support

One of the most important things for you to do after leaving your abusive lover is to contact a mental health professional and get emotional support. The benefits of both individual and group support during this period cannot be overstated.

During the first few weeks and months after leaving your batterer, you may experience emotional swings like never before. You may feel lonely and depressed, missing your ex-lover, then suddenly be angry and disgusted with the way he treated you. Feelings of intense relief that you finally managed to escape may be interrupted by the intense fear of more violence. You may feel very sad that the future you once envisioned with him will not happen, and a moment later experience joy and exhilaration that you are free of him. Guilt will surface again and again, both for staying with him so long, and for leaving him to fend for himself. The shame and self-blame associated with victimization can also be overwhelming and painfully slow to pass. Furthermore, friends and family, whose support you may desperately need, may not only be nonsupportive, they may be angry, indignant, compassionless, and blaming. For the sake of your own safety, you may also have chosen to be cut off from your usual support network of friends. In short, these can be extremely difficult times for you.

The powerful emotional turmoil you may experience needs to be dealt with, and taking care of yourself, or bending the ears of your one understanding friend will probably not suffice. Emotional support at this phase of your new life as an ex-victim is critical in helping you to stay out of your relationship with your violent ex-partner and begin to heal.

Since there are no shelters for battered gay men, and since many lesbian and gay therapists have little or no experience and training in working with gay male victims of domestic violence, you may have to shop around for appropriate counseling. Remember, too, that an effective counselor for you need not be gay, but she or he must at least be knowledgeable, understanding and sensitive to gay issues. Since many of the victimization issues are similar for battered women and battered gay men, a straight woman therapist who has worked with battered women may work perfectly with you. (See the section on counseling in Chapter VIII.)

For those victims who may feel deeply ashamed and responsible for the abuse they have experienced, we encourage you, too, to muster up all of your courage and contact support services. There are people who care and understand, who will believe you, and who will not blame you, ridicule you, or encourage you to go back. The sooner you contact help for yourself, the sooner you can begin to deal with the massive changes you are experiencing as you regain control over your life. People are there to help you. Contact them.

Living in San Francisco, I was fortunate enough to be able to participate in a 13-week therapy group for battered gay men. The group started about four weeks after I left Stephen, and quickly became my emotional life-support system. The six other group members and two wonderful therapists were instrumental in helping me stay out of my relationship, learn to accept the violence I had experienced, and grow stronger in my life without abuse.

In one of the last sessions, another member pointed out that he could see I had grown a great deal, because, as he said, "For the first two months, Patrick never smiled." I smile and laugh a lot now, in part because this group was there for me when there was so little to smile about.

3. Get a Restraining Order

We cannot underscore enough the importance of obtaining a restraining order to protect you from further harassment from your abusive ex-lover. Restraining orders can be invaluable, and they serve several significant purposes.

First, it is crucial that you have a restraining order in order to get the wheels of the criminal justice system turning for you. A restraining order is your legal protection, and the police and criminal justice system act according to its dictates. For example, a restraining order can prohibit your batterer from coming within a specified distance of you (say, 150 yards), from telephoning you, from coming to your place of work, or where you work out, or where you do volunteer work, or from contacting members of your family. You can, theoretically at least, prohibit him, by law, from contacting you. Remember, he will try more than anything else to "contact" you. More accurately, to quote Del Martin, he will stalk you "like a hunted animal," and you will probably need all the protection you can get (Martin, 1976, p. 78).

A second invaluable attribute of a restraining order is that it sends a loud and powerful message to the abuser: He is breaking the law. Violence against you, like violence against any other person, is illegal, and if your ex-lover insists on contacting or harassing you, he will have the law to contend with and will suffer the legal consequences of his actions. Without a restraining order, it will be almost impossible to get the police or any court in the country to take action against your abusive ex-lover to keep him away from you. Thus, not only do batterers learn that their abusive behavior carries serious legal consequences, but they also learn that you are serious about ending the relationship and the violence that goes with it.

A third powerful incentive to obtain a restraining order is that it can help provide the ex-victim of domestic violence with feelings of strength, security and empowerment. To someone who has been criticized, harassed, punched, and slapped for months or even years, feelings of strength and security may be totally foreign. Domestic violence depletes the strength of its victims, erodes their self-confidence and self-esteem, and leaves them feeling weak and powerless. Restraining orders can play a part in helping to rebuild that strength. They provide tangible evidence that the ex-victim has taken a stand, that he will not tolerate abuse, that he is putting a stop to the violence, and that the law is on his side.

My restraining order, painful as it was to obtain, quickly became my best friend. David had a copy reduced and laminated for me, so that it fit neatly into my back pocket. I felt secure when I had it with me, and fearful the few times I left it at home. It was shown to countless police officers as Stephen again and again violated its dictates. It was, for me, power. It was my legal protection and a document that the police took seriously. It was my ticket to safety. Do not think for a minute that Stephen was unaware of its power. After a long absence he resurfaced again and began harassing me the week before my first restraining order was to run out. He knew that in a week's time my legal wall of safety would come tumbling down. What he did not know was that I could, and shortly thereafter did, obtain a second one. This one, reduced, laminated, and in my back pocket again, is good for three years. My legal wall of safety is still around me. Stephen is not.

4. Develop Crisis Rules

It is likely that after you leave your battering partner, he will pursue you with a vengeance. If you have left him before, you may know the ruthlessness with which he will try to track you down. This, of course, means constant vigilance on your part against attacks from him, or any other form of contact with him. You must, somehow, always be prepared for the crisis situation when he suddenly appears out of nowhere and grabs you.

We advocate a complete cutoff from your batterer: no phone calls, no meetings, no casual conversations in the street, no messages back and forth through friends. No communication whatsoever. Remember, this time you have left him forever, and there is to be no talk of reconciliation. Our "no contact" stance is important in that it can save you a tremendous amount of confusing and unproductive emotional turmoil. You will save yourself the agony of listening to his pleas for forgiveness, his how-can-you-leave-me-now challenge; his I'm-so-sorry apologies; his I-can't-live-without-you declarations. You are effectively eliminating any phase-three behavior on his part (see Chapter IV), and you are preventing yourself from being seduced back into the relationship by your feelings of guilt, false hopes, and love. This is a difficult and necessary part of staying away.

An invaluable method to help you maintain this "no contact" stance is to develop and follow a set of crisis rules. These are rules that flash into your head in an emergency, and they are designed with two goals in mind: maintaining your personal safety and keeping you out of the relationship with your violent partner. Crisis rules should be few in number, say four or five, and should be short in length, three or four words each. When in a crisis you want to be able to go through your list in a matter of seconds. Patrick's rules, for example, were (and three years later still are) as follows:

1. Avoid eye contact
2. Never speak to Stephen
3. My safety first: taxi, run, or call police
4. If I run, run toward help
5. Tell the person I am with what is happening

Your own rules should be well-rehearsed, so that in a crisis they will come to mind automatically. What kind of crisis do we mean? The list, unfortunately, is long. Let us say that you have managed to stay away for two weeks, and here he comes walking toward you on the street as you wait for the bus. Or, you come home from work and he is on your doorstep. He telephones you. You walk into the grocery store, and there he is. You walk into a restaurant, theater, party, or friend's home, and there he is. Your boss comes into your office to tell you that he is outside demanding to see you. You run into him on the street. He is ringing your doorbell at two a.m. You are on foot, and he is following you in a car. And on and on.

Having a set of well-rehearsed crisis rules may literally save your life. One look at him and the rules come to mind, and you go into automatic pilot. Avoid his eyes, look for exits, calmly (if possible) leave the room. Do not speak to him, pick up your backpack, run like hell toward a busy street. Turn to your friend and say, "That's him," and get into a taxi. Remember, the batterer is not a healthy man. He may be madder than hell at you for leaving and determined to either get you back no matter what, or "teach you a lesson" once and for all. Do not provide him with the opportunity to hurt you physically or emotionally. Cut off all contact with him. Rehearse and use your crisis rules. Stay safe.

Finally, a last point about crisis rules. Do not be surprised if, in 18 months, you are still using them. We learn from the experience of battered women that their batterers stalk them for years. Patrick's lover, 32 months later, still harasses him and pleads for a get-to-gether, and the crisis rules still apply.

Often David's last question before he dropped me off or hung up the phone was: "What are the rules?" I would quickly recite them. They became a useful and powerful tool, saving me from panic, confusion, and even fear. I knew that no matter what the situation, I had some guiding principles, some plan to rely on. And use them I did, again and again and again. They helped me to keep away from Stephen, and kept me from worrying that I would run into him, and from panicking when I did.

5. Stay Focused

After leaving an abusive lover, the combination of conflicting emotions and tough decisions can be so bewildering that they too, like the batterer once did, can leave you feeling helpless and overwhelmed. However, there are steps you can take to help yourself, and they all involve staying focused on your goal: to stay out of the relationship. Staying focused means concentrating on what you know to be the best for you. It may be difficult for you, at times, as an ex-victim of gay men's domestic violence, to believe in yourself and to focus on your own plan of action, despite what other people say, think, or feel. After being told by your batterer a thousand times that you never do anything right, you may have been conditioned to doubt yourself or your decisions and abilities. So when a friend, who simply does not understand, encourages you to go back, stay focused on your goal. In difficult periods, you can start out by focusing on the courageous right-things you have done so far, such as escaping from your apartment, stopping the violence in your life, opening your own bank account, or whatever positive steps you have taken to help yourself. There may be times when it feels as if only you know that leaving and staying away is best. Trust your feelings, believe in yourself, stay focused on your goal.

One technique to help you build strength and stay focused is called "changing the tapes" that you play to yourself. Tapes, here, are the messages you may have received so often from your batterer (or from other sources) that they have become part of your belief system about yourself. For example, if your batterer tells you repeatedly over months or years that you are "too thin," or "clumsy," you will eventually play those messages to yourself. These demeaning, critical, or blaming messages are psychologically abusive and can contribute significantly to your own victimization.

Take heart, because the time has come to change the way you talk to yourself about yourself. You are encouraged here to start playing positive, affirming messages to yourself about the good things you do, about the wonderful aspects of your personality, and about your strengths. Make a list of five things you like about yourself. This is your first new tape. Here are some examples:

- I am intelligent.
- I am a good cook.
- I am a talented artist.
- I am witty.
- I know a lot about politics.
- I am a great dancer.

- I am a good swimmer.
- I am a loving person.
- I am strong.
- I am a good listener.
- I am a good softball player.
- I am good-looking.

Create a short list, with five of your positive attributes, and say it again and again to yourself. Remember, years of criticism and cruelty will not vanish overnight, but before long your new and positive messages will replace the others in your self-concept. Recite your list all the time: in the shower, on the bus, as you walk to work, as you cook dinner. Remember, this list is to help you stay focused and will be particularly helpful in difficult situations. When someone says you were "stupid" for staying, silently recite your list. When you need strength to face the police after another restraining order violation, recite your list, build yourself up. When you have that fleeting fear that you will never find another lover, recite your list.

As time goes on you will become even more skilled at detecting the often very subtle, negative, and demeaning messages you tell yourself. Change them, and develop a repertoire of affirming and empowering messages. You will slowly and methodically eradicate victim-thinking and the victim role from your life, making it easier for you to stay away from your ex-lover and to remain free of abuse.

Another powerful way for you to stay focused on your goal is to keep in mind the violence you have experienced. Do not allow yourself to put it aside, unpleasant as it may be. Do not deny or minimize it. In fact, remembering the violence as vividly as possible may prove to be your strongest incentive to stay out of the relationship.

As most victims know, time passes and bruises heal. Ripped clothing is mended. Broken furniture is repaired. A loving period begins . . . and violence is put aside, diminished, "forgotten." This pattern, characteristic of the cycle of violence, must be broken. Do not allow yourself, once again, to slip into complacency and dream that violence will not happen again. Instead, remember what has happened. Write down in considerable detail the violence you have experienced. Be specific. What did he say? Where did he hit you? What did it feel like to be hit? Remember the details. What was broken this time? What "caused" the argument? How long were you in shock when it was over? What did he look like when he hit you? What did you have to do to protect yourself? Put it all down on paper. At some point in the future when you are lonely and miss him, read it. You will help yourself to remember why you left, and why you must stay away. As time passes, you will remember more of the violence. Write it all down. Remember it.

You, too, can make a list of the violent acts you have experienced similar to the list of violent acts in Chapter I. Think hard and include every single one, no matter how insignificant it might seem. Chances are, like most victims, your list will be long. Every so often read your list. When a friend encourages you to go back, read the list to him or her. Remember what each act of violence felt like. Remember your humiliation when he screamed at you in a restaurant. Remember how you felt when he threw your spaghetti dinner onto the kitchen floor. Remember the scratch marks on your arms and neck. Remember each one, and you will strengthen your resolve to stay out.

We know of one victim of gay men's domestic violence who, over the years, collected hundreds of dollars worth of "vintage clothing" from the '20s and '30s. He was a dazzling dresser. One night in a rage his lover cut up all of his clothing with a pair of scissors. Lest he forget the violence, the victim kept shreds of his clothes all over his room. He never forgot why he left. The remnants of his wardrobe forced him to focus on his goal of staying out. It worked.

Staying focused will help you ride out the storm that follows leaving a violent lover. At times staying out may seem like more effort than it is worth. At times you may sorely miss your lover/batterer. At times you will be exhausted and just want to "go home." It is during these periods that staying focused on your goal is most crucial. Remember, this time you have left for good. Going back now means going back to more violence.

When I made my first list of violent acts there were 31 items on it. At first I was absolutely appalled and thought surely I had exaggerated. I hadn't. I cried, felt rage, and knew that I could never return to that kind of life. I have since remembered four more. Three years later, abuse that I had long "forgotten" comes to mind. Remember, yes. Go back, never.

YOUR LIFE WITHOUT ABUSE

Congratulations. You have just done what is perhaps the most difficult thing you will ever have to do in your life: You left the man you love, who battered you. People may not be congratulatory, now or ever, but you certainly deserve praise. It takes strength, courage and determination to leave an abusive partner and to stay away. Pat yourself on the back, because you have just climbed a mountain in your life.

As you probably know only too well, your troubles, unfortunately, are not over. Financial and emotional hardships are most likely coming your way. Stay out of that relationship and you will find strength and energy you never knew you had to deal with things. Loneliness and fear may be your traveling companions for a while, and that is natural. They are the by-products of leaving someone you care about, and of trying to protect yourself from violence. Eventually they too, like your ex-lover, will pass out of your life, and you will be healthier, stronger, and safe.

You may experience feelings best described as, pardon the cliche, "freedom." You may notice, with great pleasure, the absence of fear in your life, the absence of stress and anxiety. You may wake up morning after morning and smile in disbelief: "I really did it. I don't have to deal with him anymore. It's really over." The freedom and sense of accomplishment will stay with you for a long time.

Of course, your new bed of roses has its pricks. You may have left everything behind, and at the age of (however old you are) you may be starting over, again. You will have to make new friends, because you will no longer have some of the old ones. You will probably be very busy reorganizing your life. Nevertheless, you are in a bed of roses that is soft and sweet in contrast to the bed you just left.

I think it was at least six months before I began to relax and feel free from my ex-lover. Even while he was still around and harassing me, the hardest part was over, and I knew I would never go back to him. Six months may not sound like very long, but they were certainly the longest six months of my life.

Somehow my fear of violence from Stephen was generalized to a fear of, it seemed, everything. I was afraid of loud machinery. I was afraid to operate a dishwasher. I was afraid of any sharp objects or weapons, and even of household tools. I was afraid of rude or angry people – and in particular, oddly, angry waiters or waitresses. When these fears eventually subsided, I began to feel free. I laughed and smiled more. My appetite tripled, and I put on a lot of weight. I began working out and getting stronger. I began to manage my own life. I began living as an ex-victim of gay men's domestic violence.

It was probably a whole year before I began to accept that my new freedom was not, somehow, temporary. I was afraid for a long time that my abuse-free life would come crashing down, and that I would be left in the rubble: cowering, bleeding, battered. Thus, even freedom was hard for me to trust. That fear, though, like the others, passed. I know that I am free now, and I always will be.

A formerly-battered woman sums up this feeling of a new life in the book, *The Ones Who Got Away.* She writes, "Life is marvelous now. I enjoy everything because I don't have this cloud hanging over me. I go for a ride and look at the tulips. Now I'm free. I really love the freedom. I can do the things I want. The freedom is great. At last I'm free. No one is looking over my shoulder. I'm free, I'm free, I'm free, I'm free" (NiCarthy, 1987 p. 325).

CAN YOU TELL IF HE IS A BATTERER BEFORE YOU BECOME A VICTIM?

Contrary to what many people believe, victims of domestic violence do not "seek out" violent partners. They are not masochists who want or need abuse. Yet, victims are often told that they got what they deserved because they "should have known better" than to get involved with a violent man. Unfortunately, these beliefs are based on ignorance about domestic violence, not facts.

Most victims of domestic violence could not have predicted that the men they were getting involved with would later batter them. One reason is that most domestic violence does not occur until *after* the partners are involved. In her book, *When Battered Women Kill,* Angela Browne explains that, "Typically, in 72 to 77 percent of the cases, violence occurs only after a couple has become seriously involved . . . or is living together; rather than in the early, more casual stages of dating" (1987, p. 42). Victims usually do not know that the potential for violence exists until it occurs. Remember, men who batter do not show up for dates carrying boxing gloves. Their violence is usually a well-kept secret.

Men who batter are often first perceived as charming and enter-taining, rather than as abusive. In virtually all of the relationships Browne studied, victims described their partners, in the early stages, as the most romantic, attentive, and passionate lovers that they had ever had. Descriptions such as charming, sensitive and caring were common, and the men were viewed as intensely com-mitted to the relationship. Most victims described the first incident as "out of the blue" (1987, p. 47), and had great difficulty making sense out of violence perpetrated by someone they knew and loved (1987, Ch. 3).

No one can predict for sure that someone will be violent. No one can predict just when a violent person will be abusive again. Not until your boyfriend or your lover has actually hit you, has de-stroyed some of your property, or has intimidated, harassed or frightened you will you know for sure that you have an abuser on your hands. Yet there are signs of potential violence in a man, pat-terns to look for under the charm and intensity of your new partner.

Learn to trust your own judgment about how you feel and what you notice. Are you uneasy around him but do not know why? Is there a fear inside you? Listen to it. Give yourself the benefit of the doubt. When you feel it, it is there. Your judgment is valid.

If you suspect that your lover or the man you are dating may be a batterer, you can take some steps to find out, that may protect you from abuse later on. If you have any reason at all to think that the man you love might be a violent man, do something now. Do not wait until you are lying in the hospital recovering from a violent attack wishing you had acted earlier on your hunches. Think about it, then take action.

Consider the following suggestions.

1. Ask Him If He Has Ever Been Violent and Observe His Reactions

We strongly encourage you to talk to your partner about his past relationships. You need to know if this man has a history of violent and abusive behavior. A history of violence is the best predictor of future violence, so if your boyfriend reveals having been abusive or violent with his partners in the past, do not wait around to be his next victim.

Keep in mind that it is in your partner's best interest to keep any violence in his past a secret. Nobody would date the man who freely admitted having beaten the daylights out of his last two lovers. Therefore, you can expect that you will be lied to when you ask directly about battering. Or, if he does admit to some violence, assume that he is minimizing the seriousness of it. Do not be deterred from asking anyway, because how he responds to your questioning may be as revealing as the answers he gives.

Remember, you have a perfect right to know the answers to these questions.

- Have you ever been violent? Have you ever hit anyone? Who? When? What happened?
- Have you ever wanted to hit me?
- Have you ever been so angry that you broke things, or put your fist through a wall?
- Have you ever been really drunk and not remembered how you hurt somebody?
- Is there something you think I could do that would be bad enough for you to hit me?
- Do you ever have trouble stopping yourself from doing something violent?
- Have you ever hit a boyfriend of yours?

The way your partner answers these questions is just as important as the substance of the answer. Observe his responses, and trust your gut. If he brushes aside your questions with, "That's a ridiculous question. I won't answer it," or, "My past is none of your business," then you already have your answer. He may not be violent, but he is still to be avoided because he will not respond sensitively to a concern of yours. Now is the best time to put a stop to that relationship.

If he does answer these questions directly and without hesitation, thank him for being honest. Or if he is open to the topic, and willing to talk about violence in a relationship, and how it should never happen again, thank him for being honest. But keep your eyes open, and watch for minimization and denial. Does he answer, but change the subject too quickly? Does he talk fast and hurry through the answers? Does he get defensive, or try to turn the conversation back onto you? Trust your instincts. When in doubt, get out.

2. Observe Him Carefully When He Is Angry

The reason you want to observe your boyfriend or lover carefully when he is angry is that batterers characteristically have a lot of trouble managing and controlling their anger. In the old days, it was called "having a bad temper." Not all batterers' anger problems are easy to spot, because many men are able to keep them effectively hidden.

We know that abusers and batterers are very angry and desperate men inside. They tend to hate themselves deeply, and they strike out at their loved ones as a way of coping with their self-hatred. Consequently, if you want to find out if the man you love is also a batterer, it makes good sense for you to observe very closely when he is angry. What does he do? What does he say? What does he look like? Watch to see how hard he struggles to stay under control when some little thing (little to you) has triggered his anger or rage. Note the kinds of things that trigger his anger. Is it you, your comments, your opinions, your independence? Is it traffic? The weather? Television? Stupid drivers? Forgetting something? Is it little tiny frustrations, like burnt the toast, dinner that is late, or laundry not folded?

Watch for nonverbal cues. Watch his hands. Does he clench his fists? Does he pound on the table or the steering wheel? Does he tap his feet or fingers just before an angry outburst? Does he put his hands on his hips, turn and square off at the object of his anger?

Listen to the words. Does he start off his angry outburst with a tirade against the person or the situation? Listen to the volume and tone. How loud does he get? Does his tone change and become mean-sounding? Do your ears hurt?

If you watch him carefully when he is angry, you will begin to see patterns. These patterns will tell you about your man, and you will be better able to judge whether or not you are going to be the target of his violence and abuse when he is angry.

3. Talk Privately About Him with People
He Is Close to

These conversations are difficult and not recommended unless you have no other sources of information and can be assured of your own safety and of confidentiality. The people closest to your lover will be able to give you the most reliable information about him, unless they are protecting him.

You must keep in mind that these people may be reluctant to talk with you about abuse. First, no one likes to talk about violence. Second, these individuals may fear retribution from your lover if he ever finds out that they have talked with you about him.

Sometimes, however, these conversations with his close friends or relatives can be easier than you imagine. We advise being straightforward. Tell the person that there is something about your new boyfriend that bothers you. You are wondering if they have any good advice for you on how to handle him. Has he been abusive in other relationships? Have they ever seen him quite angry? Do they think he is capable of striking out in anger? Have they ever seen him break things, destroy property or hit people?

4. Take Note of His Habits and His Interests

Does he collect guns? Does he ever talk about "wiping out" people? Does he laugh at violent scenes in movies? Does he seem to prefer violent movies? Violent TV? Does he think people are wimps who do not enjoy fighting and conflict? Does it seem to you that some of his interests are in support of violence and violent means to solve people-problems?

5. Notice How He Handles Stress and Disappointment

There are many uncontrollable forces in the world that cause us stress and tension at times. The weather, the traffic, and the behavior of other people are such forces. How one handles them is a tip-off to one's mental health, and the stability of one's personality. Batterers generally do not handle stress and ordinary disappointments very well. They overreact and act out. They get loud and

physical, and they can become violent. If you wonder whether or
not the man you love is also a batterer, it is important that you note
his reactions to what most of us think are just ordinary, expected
stresses and distresses of life.

How quickly and how frequently does he lose his temper over
small stresses? What does he say and do when it rains on your
picnic, or while you wait in line for a movie? Does he ever blame
you for situations that you cannot possibly be faulted for?

6. Take Note of How You and Your Partner Settle Disagreements

This point is very important since small disagreements are the
fuels that stoke the fires of domestic violence.

For instance, you have eaten out in a nice restaurant. Your lover
wants you to leave no tip because he judged the waiter to be incompetent. You want to tip the waiter the usual 15 percent. How do you
and your lover resolve this difference of opinion? Is it important to
you to keep him from getting angry?

You are grocery shopping for dinner with the man you are dating.
You notice that every time you add an item to the shopping cart he
questions or criticizes your choice. You also notice that if you question anything he puts into the cart he reacts very negatively. He
wants to control your choice making, but does not want you to
control his.

These are but two examples of hundreds of ordinary activities
which can reveal clues that the man you are falling in love with may
be trying to coerce or dominate you. Ask yourself: "If he controls
what kind of bread I put in the shopping cart, won't he want to
control when we have sex, how much money I have in my wallet,
and whether or not I call my brother?"

7. Listen to How He Talks About You, Especially When He Is Critical

Words hurt and can be abusive. Notice if your lover or your
boyfriend uses cruel, mean, or overly critical words when he talks
to you about you. "You're so bony." "You're getting too fat."

"Your hair looks awful tonight." "You're ugly, and no one else would want you." "I hate your mother." Also notice if your boyfriend uses insulting humor about you in front of other people, putting you down or embarrassing you in public. When you tell him that the things he says hurt you, does he say, "Oh, don't be so sensitive!" doubling the hurt and insinuating that there is something wrong with you for feeling badly? Remember, words that hurt are a common form of psychological violence.

Most batterers are quick to criticize and very slow to praise. If your lover only rarely praises you for something specific that you have done, think about how you are being manipulated or taken for granted.

When the praise comes, you may find yourself wondering what his motives are, because it is so rare. This also deserves your attention since it is a cue that manipulation is occurring. Trust your feelings. If you think you are being manipulated, or criticized too much, you probably are.

Many batterers will heap verbal abuse upon their partners until they see the devastation they have brought. The partner crumbles under the avalanche of criticism, breaks down and cries, or just withdraws into silence. Then, the batterer showers the victim with verbal "gifts" to make up. This is the cycle of verbal violence: tranquility-criticism-make up-tranquility. Look for it.

8. Find Out from Your Lover About All of His Past

Find out about all of his past, not just his past relationships, but his jobs, his educational record, his upbringing, his finances, his activities in life.

Did his father beat up his mother and did he see it? Did his father hit him a lot? Had he been in a lot of fights with friends when he was a teenager? Has he ever been in jail for disturbing the peace? Has he ever owned a gun? Has he ever had any bones broken as a result of violence?

You have a right to know if he has been abusive, or if he may abuse you. If he won't tell you about his life, get him out of yours.

9. Observe How Jealous and Restricting He Is

This is particularly important. Batterers are known for their extreme jealousy and for their desire to restrict your scope of activity outside their company. Some batterers are ferocious in their need to control all of the activities of their lovers.

Does your boyfriend expect you to spend all your free time with him, or to keep him informed of your whereabouts? Do you get quizzed closely when you get home? Does he want to know exactly where you were and whom you talked to? Is he constantly accusing you of being interested in, or having sex with, other men?

The intense interest that new lovers show in each other is normal and healthy. Do not let your mutual infatuation blind you to controlling behaviors he may already be showing. "Overkill" is the clue (Walker, 1979, p. 37). In your opinion, is he overly interested in your activities? Is he too jealous of your friends or family? Intense jealousy is a red flag, so beware. Jealousy and the need to restrict your activities go hand in hand, and both are part of a controlling, domineering personality.

10. What He Has Done to Others He Will Do to You

Do you see your lover treat other people and objects badly but then think to yourself that he will not treat you that way because he loves you so much?

Many straight battered women report that they knew their husbands had hit other women but thought the previous women had provoked the violence. These women thought for a long time that somehow they were different and would not be abused. How wrong they were. Remember, domestic violence has nothing to do with a batterer's partner. It has everything to do with the batterer himself. Do you think that your lover will never abuse you because somehow you are special and different? Think again. If he has abused before, he will abuse again. If he is abusive to others, he will be abusive to you.

11. Observe How Rigid and Controlling He Is

Many batterers are extremely rigid and inflexible. You are cooking dinner and it is to be ready at seven. At ten past seven you call him to the table and he is furious because it is late.

There are hundreds of examples of rigidity and controlling behavior. The table has to be set just so. You have to drive at exactly 60 miles per hour on the freeway. He always has to shower first in the morning.

Look for signs of rigidity. When he is rigid about your activities, then he is showing you his inclination to control you.

12. Note His Ideas About Sex-Roles in Relationships

It is possible that gay male batterers place significant value on traditional male/female sex-roles. We know this to be true of heterosexual batterers. These men believe that women ought to behave only in certain "wifelike" roles that are strict and limiting to most women. Gay relationships, generally speaking, are more egalitarian, as gay men tend to place less value on the role-bound behaviors of heterosexual relationships. Gay male batterers, however, may share with their heterosexual counterparts the deeply socialized patriarchal concepts of gender roles.

Does your partner think that women should submit to the authority of men? Does he think that wives are husbands' property? Does he think that women should be tender and nurturing, and that men should be tough and not show their emotions? If he has rigid ideas about the way men and women should behave, he may also have strict ideas about how you should behave in a relationship with him.

Listen to what he says about women and about married couples. Check out his ideas about the roles he expects both you and him to take when you are a couple. Evaluate carefully whether or not he behaves in accordance with the way he talks about roles.

AND STILL HE PURSUES ME

Thirteen months after I leave Stephen he is still harassing me. Though no physical violence has occurred since I left him, the psychological harassment goes on and on. He sends me letters and packages; he appears at my workplace; he chases me down streets.

I have not uttered one word to him for more than a year. I have taken him to court twice and have been granted two restraining orders totaling four years of protection from him. I have already filed five police incident reports for restraining order violations and have contacted his lawyer after each one. All this and still he pursues me. In doing so, Stephen continues to create a climate of fear and intimidation that I, like so many victims of domestic violence, live under. What will happen next? How long will I keep having to look over my shoulder? Will I ever be safe? Is he going to show up at my front door? Will he be outside work today, waiting for me? Will this ever end?

One night in October, 1988, I am out on a date with Dennis, a man with whom I feel safe. I have told him about the relationship I have left, and that my ex-lover is still "on the loose" and bothering me. Despite this, we take a risk and go to a restaurant in the Castro for dinner. During dinner we decide that dessert at a spot called Sweet Inspiration, about two blocks away, would be nice. Later, as Dennis and I walk arm in arm into Sweet Inspiration, I spot Stephen sitting at a table by the door. I stop, turn to Dennis and say calmly, "I know, let's go someplace else." He catches on immediately, and we abruptly turn around and walk out.

I wait until Dennis and I are about a block away before turning around, and am then completely surprised to find that Stephen is nowhere to be seen. However, as we turn the next corner, en route to the second dessert spot I see Stephen running down the street toward us. By the time we enter Just Desserts, Stephen is right behind us. So now Dennis and I are standing at the counter in Just Desserts, and Stephen is standing in the doorway, his chest heaving from running. At this point, I feel both anger and hopelessness; the anger, obviously, directed at Stephen for following me, for not leaving me alone and for not getting out of my life once and for all (". . . and now he has really fucked up this date . . ."); and hopelessness, believing that it may never end, believing that he will haunt me until, finally, he is able to get at me again . . . and then what?

In anger and disgust and disbelief, I glare at him, breaking a long-abided-by rule. I turn to Dennis and say, "You won't believe this, but that's him," and I gesture toward the door. Dennis asks, "Where, Patrick?" I look and Stephen is gone.

The next morning I spend half an hour in the police station, filing an incident report for the sixth violation of a restraining order.

"And Still He Pursues Me" underscores a major point made throughout this chapter: batterer tenacity. It is serious enough when an abuser pursues his ex-lover two months after the victim has left him, but tenacity takes on another menacing dimension when the pursuit continues 13 months later. In this case, tenacity may have become an obsession. The lesson for the ex-victim is never to reduce his vigilance for possible pursuit by an abusive ex-lover. The ex-victim can make and rehearse plans for such possibilities and for the potential danger (or, at the very least, embarrassment) that may follow. An ex-victim should rehearse how he is going to tell his date that the "man staring at us through the doorway" is his abusive ex-lover.

Understanding why a batterer still pursues the ex-victim after so many months is important. Many victims seek help to deal with the abuse they have experienced and to get out of the victim role. Not so with batterers. It is much harder for batterers to admit that they need help, and it is very likely that Stephen, even thirteen months later, is still in the same psychological space he was in when Patrick left him. A batterer may also desperately desire the opportunity to make contact with his ex-victim, in hopes that the victim will forgive him, absolve him of the depravity of his actions and "help" him, thereby, to move on with his life. All of that, of course, is ridiculous, as well as dangerous for victims. It does explain, somewhat, why Stephen may still be pursuing Patrick. Stephen may believe that if he has "just one more chance," then perhaps everything can be worked out. That, too, is false. Research indicates that batterers continue to batter unless they seek long-term treatment, and even that is no guarantee that the violence will stop.

Finally, another possible explanation for Stephen's behavior is that he may be dumbfounded that after all these months of his waiting for Patrick to return to him, here is Patrick actually out on a date with another man! Some gay men who abuse their partners may not be able to accept that their partners hated the abuse, and they may look on in disbelief when their victims finally reject them.

Chapter VII

How Do You Help a Friend?

SARAH "HELPS OUT"

Following several months of periodic and escalating violence, I leave Stephen in March of 1985, and manage to stay away for almost three weeks. For most of that period, I stay with a friend who lives about 250 miles away; I am safe there. During this time, I maintain contact with only one friend, Margo, who reports to me that Stephen is "on the hunt," looking for me everywhere, calling all of our friends day and night. Some he accuses of hiding me from him, others of always interfering between us, and from still others he demands that they help him track me down. Except for Margo, I have told no one where I am staying.

After about two weeks away from Stephen, I am feeling better and stronger, and ready for what I believe to be inevitable: facing him, seeing him again, talking. After a lot of urging from our mutual friend Sarah, I agree to meet Stephen at her house, as long as she stays there with us. I absolutely refuse to return to our apartment to talk with Stephen, certain that only more violence will take place. I refuse even to meet him in a public place, like a restaurant or bar, as he has been violent with me in pubic places before. Somehow, though, Sarah's house seems to be a safe place. We both love and trust her, and I believe that with Sarah there Stephen will not get violent. I am wrong.

We have been sitting around Sarah's dining room, the three of us, for about ten minutes, when the tension begins to build. I am talking about the way things have been going between Stephen and me, and I make a comment about not being sure that I want the relationship to continue. Suddenly Stephen strikes. The punch comes full force, in the face. He hits me so hard that he knocks me over backward, the back of my chair hitting the floor. He is on me in a second, grabbing me by the shirt collar, shouting, "What did you say! What did you just say?!!" He is pounding my head against the floor as he yells. I am trying to get away, slowly crawling under the table with him on top of me. Sarah finally manages to pull him off me, shouting all the while, "Stephen!! Leave him! Leave him alone! Stephen!" I crawl out from under the table and run out of the room, the nearest exit being to the back garden. When Sarah comes out a minute later I am shaking with anger, fear and rage, and I am crying. "Why does he do this?! Why does this happen?" I begin to sob on Sarah's shoulder.

And then another very bad thing happens. Sarah begins to defend Stephen, trivializing what has just taken place. "He's so upset, Patrick. He loves you so much he can't bear the thought of losing you. When you say things like that he . . . reacts." She then "assures" me that many men hit their partners, and says, "It's not the end of the world." Why even she has been hit before (she says), and **she** *stayed with* **her** *husband.*

And again, yet again (as I write this, I shake my head in disbelief), I listen, and nod, and believe. It is as if no violence has just taken place. Or perhaps, worse yet, Sarah and I blame the violence on me; it is what I said that caused it. And here is Sarah, a close and trusted friend, telling me that the man who has just knocked me to the ground with his fist, and then pounded my head and shoulders into the floor, did this because he can't bear the thought of losing me. "And really it wasn't so bad, Patrick." By the time we return to the house Stephen has left. Apparently no further "conversation" from him is necessary. He has said (done?) what he needed to. I leave Sarah's shortly after, and a week later I move back in with Stephen.

This incident clearly and poignantly illustrates four crucial points about domestic violence. First, in this incident Patrick makes the grave mistake of assuming that he is safe because with Sarah there Stephen will not get violent. As pointed out earlier, domestic violence can occur anywhere, including at the houses of and in the presence of good friends.

Sarah also makes the mistake in this incident that countless people make when dealing with victims and batterers: She encourages them to get together. Victims of domestic violence need to be treated like victims of other crimes who are never expected to meet with their attackers.

Sarah's error in getting Patrick and Stephen together also demonstrates the ineffectiveness of the role she attempts to play as mediator. In fact, mediating in and of itself is always a mistake. She could have helped Patrick more by saying, "There is no justification for violence, Patrick, ever. I'll help you however I can, but concentrate first on your own safety."

Finally, this episode illustrates the pervasive pattern of blaming the victim. By the time they walk back into the house, both Sarah and Patrick believe that Patrick has "caused" the violence by what he said. As has been reiterated again and again in this book, violent behavior is the responsibility of the violent person. The victim's responsibility is to choose to leave the relationship.

HOW FRIENDS AND RELATIVES CAN BE SUPPORTIVE

People do the best they can, the best they know how. They mean well. Most friends and relatives of ex-victims of gay men's domestic violence have good intentions and are perfectly decent people.

Why is it, then, that sometimes they fail so badly to be helpful? Why do they arouse resentment and fear in the ex-victim? Why are they so confrontational, and, at times even abusive to the ex-victim? Why do they come on so strong?

Friends and relatives of ex-victims of gay men's domestic violence have two major, interrelated problems.

First, they probably do not understand at all what the ex-victim is going through during the first weeks and months after he leaves his abusive partner. During this period, the ex-victim is a psychological and emotional mess. Friends do not quite see this clearly. He looks normal to them. Relatives, of course, do not want to see it. The result is that they collectively respond to him as if he is fine! The fact is, he is not fine; he is in serious distress.

Second, they have not thought much about what they say to him and do with him, and they have not practiced the behaviors they need in order to help. Understandably, it just does not occur to most lay helpers that being responsive and supportive to a gay man who has just left his battering lover requires a far different set of being-a-friend skills than those they use when talking with a buddy whose date just stood him up. People genuinely try to be helpful and supportive to an ex-victim, but they can easily get in over their heads if they fail to keep in mind the plight of the victim. Being supportive to a person in distress, though not particularly hard, does demand well thought-out actions. To solve the problems, we make two suggestions:

1. Believe the Ex-Victim

That's all you have to do. He probably wants to tell you how awful it was. Let him. Do not ask why he did not tell you sooner. He is telling you now! Honor that act. You do not have to do anything except sincerely, genuinely believe him. Curb your tendency to doubt him. He is probably minimizing the violence and the trauma anyway. Assume that everything he is telling you is true. The essence of supportiveness is a tender, caring belief in the individual. If you cannot believe him and believe in him, for goodness sake, please temporarily excuse yourself from conversations with him and from the man's life. Otherwise you will harm him. "Do no harm" must be your guiding principle as you deal as a friend or relative with an ex-victim of gay men's domestic violence.

2. See the Distress

The ex-victim is probably suffering from Post-Traumatic Stress Disorder, a temporary mental disorder. His act of leaving an abusive partner was extremely traumatic. He is more stressed and distressed now, and will be for a certain period of time, than he was while he was in the relationship. He just left the man he loved. Worse, he may now actually fear for his life. He does not know what his now-angry ex-lover will do next. He realistically fears retaliation and more and worse violence than before. Consequently, he is extremely anxious and in need of lots of affirmation and comforting, but NO confrontation. When a man is severely distressed, that is not the time to begin confronting him, challenging him, or criticizing him. It is the time for calm, for gentleness, for listening.

It is the time to tell him softly that he is doing the right thing by leaving his abusive lover and that his safety is your primary concern, too. It is the time to put your arms around him, hold him tight, and tell him that you like him and care about what happens to him. That is what it means to be supportive. Do not give him advice. Do not try to solve his problems. Do not defend the abusive ex-lover. Do not offer your opinion, unless asked. Most importantly, do not tell him to go back.

HOW DO YOU HELP A FRIEND?
BASIC TIPS FOR THE LAY HELPER

When you decide to help a friend get out of a relationship with a violent man, you have made a commitment. You cannot comfortably stop assisting him until it is over. That may take many months. You may get tired of the whole thing, and you may feel like giving it up before it is over. Make your calendar flexible. Inform your friends and family that you may be unavailable at times. Fill your refrigerator. Helping an ex-victim of gay men's domestic violence takes time (and sometimes, a lot of food). You will talk with the ex-victim all night some nights, and then, exhausted, you will still have to go to work. You may receive a call at your workplace and choose to leave at midday to attend to your friend. You may have to cancel your appearance to a social event. There may be a new stocking hanging on your fireplace at Christmas. Of course, you must not restructure your life around the ex-victim, but, there will be important demands made on you, and since you have volunteered to help, you need to respond to them. Often, the helping process will not be any fun, and you may wonder why you are doing it.

But, I remember the night, the spot, the exact moment when Patrick turned, looked at me and said, "David, I believe it's over. I'm out of my relationship with that abusive man. I don't have to go back to Stephen. I don't want to go back. I'm really out! No one will ever do that to me again!" He was laughing and smiling, his brown eyes shining with pride and accomplishment. Months of work had paid off.

1. Hopefully, the Batterer Is a Stranger to You

It works best if you, the helping friend, do not know the batterer. Then, you do not have that other relationship baggage to pack around and deal with. When the batterer is a stranger to you, you are more able to be supportive to the ex-victim. There is no need to defend the abuser. You can be as cold and as logical about him as necessary. This tip is really for a victim: choose a friend to help you who does not know your battering lover.

I never knew Stephen, and I am glad of that. I saw him many times on the street, of course, and in court. I personally served court papers on him twice. I was named on Patrick's second restraining order as an additional person Stephen had to stay away from. But I did not know him, and I did not want to.

2. Choose a Side

By agreeing to help the ex-victim, you have accepted his decision that his relationship with his abusive ex-lover is over. Therefore, you have taken the side of the ex-victim. That means that if you know the batterer, you, too, should probably terminate your relationship with him. You may feel that this action is ruthless. Do not return his phone calls. Only nod a greeting, without a smile, when you see him in public. Do not welcome him in your home. You will never have another conversation with him. Tough? You bet. Necessary? Unquestionably.

The reason for taking a side is your new role with the ex-victim. You are no longer just his friend. You are his protector and advocate. Your role is never one of mediator or go-between. That never works. You must not provide shuttle diplomacy between them. Not once. Your function is not to help them work it out. By agreeing to help the ex-victim, you have committed yourself 100 percent to *his* goal of staying out of that relationship. It is not possible to give effective empathic support to the ex-victim with his abusive ex-lover hounding you (as he will) for information and pressing you (as he will) to hear his story of denial, minimization and falsehood. You, too, must adopt a position that the batterer and the ex-victim are never to see each other again. You can never waver from that position.

In the weeks and months right after his escape from Stephen, I observed several of Patrick's friends trying to be helpful to him, while remaining steadfast friends with Stephen. In every single instance, tension was created, ill-feelings developed and, in the end, no one was ever helped. Friends who want to help have to take a stand, on the side of either the batterer or the ex-victim, perhaps neither, but never with both.

3. Believe What the Ex-Victim Says About the Violence

Believing is the essential ingredient in being supportive. Accept his descriptions at face value. Never challenge the ex-victim about whether or not some particular episode of abuse, some detail, or intensity of violence occurred. It is not your place or role to challenge or doubt. The ex-victim will never trust you (for good reason) if you do not believe him.

I learned quickly when talking with Patrick about the abuse he experienced that his anxiety decreased in my presence and his trust in me increased when he began to realize that I was not going to challenge him. I never once said to him, "Oh, Patrick, it wasn't that bad, was it?" Because nearly everyone else he talked with (except some mental health professionals) challenged the truth of what he said, or, criticized and disbelieved him. He did not trust those doubters. I knew I had to act differently. I had to believe everything. It was easy. There was nothing to doubt.

4. No Gossip

When you commit yourself as a friend to help an ex-victim of abuse, you must be careful about how chatty you are with others and how much you disclose about the details of the ex-victim's life.

Never talk about the ex-victim's life and anything he has related to you with anyone, including his and your friends. The violence *he* experienced is not an appropriate subject for your conversations. It is confidential. Get permission from the ex-victim first, if you have a need to disclose anything about him.

If you and the ex-victim are together in a conversation with others, then it is entirely his decision whether or not to disclose anything to them about his situation.

For the first year of my involvement as a helping friend to Patrick, there were many occasions when I discussed him and his problems with others in his presence and out of his presence. Patrick always knew to whom I talked and what was discussed, because I always asked him first. He would think about it and then either give or withhold permission. Because I was careful to check with him first, Patrick grew to trust my handling of the knowledge I had about him. He was always the decision-maker about disclosure. Some months later, he gave me general permission. He put it this way. "David, you can talk to anyone you want to about me without asking me first. I trust your judgment, and I know you will keep my best interests in mind." Most of the time, even today, I still ask him first.

5. Assistance Not Dependency

When appropriate, it is helpful to offer the ex-victim some material resources. He may need to use your typewriter or telephone. He may need a place to sleep or shower. Offer your garage to protect his car. When you are together and mealtime approaches, invite him to eat with you. You may want to accompany him on emotionally difficult errands, which he inevitably will have to run, such as going to the police station to file a report of a violation of the restraining order against the batterer or going to the courthouse to file papers. However, be careful about giving the ex-victim money. Money transactions complicate otherwise smooth-running relationships. Your relationship with the ex-victim needs clarity and simplicity with a no-strings-attached independence. His achieving independence is crucial, and that is just one reason you should consider offers of money carefully. If you do offer it, make it a one-time gift or a businesslike loan with a timetable for repayment. Remember that the victim has just emerged from a disastrous relationship in which many destructive forces were operating. The last thing the ex-victim needs is to find himself in a relationship with you with a funny dependency issue operating. Talk frequently with him about his reliance on you and his independence from you. You will have to bring up the subject.

In Patrick's case I frequently offered rides to him, since at that time he did not own a car. Early in his stay at my home, I would drop him off and pick him up at his job on my way back and forth to work. This was necessitated at first because Patrick was afraid to ride public transportation (for fear of being pursued or attacked by Stephen), and taking a taxi was too expensive.

I never gave him money. I was a friend helping out, not a suitor seeking his favor. I did not do things for him. I did things with him. He knew and I knew that his independence needed to be established as a foundation for rebuilding his self-concept.

After I knew Patrick well enough to trust him, I co-signed with him on a credit card so that he could obtain an independent credit record, a relatively risky thing to do, I thought. As soon as his credit was established, I withdrew my co-signature. We frequently talked at length about the steps we were taking to keep our developing friendship free of dependency forces.

6. Advocate Work

Never foster in the ex-victim an irresponsible attitude about going to work. This advice grows not out of a puritan work ethic but rather out of two other important principles: Work is therapy, and work sustains independence. Steady work is an indispensable factor in restoring mental and emotional stability in addition to providing some overall daily purpose and, of course, funds. Your role, as the helping friend, is to advocate his going to work on time every day without fail.

7. Your Work, Your Calendar, Your Friends

Be able to change your calendar when necessary. There will be a few times when he simply needs to talk to you or needs your help with something. The concept is access. The ex-victim needs access to a secure and safe person. Access to you is an anchor for him. Remember, his life has just been dismantled. He has left his lover, his apartment, and all of his belongings. He is anxious and afraid. He is in need of a steady, calm contact. He needs the certainty that there is someone out there on whom he can rely. That person is you. The importance of your being accessible and predictably calm cannot be overestimated.

Prepare the people at your workplace for interruptions and contact by the ex-victim. People there need to be advised that, for a certain period of time, if the ex-victim you are helping calls or appears, you are to be located. You do not have to provide many details, unless your supervisor or manager needs them. Instruct the individuals what to expect and that the ex-victim is in a crisis and needs access to you on rare occasions.

If you sense danger to yourself, such as an attack by the batterer in retaliation for your helping the ex-victim (a common occurrence), you should also prepare the people you work with for that emergency. You should show receptionists, co-workers, and security staff a picture of the abuser and ask them to warn you and to call the police if he should appear.

Since I was a business owner then, I had some leeway in my schedule. At the office, my work could be interrupted for important family and personal matters. The list of people who had immediate access to me was short: my mother, my sister, my two sons, and Patrick.

As it turned out Patrick seldom contacted me at work. He appeared there several times as we prepared for court appearances or debriefed after them. His lawyer was one of our employees, and our company donated the lawyer's time and mine to assist Patrick.

8. Encourage Legal Action

Battering your lover is a crime. Because of that fact, it is important for the lay helper to encourage a victim of gay men's domestic violence to take every available legal step for his protection and safety. Using the police, the courts and all other appropriate government agencies is not only a right of all citizens but an obligation. Our justice system must protect *every* citizen from harm. A gay ex-victim may not realize, however, that if he wants the system to help him, he has to go to it and ask for help, and sometimes even fight for it. It is a lot of trouble. Sometimes it is slow. Gay men are afraid that they may be ridiculed, ignored, or further victimized by the legal processes. They often are. However, all gay men, especially victims of violence, must insist that the system treat them as it was designed.

It is very important for the lay helper of an ex-victim of gay men's domestic violence to be positive and not cynical about taking legal steps. Never discourage a victim from taking proper legal steps. The common legal steps are: obtaining a restraining order; reporting all violations of a restraining order; following up all police reports with statements and any photographs that may be necessary; obtaining a warrant for the batterer's arrest or a contempt of court order if the restraining order is violated; and prompting the district attorney to prosecute the abuser when violations occur. Starting criminal proceedings against a battering lover or ex-lover is also one way to secure his attention to the fact that the ex-victim will not tolerate violence.

If he can afford it, encourage the ex-victim to obtain the services of a good attorney, some of whom are available at low cost or for free at community legal service agencies. Perhaps you can help him to locate one. Some communities have low-cost gay attorneys who are helping people with AIDS. These men may also be available for your friend. Join in meetings with the attorney and ex-victim so that you stay abreast of all of the legal developments. Help the ex-victim keep track of all of the legal activity he has generated. Help him keep commitments, court dates, and his resolve. Your attitude about legal processes is one of the most important influences you can have. Your attitude has to be upbeat and action-oriented.

At first, I believe I was more insistent than Patrick was about involving the police, a lawyer, the courts, the district attorney, and other appropriate government agencies. It wasn't that he was re-luctant. Instead, he dreaded the ordeal ahead of him and felt embarrassment and great sadness in anticipating going through the procedures. He had no idea how it all worked. But most of all, at the beginning, he didn't want to hurt Stephen.

I recall that filling out the forms to request a restraining order was particularly wrenching for Patrick. In California, to justify a request for a restraining order against a person for domestic violence, the history of the abuse must be written down for the judge to read. It took Patrick two full days of agony, with several false starts, periodic avoidance of the task and intermittent fits of rage and tears, finally to draft the chronological history of Stephen's abuse. I typed it on the forms while Patrick made last-minute addi-

*tions and corrections. Just remembering it all was painful. Writing
it down was worse.*

*As time went on and as Patrick learned how to use the available
services, his own enthusiasm and momentum took over. Today, he
is a zealous proponent of legal action for all victims. Without the
assistance of the law enforcement and judicial branches of our government, Patrick would not have felt the power and security that
enabled him to protect himself from Stephen and to get on with his
life.*

9. Encourage Psychological Help

Every ex-victim of gay men's domestic violence needs to receive
competent, professional psychological help. While we believe that
most gay men exiting relationships with abusive men suffer from
Post-traumatic Stress Disorder (temporarily) and require treatment
for it, the bigger question is, can they find appropriate therapy at
all? Most therapists have not been trained in this field, and no theory of treatment for gay male victims exists. Many existing therapeutic approaches are inappropriate and may even be harmful.
Nonetheless, the lay helper of an ex-victim must encourage the ex-
victim to seek out mental health services.

You may have to help the ex-victim learn how to screen therapists. Show him how to question the therapist (during what may be
a free intake session) about his or her experience, philosophy, approach to gay male victims, and his or her training. Help the ex-
victim to rehearse the questions to ask the prospective therapists and
to evaluate their responses. (For more detailed information about
appropriate therapists, see Chapter VIII.)

Just as your attitude about legal action is crucial, so is your attitude toward obtaining the right psychological help important to the
recovery of your friend.

*Patrick was lucky. At the time he left Stephen, San Francisco had
public funds available to help victims of gay men's domestic violence. He obtained both individual and group therapy during the
critical weeks after his escape. The therapists were gay, competent,
and experienced in gay male victim issues. Every contact he had*

with these dedicated professionals was instrumental in his healing and his gaining insight.

My role was to be supportive of his therapy, to help him integrate his learning, and to reinforce his progress. I usually picked him up after group. Together we would debrief the session. Sometimes I merely affirmed what he had just experienced and told me. And, sometimes I pushed him farther, asking him to explain to me what something had meant to him. Our discussions were always feeling-oriented and focused on what Patrick got from the session. It was important for me to understand the content of his therapy so that during the rest of the week I could support what the therapists had asked him to work on, and so that I could understand his frame of mind.

10. Listening

Listening is your primary job. Not talking. Not doing things for him. Not giving him hugs. Listening. You listen. He talks. Let him know that however long it takes him to talk about it is okay with you.

You will receive an avalanche of tears, fears, rage, and confusion. He will be furious with his abusive ex-lover while at the very same moment sorely miss him. Although the feelings an ex-victim expresses are powerful and startling, you can avoid feeling overwhelmed by them if you quietly allow him to express them. Just be sure you do not try to stop his expressions.

There are two main reasons for your emphasis on listening during the first weeks. First, most ex-victims have been out of touch with their feelings for so long that they hardly know what they feel any more. The victim has been focusing on everyone else's feelings, especially the batterer's. That is how he survived. You may be the first safe person in whose company he has been for months or years. It is your job to give him time to think about the abuse and express his feelings about it. Assuredly he will come to feel outrage toward his ex-lover. The abused man must get back in touch with all of his feelings, especially his rage, and express it. Without that expression of feeling, he will never heal.

Second, he needs the opportunity to tell his story. The story of abuse has probably been bottled up for months or years. The telling of his story of abuse requires an avid, safe, non-challenging listener. That is you.

Patrick's story was inside him for about two years. He had hardly told anyone about the abuse until he told me. My recollection is that the telling of his story took about a month, although I recall that I was learning new facets about what had happened to him well into the second month. That first month's conversations, I estimate, took upwards of 100 hours.

I would frequently ask Patrick, as he related an episode of violence to me, "How did you feel then *when that happened?" Soon after, I would also say, "That's interesting, Patrick. How do you feel about it* now*?" It is important to encourage an expression of feeling about the past* and *about the current view of the past. In this way, I helped Patrick to uncover hidden feelings, such as his rage, and to integrate his past and present feeling states into an action plan that validated his decision to leave Stephen.*

11. Keep Your Goal in Mind

Remember what you are doing: You are helping your friend to get out and to stay out of a relationship with a violent man without abusing him in the process. His goal is freedom. Helping him to freedom is your goal.

12. Don't Chicken Out When the Going Gets Tough

"Okay, tell me more about it." That was often my answer as the lay helper to Patrick. There were times when I actually wanted to and did say, "I'm tired. Don't say another word."
When did the going get tough?

- *When I had heard* **that** *story six times.*
- *When I was extremely tired and did not want to talk any more.*
- *When Patrick did not get done what he said he would.*
- *When there were delays in the legal system.*
- *When I was frightened about having to serve papers on Stephen.*
- *When I thought there had been no progress for 2 months.*

- *When Patrick talked about how wonderful he remembered Stephen to be.*
- *When Stephen decided to show up in court to contest the issuance of a restraining order against him.*
- *When, after months and years, Stephen still continued to harass Patrick.*
- *When Patrick's relatives didn't seem to understand.*
- *When he became depressed one more time.*
- *When it just seemed endless.*

To lay helpers, I say, "Don't give up. Don't chicken out. Keep on supporting your ex-victim friend. Get help for yourself if you need it. Your effort is worth it. He is one more person who will never again be battered. It may be the best thing you ever did."

SAFE HOUSE GUIDELINES

1. Your House as a Safe House

The concept of a "safe house" for victims of domestic violence is not new; it goes back to the annals of political asylum and of concealing fugitives and refugees. More recently, the battered women's movement in both Great Britain and the United States has reinterpreted the concept and developed group homes for survivors of domestic violence and their children. For gay male victims of domestic violence, we, too, suggest safe houses. Our application of the concept, however, prescribes only one gay male victim per home. (See Chapter VIII for further details.)

If your situation permits, you may want to consider that your home can serve as a safe home for the ex-victim you are helping. What this means is that your friend moves in and lives in your home for an indefinite period of time. When this happens, your level of involvement with the ex-victim obviously increases significantly. You will spend much more time with your friend. Both he *and you* may be in danger from attack by the ex-lover.

Precautions need to be taken. Be sure you know where all of the keys are to your home. If too many people have had keys recently, change the locks. Make sure that all of the windows can be locked.

Privacy and safety are all-important to the newly-escaped victim of gay men's domestic violence. He must be able to feel safe. He is the sole judge of his safety. If the batterer does not know who you are or where you live, all the better for the ex-victim. Keys to a safe house are a symbol of freedom from and defiance of the batterer. Keys to a safe house are symbolic for another reason. Since the ex-victim needs to learn how to trust others all over again, being trusted is one way he learns about trust. By giving him keys you demonstrate that you trust him; by accepting them, he takes a small step toward trusting you.

If your home cannot be used as a safe house (because you just do not want to, or your house is too small, or you have a lover, roommate, or landlord who objects), then you can help your friend locate one.

Some ex-victims succeed in forcing the assailant to move out of their home. This is rare, but it does occur. In that event, the ex-victim must transform his own apartment or house into a safe house. Locks should be changed. A new roommate should be found. During the first weeks and months after the breakup, we believe an ex-victim should not live alone in the old apartment where all the battering occurred. The memories are too painful. Spending a lot of time by himself can make the ex-victim yearn for his lover. In addition, he is virtually guaranteeing harassment by staying there. It will be difficult for him to protect himself adequately from being harried by the batterer or from his own worry and anxiety about harassment.

When your home is a safe house for your friend, make sure he has his own space, if possible, or at least room for his belongings and access to all living areas. It is important that he comes to feel at home as soon as possible. He needs the comfort and security that your home can provide him.

When Patrick came over to my home on the evening of September 8, 1987, to talk, neither he nor I had any idea that he would stay for more than two hours, let alone for four months. But, as it turned out, he had no other place to go and he chose not to return to his own home. He had many friends who would gladly have let him stay. Patrick's brother and his wife also lived in San Francisco only about two miles away. But Patrick reasoned correctly that if he went to any of those homes, Stephen would locate him in a flash.

*Patrick needed time in which, isolated and hidden, he could orga-
nize his plan of action. He would not be able to begin the difficult
steps he knew lay ahead with interference from well-meaning
friends who would reveal his whereabouts.*

*After considerable discussion we concluded that it would be best
if he stayed the night, to sleep if he could and to get grounded. The
next morning as I was preparing to leave for work, I spontaneously
and somewhat nervously handed Patrick a set of keys to my home.
Since I didn't know him very well, I was uncomfortable. I did not
know if I could trust him. Patrick was so moved by my gesture that I
decided that the risk would be minimal. There was no risk, of
course, and, all things considered, my hesitant action of giving
Patrick the keys to my home that morning was probably the single
most helpful thing I ever did for him.*

*In many ways, my San Francisco apartment proved an ideal safe
house. It is the top floor of a modern, three-unit building. The only
ways to enter are through the garage doors and the front entrance
to the building. Two keys are required. The apartment is large and
two of the three bedrooms face an enclosed back yard, two floors
below. The living room and dining room face the street at the other
end of the house, and 30 feet of floor-to-ceiling glass open onto a
full-house-width balcony, overlooking the street, a large city park,
and downtown San Francisco. From the balcony, the park, streets,
and city can be viewed for blocks. Thus, though open and bright, it
was secure and private. It was a perfect place for someone who
needed to be vigilant and safe. The third bedroom was unoccupied
with plenty of room for Patrick's belongings.*

*Three weeks later, we returned to Patrick's apartment under
court protection (and Stephen's required absence), loaded up my
Bronco full of some of his things (he left most behind) and placed
them in my home. The safe house concept for Patrick was then fully
operational.*

2. Reinforce His Decision to Stay Out

Because you have daily, close, and extensive contact with the ex-
victim, you become a significant influence. That means that when
you tell him what you think and how you feel about what he is
doing, you will be a reinforcing agent to his decisions and actions.

Therefore, in the beginning days and weeks, be sure to tell your friend that he is doing the right thing by leaving his abusive ex-lover, that you feel proud of him and that you know he is in a big struggle. Encourage him to file a restraining order. Encourage him to find the strength to resist going back. Encourage, but do not insist, and do not tell him what to do. Keep *his* goal of getting out and staying out in your mind at all times and encourage him to keep his goal in view.

In the first weeks, Patrick occasionally lost sight of his own goal. That happened when he would become depressed that he would never see Stephen again. Violence had been a periodic, and disastrous, but not constant, part of Stephen's personality. Indeed, Patrick still loved Stephen. When his tears stopped, I would say to him, "What is the main thing, the most important goal you're trying to achieve during these weeks?" He would inevitably answer, "To get out and stay out. To keep Stephen away from me. To be safe. To keep me away from him."

And, I would say, "That's exactly right. It is painful and hard and you are putting an end to that relationship." He might cry some more, but the crisis had passed.

3. Believe in the System

The ex-victim has to believe that agencies and people and "the system out there" will actually help him. Your friend will easily pick up your attitude about "the system" as you and he talk about his daily activities. A cynical attitude on your part about the police, therapy, or the courts will foster a negative attitude. It is crucial that he develop a positive approach. He has to believe that things will get better, that the abuse has ended, and that some people in his community will protect him.

It is up to you to reinforce positive attitudes about the legal system and the helping agencies. You have to believe the system works in behalf of victims and those in trouble, and tell your friend so. For example: "Even though it's hard, I think you really need to file that police report. I know they've given you a bad time, but they won't be able to prosecute Stephen unless there are reports on file of his violations. Maybe a new approach would help. What do you think your reception at the police station would be if you showed up in a coat and tie?''

You can express wariness about the police and their homophobia and at the same time you can show your ex-victim friend that he deserves their protective services. The same holds true for psychological services. Even if these services are not particularly on target or sophisticated, you can help your friend insist that the helping agencies do the right thing.

"Patrick, the court is obligated to help you," I said to him one day. "That's its function. You may not get everything you want in your restraining order, but the court will grant it to you. They have to. You are a citizen of this country who is being threatened by a violent man. You have a right to protection under the law. You must insist on that right. The legal system exists just for you in this matter. I will stand beside you in court. We will make it work for you."

I, too, am named on Patrick's second, three-year restraining order. Patrick's abusive ex-lover is prohibited from coming anywhere near me or my home. I carry the restraining order, too. I have felt fear and intimidation from Stephen, who followed me one night on a street near the Castro in San Francisco. My attitude about the law and the police in San Francisco has been reinforced. They are there to serve me, and they will serve me when I need protection.

4. Encourage Him to Keep a Diary

Tell him to write it all down, even if he is not a person who feels comfortable or competent writing. It is important that everyone who goes through traumatic experiences develop some understanding of what they experienced. Keeping a diary is one method to accomplish that. A diary shows change over time, just as a photo album does. Writing in a diary can help one think clearly about the experiences. Talking is transitory and the words are forgotten. Writing is permanent and it can be reread, reviewed, and shared. Writing a diary is also an important release, a kind of catharsis. The ex-victim can feel cleansed or purified from a session of writing in his diary. It clears out the mental debris of constant thought about his problems. Keeping a diary is also a good substitute for talk. Many times, the talking can be much more productive *after* the ex-victim has collected his thoughts by first writing them down.

5. Help the Ex-Victim in Self-Grounding Activities

It helps to remind the ex-victim about the safety rules that he has developed. These are the basic rules about what to do in emergencies, for instance. In reminding him about the rules, however, you must be careful not to nag. The essence of your participation is helping him ground himself as he embarks on a new activity.

With Patrick, I often started this kind of conversation just as he was leaving the house, getting out of the car, or starting on a new adventure. I'd say, "Hmm, has anything changed, Patrick? Or do the same rules operate today? Is there anything you think you need to remind yourself of? Is it possible that Stephen will show up? Which of your rules do you think apply?"

Patrick would click off the replies. "No eye contact. Never speak to Stephen. Check for exits."

I'd say, "Great. That sounds right." I may add, "Well, what about phones? Will there be phones there?"

Finally, one of us might say, "And, the big picture? What is the big objective?" If the moment were right, we'd both laugh and say, simultaneously, "To suck dick!" But then, just as quickly, both again, "To stay away. To stay safe."

6. Be Prepared for the Victim to Collapse

It is normal for an ex-victim, when recovering from the shock of leaving his abusive partner, to feel completely devastated from time to time. You, as his helping friend, should not be shocked, upset, or disappointed when it happens. To crash is not a setback. It is not weakness. It is normal for an ex-victim to have periods of depression and crying. Your attitude about your friend's "crashing" is as important as your verbal response to it. It may be up to you to provide genuine comfort, to listen sincerely, to draw him out in conversation and to be able to respond to what he is saying and not be thinking about yourself. After a crash, you can talk with him about this and his most recent depressed periods. Help him to look for patterns and observe their frequency. Crashes are bound to be repeated with little progress unless the ex-victim learns from them. You can help him learn the lessons that they teach by accepting them as normal and helping him see them as opportunities to learn.

Patrick and I had many conversations about how often he was

*crashing, what the crashes were stimulated by, how long they
lasted, and how quickly he recovered from them. I was intent on
Patrick learning to monitor his own depressed periods and learning
about himself from them.*

*A number of times, I said to Patrick, "What did you learn about
yourself and the progress you are making as an ex-victim?" Sometimes, Patrick would look at me, smile, and say, "I knew you'd say
that, and I already have the answer. (Then, he'd tell me.) What do
you think, David?"*

*It didn't matter what I thought. I often would tell him what I
thought, but it didn't matter. He was perfectly capable of doing his
own thinking, and he and I both knew this. What did matter was
that he was increasingly taking his depressions as an opportunity to
learn about himself and his mental world. He learned how to profit
from self-monitoring and reflection.*

7. Do Not Advocate Activities Beyond
the Ability of the Ex-Victim

Restrain yourself from overwhelming the ex-victim with too
many "happy" things to do and with too many suggestions. Take
into consideration his mental state. He might still be frightened of
physical acts of violence, cringing even when he thinks of violence.
Therefore, you would not want to encourage him to see a violent
movie, because the stimulation from it might push him beyond his
current emotional boundary.

8. Initiate Conversation About What Is Going On

Do not wait for your ex-victim friend to get around to telling you
what is happening to him and what is on his mind. Ask him. By no
means, however, do we suggest that you should constantly talk with
him about his relationship or about his leaving it. On occasion, you,
the lay helper, can start constructive talk with him about the "here
and now." You achieve this by shifting the conversation to the
present moment. Ask him how he feels talking to you right now and
what is happening inside his head right now. The ex-victim needs to
update himself on his current mental state and to bring his uncon-
scious thoughts to the surface so that he can remain focused. Such

monitoring is one more element in his regaining control over his mental life.

SPECIAL ADVICE FOR LAY HELPERS IN DAILY CONTACT WITH EX-VICTIMS

For those lay helpers who become involved on a daily basis with ex-victim friends who have left abusive partners, there are many additional ways you can help. The following special tips are intended to help you understand what is happening to you and to help you to help your friend effectively.

1. You May Not Be Trusted

Prepare yourself for a potentially troubling experience: You may not be trusted by the ex-victim. Remember, your friend has been conditioned by his abusive ex-partner to be on guard at all times. He did not know when the violence would occur. He did not know what simple event might precede his getting bashed. It does not take long for that kind of daily existence to erode trust. By the time he reaches your safe house, the ex-victim may not trust anyone. He also desperately wants to trust someone and vacillates back and forth between trusting you and not trusting you. He may not speak about it, however, because he is in the throes of a dilemma, needing to trust you but perhaps not knowing you well enough to. And, even if he did, he may fear that you too will victimize him, abuse him, hit him, or try to control him. He is on guard. Everyone, including you, is suspect. This may be a shock to you because you probably view yourself as trustworthy and incapable of hurting a fly. You may have lived your 30 or 40 or 50 years without ever being hit or hitting anyone.

It was a shock to me, one day, when Patrick took three steps backward and said, "David, when are you going to hit me?" I had expressed mild anger to him and he had been so trained by his batterer to expect anger to result in physical abuse that he was sure I would hit him. He was also frightened that he might hit me. I learned that it would take a long time for Patrick to rebuild trust as a result of his ex-lover's abuse.

2. Rehearsed Behavioral Responses

To help the ex-victim properly in emergencies and in regaining control over his behavior, you may want to consider helping him to build behavioral answers to questions that start with these words: "What are you going to do if . . . ?"

First, behavioral answers are those answers to questions that have action responses in them. "I'm going to find a phone and call the police." "I'm going to run into a very busy, people-filled place."

Second, help the victim to identify and anticipate the crucial events that might happen to him, events which involve the ex-abuser. These events need to be listed, discussed, and analyzed. Optional answers need to be thought of, and the most logical ones chosen as the preferred behavioral response. Then, the responses need to be rehearsed.

The most important result of helping the ex-victim answer such questions is that the victim begins to understand that he is in control of what happens to him. The victim must reverse the feeling of helplessness that has damaged him for so long. Learned helplessness has badly eroded the ex-victim's self-confidence. For too long he has thought that he cannot handle himself in the presence of his abusive ex-lover. He must regain that confidence. He must never again find himself in a situation with his ex-lover that he has not already thought about. Such preparation will enable him to be in control of his options. One way for him to achieve this control is to anticipate in advance all of the kinds of situations that might occur. Then, he rehearses, memorizes, and practices his responses. The ex-victim then knows what to do. His response to any situation will be a practiced reaction. He will not have to think, "Oh, God, what do I do now?" He will have already thought about it and then simply have to put the plan into action.

For Patrick, examples of such events that needed answers and rehearsal were as follows:

- *What are you going to do if Stephen shows up at work or has flowers delivered again?*
- *What are you going to do if he chases you on the street?*
- *What are you going to do if you are walking down a dark street and Stephen spots you and approaches you?*
- *What are you going to do if you and he are riding on the same bus?*
- *What are you going to do if Stephen knocks on the door to your house some night?*
- *What are you going to do if the police do not come when you have called them to protect you from Stephen?*

The importance of rehearsing behavioral answers to these questions proved important time and time again in Patrick's ability to deal with problems that actually developed with Stephen. A key behavior that Patrick used with great success many times to stay confidently in control, when unexpectedly in the presence of Stephen, was never to make eye contact with him. Only twice since September 8, 1987, the day he left Stephen, has Patrick ever held eye contact with him. The power of Patrick's control over his own behavior cannot be overemphasized in explaining how he successfully communicated to Stephen that he never again wanted anything to do with him.

3. Keep Track of Everything

One thing you will learn quickly when you help someone escape from a violent partner is that there is much to do. Sometimes, there is just too much for the ex-victim to remember. You may find yourself functioning as a "general secretary" to your ex-victim friend, helping him keep track of everything and helping him to review the big picture. You will start conversations about his activities and play an important, quiet role in his keeping his main objective in mind: getting out and staying out.

I functioned as Patrick's "executive secretary" for a short while to help him keep track of actions and decisions that he had taken, planned to take, or was thinking about. Patrick, similar to many ex-victims, wasn't sure if he could stay away. He hated his job, but he needed it. He was thinking about graduate school. He needed to reestablish relations with his family. He was lonely. A lot was happening all at once. I was able to stand back and watch it, whereas he was in the middle of it. It wasn't nearly as complicated for me, an observer, as it was for Patrick.

Patrick never really lost sight of his goal, in part because we had many conversations about what was going on, what was pending, what had just been accomplished and what needed to be decided. We were an effective team. Frequently we reviewed and planned and recapitulated. We never let the business of getting out and staying out get so stale that we couldn't remember everything that had to be done.

4. Encourage Efforts to Lead a Normal Life Again

Never discourage a return to normalcy. Never deflate an idea of the victim's to act like a normal gay man, such as going to see a movie, taking a bike ride, reading a book, talking on the phone, planning a trip.

Three weeks after Patrick left Stephen, he attended a dinner at my home with many people present. It was his first social function since leaving Stephen, and my impression was that he was rather uneasy. But in the long run, it was good for him to interact with strangers. The lesson for him was that he could function perfectly well in a social environment with people who did not know anything about him. It was another way for him to regain control. He was able to resist the temptation to tell everyone about his problems. That was normal.

What is a normal life for an ex-victim? When, for instance, does an ex-victim begin dating again? Some ex-victims of domestic violence become very promiscuous, as if seeking love and sexual gratification with presumably non-battering lovers to make up what they did not have for so long. We think that the ex-victim should be encouraged to begin dating slowly. Gaining control seems an obvious objective, but it is elusive. As the lay helper, you need to encourage a return to a normal existence. Also, you need to encourage clear thinking and sober reflection on the lessons learned. There should be sufficient time for reflection and therapy between the end of the relationship with the batterer and the beginning of a new

relationship with a non-abusive man. We think an ex-victim generally is not ready for a new relationship for a long time. A minimum
of two years (and perhaps three to four) should elapse before a gay
male ex-victim of domestic violence commits to a new lover relationship. For an ex-victim of gay men's domestic violence to move
too quickly from a relationship with a violent man into a relationship with a new lover is an invitation to fail. Insight, growth, time,
healing, learning how to trust, centering, therapy, making new
friends, and accepting the past violence all must happen between
relationships.

How about new friends, family, and resuming old relationships?
In contrast to how the pursuit of a new lover should proceed slowly,
the pursuit of new friends and reestablishing broken or damaged
family ties should start quickly.

*Patrick's workplace became a source of new friends. So did
graduate school. And so did my own family and circle of friends.
When I encouraged Patrick to work on reestablishing and strength-
ening relationships within his family, he found it difficult, because
some members of his family were judgmental. To continue to encourage him to approach some of his family members became difficult for me when he reported to me how unrewarding the contact
was with them.*

Returning to a normal life also means to have fun, to take vaca-
tions, to go to movies, read, write letters, watch TV, cook, and do
the laundry.

*A clear theme in my early talks with Patrick was: "Get on with
life." Thus, it turned out that doing ordinary things and reactivat-
ing old interests was another way for Patrick to heal. Free of
Stephen's drain on his finances, Patrick replaced his previously
stolen bicycle within two months. In so doing, he regained a sense
of his old self. He suddenly had a freedom that he had not had for a
long time. It was a safety measure, transportation, and a way to
exercise. The return to normalcy it represented was crucial. Few
symbols from that time period stand out as more important. One
day he said to me, "David, I took a long ride to the beach and back
today. I thought a lot about how angry I am at Stephen. I raced
through Golden Gate Park so fast I almost ran over some people.
David, I was crying while I was riding and whizzing past the euca-*

lyptus trees. I was so mad. When I got to the beach I just sat on the concrete wall and sobbed. I feel much better now.''

Whatever the ex-victim's enduring and fulfilling life patterns are, help him to rediscover them. Help him to make the decision to bring them back to life again. Encourage that old normalcy.

5. That Big Word "And"

Throughout the first few months of separation from the abusive ex-lover, the battered man often will feel a deep love-loss. One way or another, the victim will say: I miss him. He was so handsome. I loved him so much. I just want to take him in my arms and hold him and tell him to get help. We had lots of really good times together. I don't know if I can stand it, not being with him. He was a great cook. I'm worried about him. We had great sex.

And on and on and on. The listener (often just a friend) feels concern and fright. The listener may well say to himself, "How can he be talking about missing that bastard who used to hit him? It does not make sense. Maybe he will cave in and go back! Maybe he will go back tonight. What can I do to stop him? Should I do anything? How can he miss that son-of-a-bitch?"

I remember listening to Patrick talk about Stephen. You'd think that they had had the "ideal relationship." Stephen's body was tight and youthful. He was smart. He knew everything about anything. Melancholy memories by the battered for the batterer and in such vivid descriptions are really very good for the battered man to experience and express. No healing will occur until the memories (and the fantasies) are brought back, played over and over, and forged into a new realistic balance.

What is a realistic balance? And what was the true nature of the now-ended relationship? In many ways, the former relationship was good: healthy, happy, interesting, and fulfilling. All of the literature on battered women suggest the truth of this. Angela Browne, in *When Battered Women Kill*, reports that in virtually all of the relationships she studied (42 battered women who killed their abusers and 205 who did not), the women described their partners, in the early stages, as the most romantic, attentive, and passionate lovers that they had ever had (1987, p. 38). For a battered person, much of the relationship and much of the personality and style of the batterer were positive. Those are strong and real memories.

Probably most of the time, that old relationship was either neutral (as when you're at work and not thinking about your lover), or positive (as when you're having a good conversation or great sex). The abuse is severe, shocking, and unforgivable, but it is not constant, although there are undoubtedly some gay men who are constantly abusive, creating a never-changing, diabolical life of terror. More typically, the abuse, the battering, and the violence are periodic. The helping friend needs to keep this in mind. Even in the face of demeaning and terrifying abusive episodes, the bulk of the memories of the violent man are good. Obviously, that is part of the problem for a victim in staying out of the relationship. The helping person needs to understand that those memories will surface and need to be expressed. Do not argue with the ex-victim about whether or not the relationship was good or bad most of the time. The helper needs to refrain from confrontation, argument, and assaults on the victim's memories and honest expressions of feelings. Thus, the helper needs to learn never to criticize the memories of the abuser.

Balance. What is a realistic balance? And what can the helper do to bring it about for the victim?

There is something that can be done, verbally, when the ex-victim begins to recount the good memories and express love for the batterer. What the helping person must do, right then, is to start assisting the battered man to reframe the memories of the abuse together with memories of the good. The ex-victim must fold in the memories of what was good with memories of what was bad and integrate the two together. Healing will not begin (and certainly will not succeed) until the battered man stops separating memories of the ex-lover into two separate sides — abusive and good. The battered man must see and feel both sides of the ex-partner as integrated parts of the same person. Then, and only then, will he be able to grow in strength to refrain from going back to the abuser. The helping person must begin, gently but firmly, to help the battered man express in immediate sequence both aspects of the batterer.

This assistance is accomplished easily with the use of the word, "and." The helping person, when the moment is right in the conversation, will say something like this:

"You mean, Patrick, that you really miss the great sex you used to have with Stephen AND Stephen used to kick you in the shins. Is that right?"

"Yes, he did. You're right. I really miss the sex I had with Stephen, and he often kicked me."

"Great. Do you see what you are doing here? You are beginning to be able to bring a balance to your statements about Stephen, because you actually have both of those feelings. They kind of come and go in waves, I've noticed. There are times when you love him because of the good memories of the excitement of great sex, and there are times when you hate him because he battered you. When you can say both of those things together in the same sentence, you can hold both of the feelings out in front of you to experience and to examine. Try it again."

And so, the helping person literally teaches the battered man to bring a balance into his feeling world, and not to overplay the importance of any one feeling, especially the positive memories. Soon, the ex-victim is volunteering the statements with the word "and" already inserted properly:

"You know, David," Patrick once said to me, "I wonder how Stephen is doing. I'm concerned about him. Do you think he's eating well? Is he losing weight? You know, he always seemed to get depressed when he had problems. I'm worried about him. I'm worried about him, and *Stephen used to choke me until I had bruises on my neck, and I had to button my collar so they wouldn't show. I hated that."*

You can see that Patrick is now thinking about Stephen in a much more balanced way and doing it by himself. The battered man must be able to state out loud a balanced reality of the former lover. "The same man who loved me, abused me. I loved him and he hit me."

The beauty of this simple approach is that the battered man's desire to return to the batterer, to take care of him, or to have sex with him is dissipated by a balanced view of him. When the battered man can keep present in his mind the facts and the feelings of being battered, in the context of the good times and happy feelings, the tendency to want to return is greatly diminished. With this small technique, the helping person can stop worrying about whether or not the victim will return and can instead start actively doing something effective to help.

6. Growing Tired of It

My involvement with Patrick as a lay helper spanned about 18 months. From time to time I grew weary of my role as helper. It would happen after an intense few days of long discussions about Patrick's problems, and often was connected to what I perceived as his wavering back-and-forth on the theme of "Poor Stephen," or, "Sometimes I miss him so."

At times I grew exasperated. I thought to myself, "For Christ's sake, Patrick, after all you've been through, you're still thinking, still considering, returning to that son-of-a-bitch?"

The pressure on the helping person is enormous. At no time can you ever behave in such a way that the victim sees you as a batterer: controlling, selfish, dishonest, unpredictable, manipulative. The helper must monitor his own behavior. To function under this weight is difficult, I admit.

The toll on me some of the time was severe. Constant monitoring: Am I Controlling Patrick? Constant vigilance: This is HIS idea, isn't it? Perpetual self-observation: Why am I doing all of this? Some of my energy at certain points in the project to help Patrick get permanently out of his relationship with Stephen was spent monitoring my own behavior and actions. Frankly, I got tired of it.

Expect it. It may happen to you, too.

Chapter VIII

Therapists and Intervention Programs

THE LETTER NEVER SENT

November 18, 1987

Dear Stephen,

I write this letter solely for my own benefit. I communicate to get things off my chest – to help me let go of some of the weight I've been carrying around. . . .

By this time I imagine you have realized and/or begun to accept the fact that I am not returning. **My** *life began on September 8, when I left that apartment, and never will I return to the life we had . . . Stephen, for so long you have underestimated me. You never gave me the credit I deserve. You always said I couldn't survive without you. Ha! You were wrong. . . . You said no one would help me. Well, CUAV, Philip, Jesse, Rick, David, Sharon, The San Francisco Police Department, and a San Francisco judge all willingly helped me. . . .*

I want to tell you about my life without you. I go to the gym whenever I want to. I shop and buy what I want and am pleasantly surprised to find nobody yells at me about my purchases . . . I bought a new bike . . . I wear some new clothes . . . I go out to dinner. . . . You see, I have more money now and realize exactly how expensive you were to keep. I can see my brother now, too, which is nice. . . .

I feel more at ease – at the movies, with friends, in restaurants, on the phone. You see, nobody shouts at me now. This actually takes getting used to. I was coming to expect people to shout at me – or hit me. Even now, writing to you, I can still hear your destructive comments, your strong negative stance about what I do, no matter what it is. I hear that voice, Stephen—and I ignore it. . . .

Do I miss you, you ask? Remember the days I couldn't shower at the gym because of the bruises? Remember when I had to wear shirts with collars to hide the marks? Remember the blood on the wall? Remember the scene on the escalator? Remember the candlestick and the tennis racket? No, I don't miss you. . . .

I'm letting go of you Stephen . . . though still you try to reach me . . . I'm already gone . . . I'm out of reach . . . I'm safe . . . I am looking after myself . . . and doing fine.

Patrick

This letter is the "homework" assignment I was given last week by the psychologist leading the group I am in for battered gay men. The assignment was to write a letter, that we would never send, to our ex-lovers, expressing anything we wanted. I jumped at the chance to do this, because there is so much I want to say (and vent), and I know I'll never speak to Stephen again. It's really an exercise in "letting go," and I guess I have a lot to let go of.

Tonight I read my letter to the group. I felt so angry reading it, thinking about the horrible things Stephen had done. I read it slowly and carefully, even repeating some of the parts that felt good. When I finished, I was embarrassed, because I had become so angry, but the group was tremendously supportive. They thought it was great. Other people said that they still hear their ex-lovers' voices in their heads, too, yelling at them or criticizing them. And one group member said he's afraid of people, because he always expects to be yelled at or hit. He thinks that because we experienced so much abuse, the fear and expectation of more abuse takes a while to go away. I felt so normal all of a sudden. They understood it, and I didn't have to explain anything.

This narrative illustrates several important points about therapy and particularly the benefits of group support for victims of domestic violence.

First, the benefits of exercises such as "The Unsent Letter" are numerous. For example, through the writing and reading of his letter, Patrick is allowed to express whatever he feels (in this case anger), without fear of retribution. For many victims of domestic violence, anger becomes an unsafe emotion. One of the coping skills they learn is not to express anger toward their violent partners, lest they suffer the potentially violent consequences. In the structure, safety and confidentiality of the group, however, Patrick's right to feel whatever he feels is affirmed and supported.

This exercise also facilitates Patrick's healing process by allowing him to communicate with Stephen on paper the thoughts and feelings that he will never have the opportunity to express in person (and, that he *must* not express in person). He has the opportunity to bring up any "unfinished business" he has with Stephen, to say what he wants or needs to, and thereby to bring psychological closure to the relationship. Everything he always wanted to say but was afraid to, the rages that come from being abused and battered, and the affirmations of his own worth are all expressed, allowing him to move forward in therapy and to move beyond the relationship he has just ended.

This narrative is also an excellent demonstration of the value of group support. Patrick is safe here among peers. The other men in the group understand the trauma, the anger, and the lingering and confusing effects of violence. Patrick's experience is shared by the group and normalized. The value of group understanding is vital because the men in a support group may be the only people present in a victim's life who understand his experience and provide unconditional support. As made clear in the following sections, we believe that therapy is absolutely essential for victims of gay men's domestic violence, and the core of good therapy and treatment for victims is group support.

HOW THERAPY CAN HELP GAY MALE VICTIMS

One of the most helpful steps a victim of gay men's domestic violence can take for himself is to get into therapy. Whether or not he is currently being battered, has just left a violent partner (and may be ambivalent about staying away), or has been away from his abusive lover for quite some time, therapy is an appropriate and necessary tool for ending the victimization of a domestic violence survivor. Therapy can provide insight and understanding, education and support, all of which are invaluable to gay male victims.

The following section provides guidelines to help gay male victims, and others, find appropriate therapy. It details things to look for and insist on in a therapist, as well as major pitfalls to be avoided. The guidelines are listed here and elaborated on afterwards:

1. Couple counseling is inappropriate and dangerous.
2. The therapist must understand domestic violence issues.
3. The therapist must be gay-sensitive and/or gay-affirmative.
4. The therapist must not use sociological and/or social learning theories to excuse or justify battering behavior.
5. The therapist must not view male violence as innate and natural.

It must be acknowledged here that gay men's domestic violence is a relatively new issue to most in the mental health profession. Heterosexual domestic violence has only been addressed by the mental health profession for about 15 years. Lesbian battering "came out" as an issue about 1982, and there is still a struggle in this country to establish more counseling services for lesbian batterers and victims. Gay men's domestic violence is just now emerging as an issue to be contended with by mental health professionals. To the best of our knowledge, there are no more than 20 gay mental health professionals in the United States who deal specifically with gay men's domestic violence. As a result, finding the right therapist will probably entail more than just opening the phone book and making a few calls. Gay male domestic violence victims will have to do some investigating and shopping around for the right therapist.

Couple Counseling Is Inappropriate and Dangerous

Theories of counseling have long supported the notion that when a couple is having difficulties they should get together to talk about them. The idea is that together with a therapist the couple will be able openly to discuss and gain insight into their problem(s). Once the problem is out in the open, each member of the couple can address his own issues related to the problem.

While the couple counseling approach may work effectively with many of the problems gay couples face today, domestic violence is an exception. Therapists should never suggest, encourage, or employ couple counseling when dealing with domestic violence.

In their book, *Confronting The Batterer*, Phyllis Frank and Beverly Houghton make clear why "couple counseling is not a viable therapeutic tool for use when there is domestic abuse between partners in a romantic relationship." They explain that treating a couple together could do any one or more of the following:

1. Endanger the victim, who may face violence or threats of violence for revealing information during therapy that is disapproved of by the battering partner.
2. Lend credence to the common misunderstanding that victims of domestic violence are in some way responsible for the violence inflicted upon them. A victim's presence in the counseling session could indicate that there is some part for him or her to play in stopping the batterer's abuse.
3. Ignore the denial, minimization, and deception about the violence that occurs when the focus of counseling is on the couple's interaction.
4. Indicate that the therapist condones violence or that the violence is acceptable or not important.
5. Ignore the victim's need to have time to exercise his or her right and responsibility to choose whether or not to save the relationship.
6. Increase the victim's sense of isolation, as he or she may prevaricate about the violence or fear to speak, even in therapy. This can have the effect of discouraging the victim from taking any other positive action to eliminate the violence inflicted upon him or her.
7. Imply that the victim has responsibility for seeing that the batterer gets help. Therapists need to be particularly wary of the manipulation inherent in a batterer's refusal of anything other than couple treatment. (Frank and Houghton, 1987, p. 63-64, cited with permission of the authors, who also gave permis-

sion to change the feminine pronouns to masculine, so as to make clear that victims are either men or women)

Separate counseling for victims and batterers is called for in domestic violence matters. By refusing to conduct couple counseling, therapists reinforce to potential clients two very important points about domestic violence. First, it is not up to the victim to help the batterer become nonviolent. Responsibility for stopping the violence is the batterer's, not the couple's. Second, battery is a violent crime, and no other victim of any violent crime would ever be encouraged to meet with the perpetrator "to talk about what happened." Nor should any victim of domestic violence ever be encouraged to do so. Frank and Houghton point out that "Couple counseling remains inappropriate even when both parties request it and/or want to maintain the couple relationship" (1987, p. 63). Given the enormous difficulties a victim of gay men's domestic violence faces in trying to get out of his relationship and stay away from his abusive partner, the worst thing a therapist can do is encourage him to contact his batterer. Domestic violence is *not* a problem victims need to "work out" with their batterers. With a victim, the role of the therapist is to help him get out and stay out of his relationship with a violent man and to start picking up the pieces of his shattered life.

The Therapist Must Understand
Domestic Violence Issues

Therapists, like the rest of us, are brought up learning and believing all the prevalent prejudices, myths, and misconceptions about domestic violence. It would be nice to believe that at some time in their education and training all therapists take classes on domestic violence, women's issues, and gay studies, or that they all do some work in a battered women's shelter. We know, however, that this is not the case. Further, the number of therapists who have received any formal education or training about *gay* domestic violence is so small they can be counted on two hands. Remember, gay men's domestic violence is just now being recognized by the mental health field. Therefore, many therapists may be steeped in ignorance about domestic violence, especially when gay men are involved.

What gay male victims must look for in a therapist is someone who understands the fundamental precepts of domestic violence. The therapist must understand that victims do not provoke the violence; that domestic violence is not mutual battery, not S&M, and not "a communication problem." A basic understanding of the dynamics of domestic violence is necessary because therapists will have to educate most victims about the phenomenon. Without this knowledge, a therapist may fail to recognize the serious and life-threatening problem his client faces by minimizing the violence or inaccurately labeling it.

The Therapist Must Be Gay-Sensitive

It is painfully obvious to anyone who bothers to look that homophobia and homohatred are alive and rampant in American society today. We live in a country that discriminates against, hates, and brutalizes homosexuals, to the detriment of all 25 million American lesbian and gay citizens. What many people may not realize, however, is that homophobia pervades even the mental health profession and may have a profound effect on the way a therapist treats a client. People who believe that therapists, just because of their training and the work they do, are somehow immune to homophobia are sadly mistaken. There are plenty of ignorant, homophobic, and homo-hating therapists in America today.

In order to receive effective and supportive treatment, the victim of gay men's domestic violence must find a gay-sensitive therapist. The therapist who believes that gays are sick or perverted will not be helpful at all and should be completely avoided. We believe, however, that rather than rabidly homophobic, many therapists are just plain ignorant about gay issues. Whatever the case, a victim should avoid therapists who are not gay-sensitive.

To be most helpful to victims of gay men's domestic violence, it is essential that the therapist have at least basic knowledge (and, ideally, extensive knowledge) about healthy gay relationships. He or she should be able to educate the victim about positive, nonviolent gay male relationships, and to refer the victim to sources of positive information. The therapist must take the position that for roughly 10 percent of the human race, homosexuality *is* natural. It is a normal, healthy, satisfying and fulfilling sexual and emotional orientation for millions of men and women. Finally, the therapist must understand and adhere to the belief that "the problem" with homosexuality is not homosexuality itself, but society's vicious bigotry toward and hatred of homosexuals.

In our view, homophobic or ignorant therapists have two options when considering serving gay clients. Choice one is to educate themselves about homosexuality and understand it as healthy and normal. Choice two is to leave the mental health profession.

Finding gay-sensitive therapists should not be a problem for anyone living in a major city in the United States. Most have lesbian and gay counseling services, or at least referral services for gay-sensitive therapists.

Outside of major cities, victims are encouraged to call whatever counseling services are available and ask questions. Do they have lesbian or gay therapists on staff? Do they have a lesbian or gay client base? Do they have gay-sensitive therapists on staff? Do they have people on staff who know about domestic violence? If the answer is "no" to all of the above, victims should ask for referrals.

A second source of potential gay-sensitive therapists is battered women's shelters, although this is probably a more difficult road to take to find appropriate therapy. Some shelters are excellent in that they are gay-sensitive, have "out" people on staff, and have great therapy referral services. Others, if they are homohating and/or anti-male, have little appeal. Wherever you are in the country, the nearest women's shelter is certainly worth a try.

No Sociological or Social Learning "Excuses"

In order to be truly helpful to victims of domestic violence, therapists must not use sociological or social learning theories to excuse or justify battering behavior. Examples of such "excuses" are as follows:

1. Men batter because men in our society have learned to relate to others through control and dominance.
2. Men batter because they were battered as children, and that is how they have learned to express anger.
3. Men batter because, as men in our society, they are isolated,

or cut off, or dependent, or are not feeling good about themselves.
4. Men batter because they are in pain and have not learned how to express their pain.

These are intelligent sounding, well thought out, and probably even well-researched explanations for male battering. They should never be used as *excuses* for violence. Therapists should never try to explain the batterer's behavior to the victim using these concepts, because they sound much like excuses to victims. Victims should not tolerate excuses for violence from therapists any more than they did from their batterers. There is one and only one reason why men batter: They choose to do so. Any excuse or justification for violence is a blurring of the responsibility that rests solely on the shoulders of the men who batter.

Victims of gay men's domestic violence desperately need clarity about responsibility as they attempt to deal with their guilt, shame, and self-blame. The proper delegation of responsibility for the violence they experience and for staying in the relationship should not be made ambiguous by a therapist. Such ambiguity may delay a victim's decision to leave a battering lover, or, having just escaped, may leave him unsure about his responsibility to stay out. Excuses or explanations for violence are not what battered gay men need. To quote Dr. Jesse Gutierrez, of Home Again Counseling in San Francisco, "Knowing why is the booby prize. You can have all the insight in the world and still have broken bones" (Kingston, 1989, p. 10).

What victims of domestic violence need are therapists who are clear on the concept of responsibility. Violence is a choice, and that is the stance therapists must take when they work with the victims of men who have chosen violence. Therapists who mix explanations for violent behavior with excuses for violent behavior are to be avoided at all costs.

The Therapist Must Not View Male Violence As Innate and Natural

It is important that victims of gay men's domestic violence find therapists who do not adhere to the sexist myth that males are innately violent. While this belief is undoubtedly widely held in America, even among gay men, we hold therapists accountable for a higher level of understanding of male violence, for several reasons.

The first reason is that the myth is just that. Men are no more innately violent than women are innately good cooks or caregivers. More accurately, men are socialized to believe they are supposed to be unemotional, strong, tough, and even violent. Violence, however, is not an inherited tendency. Unlike eye color, handedness, and sexual orientation, violence is always a choice. In reality, most men in American society are nonviolent. While the majority of violent crimes in America are indeed committed by men, they are committed by a small minority of the male population.

Second, therapists adhering to the male-violence-as-innate principle may have a profoundly negative impact on victims of gay men's domestic violence. For example, a therapist may inaccurately label gay men's domestic violence as simply "boys being boys." Not only does this label convey to the client that male violence is normal, to be expected, or even inevitable, it also grossly underestimates the seriousness and danger of domestic violence. The victim then, instead of leaving his battering partner, may return to "the inevitable" to try to prevent more violence from occurring, or to learn how to "take it like a man." Why leave, he reasons, if this is normal, and how all gay relationships are?

Third, therapists who accept male violence as innate may have great difficulty seeing men as victims. Believing that all men are by nature violent, he or she may see and treat victims of gay men's domestic violence as mutual batterers. Domestic violence may be seen as a fight between equals rather than a pattern of manipulation, control, and abuse where one man is clearly a victim. Worse yet, the victim may be treated as "unmanly" or cowardly by the therapist who believes that the normal male tendency is to be violent. Either way, the victim loses, and the therapist only further victimizes the battered gay male. Therapists should strongly adhere to the position that violence is a choice, and by no means a "normal" or healthy one.

With the gay community just beginning to face the problem of domestic violence in its midst, properly trained and educated counselors may very well lead the way in the battle against gay men's domestic violence. In the Treatment Model section we present a four-pronged intervention strategy, a battle plan, designed to provide the necessary, comprehensive help and support that battered gay men need.

A THERAPIST ACTUALLY ASKS ME TO HELP STEPHEN!

It is November 6, 1987. I have been away from my (now) ex-lover for almost two months, and have gone into "hiding." None of my friends know where I live. I taxi back and forth to work, or David picks me up and drops me off. Either way, I diligently avoid public transportation. In fact, I avoid all of the places where I might run into Stephen. I have stopped doing volunteer work. I have stopped going to the gym. I stay completely out of the Castro (the San Francisco gay neighborhood where Stephen and I lived), after one chance encounter with Stephen assured me I was not safe there. I rarely go out, except to work every day and to therapy twice a week. (David picks me up and drops me off there, too.)

I am more nervous and jumpy than ever before; somehow my fear of violence from Stephen has been generalized to everything, or so it seems. I am afraid of gay men, especially blonds (like Stephen). I'm terrified of crowds, especially if I'm alone. Loud noises cause me to jump, or turn suddenly in fear. I have nightmares, horrible nightmares of being slapped or punched or shot at or trapped in a room without doors. I have nightmares about Stephen chasing me down streets, or coming into David's house through a window, or of his grabbing my arm suddenly, as he used to do. I cry a lot, am dazed and confused, lonely, horny, sad, depressed, isolated. David and I talk daily about how I am going to get through the day. We rehearse our worst-case scenarios. We go over the crisis rules. One day at a time is our focus. I help myself get through just one day at a time.

I have come home from work today, and David hands me a letter. We are both curious about it, because it has been addressed to me at his post office box number, and few people know that is now my address, too. The letter begins,

"Dear Patrick Letellier. I am contacting you to request your

assistance . . . I am a counselor meeting with Stephen. . . . '' This counselor goes on to say that he wants my help so that he can better help Stephen. He wants me to provide a "perspective on the abusive behavior" that Stephen is unable to give him. The letter goes on to say that, "Your safety is of primary importance to us. I will not disclose information to Stephen which would jeopardize your safety." It closes with a request that I contact this therapist, or at least call and leave him a number where I can be reached.

I show the letter to David, and reread it with him. We are both shocked. After all this, they want my help! They expect me to help Stephen! I endure two years of abuse, followed by two months of hell getting away from him. I leave behind an apartment that I furnished. I lose $900 of my money that Stephen gets from the landlords. I spend about 30 hours with an attorney obtaining legal protection from this man. I go to court, only to see Stephen defended by one of our best friends, who is a lawyer. I cut myself off from everyone, hiding in fear of Stephen's finding me, beating me, killing me. And, now they want me to help him?!

I wonder aloud if they ask rape victims to come forward and meet with rapists' therapists, so as to help the rapist come to terms with his heinous behavior. Are people who are mugged expected to "provide a perspective" on the violence they experienced, so as to help the mugger heal or learn to deal with his violent behaviors? I think not. Then, why am I, a victim of violence, like these other people, expected to be there to "help" the perpetrator of the violence done to me?

I get angry because, again, Stephen has managed to get at me, only this time through a therapist. Again, I am forced to think about him, the man I have gone to such lengths to get out of my life. And now I should help him?! Will I ever be free of him? For how long will he haunt my dreams? Will it ever end?

In the midst of all of this, I feel one tiny grain of satisfaction. Through this letter, I learn that Stephen has finally admitted that what I have been saying is true: he was violent and abusive, and he is a batterer. Help him? Never. He must help himself.

In "A Therapist Actually Asks Me to Help Stephen," several important points emerge. First, the therapist's letter to Patrick is professional misconduct. Under no circumstances should any batterer's therapist make any contact with the batterer's victim. Domestic violence is a crime and victims must at all times be protected from even the appearance of contact with or by the batterer. The therapist should simply have known better.

Second, the therapist may not be trained well and may not know that there are many therapeutic strategies he can employ with Stephen, without knowing what Patrick thinks. In therapy the "target person" is not often available to verify what the client is dealing with. People have moved away, have died, or are not to be found. A good therapist can bring about the desired results in his client without contacting the person that the client had trouble with.

"Asks Me to Help" also raises an important fundamental concept. On principle, every human being is personally responsible for his own growth and development. In this case, Stephen and only Stephen alone can take on the responsibility of dealing with his problems and fixing his unacceptable behavior. Patrick has nothing whatsoever to do with Stephen's problems.

"Asks Me to Help" primarily teaches that under no circumstances should victims think for a moment that they have any responsibility to help their present or ex-abusers. They must always adamantly refuse to see, meet with, deal with, provide information about, or in any way "help." Getting over being a batterer is work that batterers must do on their own.

Partner Contact Is Couple Counseling in Disguise

There is some debate in the movement to stop domestic violence about the policy of "partner contact." Partner contact means that an agency or therapist, representing the batterer, makes some kind of contact with the victim, requesting information about the relationship, the batterer's violent behavior, and the history of abuse. Because men who batter minimize or deny the violence they commit, partner contact policies exist, allegedly, to provide therapists with more accurate information about the extent of the batterer's abusive behavior. This controversial policy is becoming less and less common, although it is still practiced by many batterer programs. In New York State, funding for batterer programs cannot, by law, go to agencies with partner contact policies. Pennsylvania may soon follow New York's lead in working to eliminate partner contact practices.

We oppose partner contact policies because they are dangerous to victims no matter how indirect or innocent the contact may appear to be. Victims often feel inappropriately responsible for their partner's violence, and partner contact, even a nonthreatening letter, reinforces this illusion of victim-responsibility. The implication of partner contact always is that victims can or should play a role in stopping the violent behavior of their partners. Both of these notions are false, and we question the ethics of therapists and agencies who participate in partner contact and perpetuate these misconceptions. There is absolutely no reason that any victim of domestic violence should ever be contacted to provide batterers' therapists, or the agencies for whom they work, with information about anything. Stopping his abusive behavior is the sole responsibility, and is within the capacity, of the batterer and the batterer *alone*. Partner contact is couple counseling in disguise, should be recognized by victims as such, and should be absolutely avoided. All partner contact policy is unethical and is a bad practice. It must be unequivocally condemned by the mental health profession and by the movement to stop domestic violence.

THE TREATMENT MODEL

No significant health problem in our society is ever adequately addressed without a large-scale, overall plan. The disastrous effect of AIDS on the men and women of America is a tragic, but perfect, example of what happens when the people in charge do not develop and enact a comprehensive plan of action in a timely fashion.

We hope that societal concern about gay men's domestic violence travels a different course from that of AIDS. To promote planning and a programmatic response to gay men's domestic violence and its victims, we outline and briefly describe in this chapter the proper elements for a Treatment Model for victims.

The treatment model specifies what services a victim of gay men's domestic violence needs, and it includes four interlinked components: the availability of therapy; the availability of community support services; the availability of safe houses and lay helpers; and the availability of law enforcement and justice system services. The guiding principle used in the creation of the Treatment Model is our understanding (and assertion) that, at the moment of exit from his abusive partner (and for an indefinite time thereafter), the ex-victim of gay men's domestic violence is in an acute crisis, requiring 24-hour assistance. The treatment model spells out the nature of the assistance needed.

AVAILABILITY OF THERAPY

Individual Therapy

The Therapist

Therapists for victims of gay men's domestic violence do not have to be gay or lesbian. They merely have to be competent. The victim should understand that just because a therapist is gay or lesbian does not guarantee that they will provide competent treatment. We believe that there are minimum competence requirements which therapists must be able to demonstrate in order to qualify as caregivers to victims of gay men's domestic violence.

1. Formal training. We believe that traditional, formal training at the best graduate schools in the country which turn out therapists can be relied on to give a therapist the best possible training and skills. This means that the ideal therapist for ex-victims of gay men's domestic violence probably has a graduate degree from a major, accredited university and has a license to practice in the state in which he or she lives. The therapist needs to be well-grounded in personality theory, counseling theory and practice, adult development, theories of development, and assessment techniques, and needs to have had a well-supervised internship under the guidance of a master therapist. The therapist should also probably have been practicing for a considerable period of time, and, hopefully, have experience in the issues and phenomena of gay men's domestic violence. We think it is important that the formal training and experience of the therapist is *not* centered on family therapy, conjoint therapy, or couple counseling.

2. Not treating batterers. We assert that an ex-victim of gay men's domestic violence will not receive the best advocacy and treatment if the practitioner is also treating batterers, or if he or she has focused on treating batterers in the recent past. We believe this because of our conviction that the psychology of the victim is entirely separate from the psychology of the batterer, and that therapists who see both, unfortunately, have a tendency to link up the two inappropriately. (We recognize that points one and two above are controversial and may limit the number of professionals currently available to work with gay male victims and batterers of domestic violence. Nonetheless, we contend that professionals who are trained in a systems approach and/or who treat perpetrators cannot provide the best advocacy and treatment for gay male victims. It is our hope that, as an emerging issue in the mental health field, gay men's domestic violence will soon draw enough clinicians who meet our suggested requirements.)

3. Expertise on gay issues. The therapist for the ex-victim has to be extraordinarily well-informed on all psychological, political, and social issues that pervade the lives of most gay men. The therapist should understand clearly how living in a society that hates and oppresses homosexuals impacts the psyche of the gay man. The therapist needs to show that he or she understands how issues of power, control, self-hatred, and homophobia (including internalized homophobia) reverberate within and throughout the life of the gay man. Understanding all of the past and current issues is important and necessary in properly understanding the ex-victim of gay men's domestic violence.

4. Expert on domestic violence. Since there is a significant literature on heterosexual domestic violence and some on lesbian battering, the therapist should be well-read on the topic and, hopefully, experienced with clients who have been the victims of domestic violence. The therapist must have made an effort to find out as much as possible about gay men's domestic violence by talking with therapists around the country and with agency people who deal with gay violence. Of special importance is a need for the ex-victim to find a therapist who will never blame him for the violence and who will accept his accounts of the abuse without challenge or minimization.

5. Victim perspective. The therapist must be a believer in the ex-victim and never an apologist for the violence of the abuser. The therapist must adhere to the 12 Principles that underlie the theory of domestic violence listed in Chapter II. In short, the therapist must be an advocate for the victim's freedom from harassment, humiliation, and abuse of the ex-lover. The therapist should have no trouble in freely expressing the point of view that each person is entirely responsible for his own behavior and that every abuser is fully responsible for the violence he rendered. The therapist should take seriously the safety needs of the ex-victim as expressed to him. The therapist should not view the gay male victim as the "wife" or as the "battered woman," but rather see the ex-victim as a man, and further, as a male victim. The therapist needs to be clear about and be an advocate for the abolition of the Myths and Misconceptions (see Chapter I) and be accessible at other than formally scheduled times to see the client.

6. Willingness to be interviewed. The therapist should welcome the opportunity to be interviewed by the ex-victim to see if the therapist meets the criteria set forth above. In all matters relating to whether or not the victim becomes a client of the therapist-candidate, the victim is the decider. Choosing a therapist will be a good opportunity for the ex-victim to exercise his newly rediscovered trust in his own intuitions about others. The ex-victim will decide if the therapist is a person who will allow him to set his own boundaries for intimacy. The ex-victim will decide on his own whether or not the therapist is a person he can trust.

7. Not a batterer. The therapist must not be an abusive person in language, style, or behavior.

8. Not a present victim. The therapist must not presently be in a relationship in which he or she is experiencing violence or abuse.

9. No homophobia. The therapist must not be homophobic.

10. Educator. The therapist for victims of gay men's domestic violence plays a unique role as educator. In few other therapy settings does the therapist directly teach the client about the presenting problem as much as he or she will with ex-victims of domestic violence. With ex-victims the therapist will and should assist the client to become knowledgeable about domestic violence.

11. No sexual interest. Finally, the therapist must not be "interested in" the victim sexually, or overly touchy-feely with the victim, and must allow the victim to set the limit for intimacy.

The Therapeutic Approach

Is there a best therapeutic approach? Probably not. The attitudes and values of the therapist are more important than his or her style of counseling. The skills of the therapist are more important than theoretical beliefs. Allegiance to victims' right to live an abuse-free life is more important than allegiance to a therapeutic guru. The therapist must unashamedly be a victim advocate, a person who first of all prizes the victim's safety and will work diligently to help the victim protect himself from further abuse. The therapist must have the ability to employ a wide variety of therapeutic techniques in order to respond to the ex-victim. For instance, the therapist needs to be able to switch from being a teacher one moment to being a supportive listener the next. The therapist will be teaching the client how to conduct self-esteem-building homework assignments and soon thereafter be engaged in vocational counseling. The therapist will find a need to remind the ex-victim that the lover he might be pining for today was also the one who beat him senseless on any number of occasions as recently as two weeks ago. The ex-victim will talk about dreams he has in which he runs from violence. In short, we know of few other client types which present a therapist with a bigger challenge to be flexible, as well as skillful, and deeply resourceful.

The first set of necessary skills in the therapist's repertoire includes proven abilities to conduct rational problem solving and decision making with the client. The ex-victim of gay men's domestic violence faces a seemingly unending array of difficult problems to solve: his safety, his finances, his belongings, his legal steps. All demand immediate solutions just when the ex-victim is most agitated. The therapist may be the only person with whom the ex-victim has contact who is capable of helping him think through these problems and make careful decisions.

The second set of necessary skills includes an ability to teach the ex-victim about many concepts of which he is totally ignorant. The therapist's obligation to engage the mind of the ex-victim cannot be overestimated. Ex-victims need to learn about, and learn how to think in new ways about, a wide array of concepts such as: provocation, manipulation, domination, victimization, learned helplessness, control, independence, safety, boundaries, and blame. Some ex-victims of gay men's domestic violence have so repressed what has happened to them that they claim not even to be victims or to know what domestic violence is. Thus, the therapist will often function as an educator, helping the ex-victim to learn about and understand what gay men's domestic violence is and how it works.

The third set of necessary therapist skills includes proven ability to perform client-centered, feelings exploration therapy. The ex-victim client may be in need of encouragement to express certain feelings, such as rage, especially as they relate to the former lover and to the battering. Through feelings exploration the ex-victim will come to understand his feeling of shame, anger, isolation, and fear.

The fourth set of necessary skills includes a proven ability to combine a comprehensive, non-exploitive support for the client with a selective reality therapy approach such that the client feels safe, cared for and validated and yet is deeply motivated and challenged to get on with the reality of re-creating his life and taking responsibility for all of his conduct.

The task facing a therapist of an ex-victim of gay men's domestic violence is enormous. The therapist clearly needs to be a "cut above": someone who is neither so inexperienced in dealing with serious, many-faceted challenges nor so attached to one therapeutic modality, that he or she is incapable of eagerly applying an individualized, diverse approach. Therapists of ex-victims of gay men's domestic violence must put their clients' needs first and adapt their methods to the objectives of the intervention.

The Treatment

Naturally, it is not possible to prescribe exact treatment goals in the abstract for hypothetical ex-victim clients. However, broad objectives and approaches can and should be described. We believe that the proper treatment for an ex-victim of gay men's domestic violence has three main overall phases: Crisis Intervention, Staying Out Maintenance, and Personal Work.

1. Crisis Intervention. In the first sessions, crisis intervention is the major task for the therapist (and all other intervention workers with the ex-victim). At this point, the ex-victim is most likely suffering from Post-traumatic Stress Disorder and needs direct assistance to reduce and eliminate the symptoms associated with the disorder. He is experiencing unprecedented anxiety, terror, and fear, and may worry about being killed. Thus, safety is his primary concern. He needs to stay away from the batterer. He needs to learn about and understand the issues involved in gay men's domestic violence. He needs to learn how to see the batterer clearly as a man who once loved him *and* the man who also beat him. He may be considering suicide. He needs to take the first steps toward regaining control over his life and its decisions, a control he may have unwittingly relinquished to his abusive ex-partner. Finally, he needs to tell and retell his story of abuse.

Outcome Measures.
   A. The client will demonstrate anxiety reduction and significant reduction or elimination of symptoms associated with Post-traumatic Stress Disorder.
   B. The client will have stayed away from or dramatically reduced contact with the abuser.
   C. The client will be able to name and discuss various aspects and elements of gay men's domestic violence.
   D. The client will have begun all first legal and other steps necessary to guarantee his safety and independence from the abuser, including but not limited to obtaining a restraining order, moving to a safe house, and establishing security precautions at work.

2. Staying Out Maintenance. After the acute crisis begins to abate, but early in treatment, counseling activities of "staying out" begin. The therapist must play a major role in assisting the client to rebuild his shattered self-concept; to rethink and reformulate his concepts concerning taking responsibility; to develop workable methods to deal with friends, relatives, co-workers, and others with whom he must interact and, at times, discuss his former abusive partner. The therapist can help the ex-victim become grounded and focused when he faces the many unpleasant tasks associated with the restraining order, the police, his lawyer and the legal system. The therapist must always keep in mind that the goals of the ex-victim include staying out of the former relationship permanently and never entering another relationship with an abusive man. The therapist has a duty to the client to help him keep that goal foremost in his mind and not deviate from it. Thus, staying out maintenance is not only the name of this portion of the treatment but its objective as well.

Outcome Measures.
A. The client will have stayed away from the abuser and have had no contact with him.
B. The client uses a workable set of crisis rules for all abuser-initiated or chance encounters with the abuser.
C. The client identifies and names himself as an ex-victim of gay men's domestic violence.
D. The client ends his isolation by taking first steps to reestablish formerly severed relationships with family and friends.
E. The client verbally acknowledges feelings of pleasure when noting the absence of abuse.
F. The client will have successfully integrated the Jekyll-Hyde personality of the ex-abuser, such that he understands that the lover and the abuser were the same man, and he accepts the reality that his ex-lover was and is an abuser. He will understand that his abusive ex-lover was intentionally and deliberately perpetrating acts of violence.
G. The client demonstrates an understanding of how he may have utilized a victim role at other time periods and in other aspects of his life.
H. The client resumes making his own decisions about career, school, living space, relationships, and other ordinary life activities.
I. The client has not entered into a new primary love relationship.
J. The client shows diminished fear about entering new love relationships and may show signs of a reemergence of trust in men and may be dating.

K. The client will accurately be able to name those acts of domestic violence which are crimes.

3. Personal Work. The final phase of individual therapy for ex-victims of gay men's domestic violence is for the therapist to conduct individualized therapeutic work. The focus will vary widely from client to client.

Some ex-victims will need to develop a greater understanding of their apparent susceptibility to dominance and control. Others will want to understand their own anger and rage, while many will want to explore gay male identity issues or their patterns of self-defeating behavior. Many will want to learn, or relearn, communication and relationship skills and others will want to acquire skills of independent living or decision making. Many will look at their life-span development history to identify specific life-stage tasks and skills on which to work.

Obviously, the list of individualized therapy work topics is as varied as gay men are. The outcome measures will also vary with the topics. However, the overall objective is integration. After the ex-victim has internalized the lessons learned from examining the abuse he suffered and has explored particular characteristics of himself in depth, he will emerge a recovered ex-victim.

Outcome Measures.
   A. The client will have established personal life goals, which are independent of all relationship contingencies.
   B. The client will be able to describe his ideas and plans about his approaches to future dating and future love relationships.
   C. The client will have demoted the former relationship to an appropriate place along with other significant life events in his personal history and not award it undue prominence.
   D. The client will have achieved objectivity about his experience as a victim of abuse and be able to describe how domestic violence occurs and how the abuse he experienced was an example of all aspects of the phenomenon.
   E. The client will be able to describe himself as an integrated person who has incorporated important new learning about

himself, especially those particular, personal aspects that have been the focus of his individualized therapeutic work.

Group Therapy

Group Structure

The group model of intervention that we propose for battered gay men is less group therapy and more group support, though ideally it is a combination of the two. The group is designed for men in crisis who fall into three major categories: men who are currently being battered by their lovers, men who have just left their violent partners, and men who are trying to leave their abusive partners but are going back and forth. We believe that group support for these men may be the deciding factor in their staying out.

The group should be lead by two experienced group psychotherapists, and should have between six and ten members.

Given the safety needs of victims of domestic violence, and the ruthlessness with which some batterers will pursue their victims, where the group meets is important. The group should meet in what is seen as a safe place by all members. A room with a telephone and multiple exits may be ideal.

The group should meet once a week, for 1 1/2 to 3 1/2 hours, depending on its size. All members should have an opportunity to discuss the events of their week, in addition to any particular difficulty or crisis they may be facing.

We believe the optimal length of the group is 12 to 15 weeks, depending on the needs of the members. Those men who may need further support may participate in a second group, not concurrently, but rather, in succession. We believe, however, that those men will be exceptions to the norm.

Therapists who work as group leaders for battered gay men should meet all the criteria listed earlier in this chapter for individual therapists. In addition, it is absolutely essential that the therapist leading support groups be an experienced group leader. In fact, extensive experience in working with groups is desirable, as he or she will be dealing with clients who are considerably distressed.

Functions of Group Support

A support group for victims of gay men's domestic violence may serve an infinite number of functions, depending on the varying needs of its members. We believe, however, that there are, at a minimum, six central functions that support groups need to perform in order to facilitate the healing of the battered gay man. These six functions serve the overall goals of group support: to help victims get out of their relationships, stay away from their violent partners, and begin to lead a life free of abuse and violence. The support group functions are listed below, and a discussion of each follows:

1. Provide a place for victims to tell their stories and be believed.
2. Help to reduce victim isolation.
3. Help members see "the victim role" in their lives.
4. Provide emotional support.
5. Allow for the exchange of helpful information.
6. Facilitate the empowerment of group members.

1. A place to tell their stories and be believed. In a support group with other victims, the battered gay man can, perhaps for the first time, unfold the story of abuse that he has experienced. For many victims who have told no one else about the violence, the group may serve as their first audience. For others, the group may be their first *believing* audience.

This group function is crucial to the healing process of the victim. In a safe, supportive, non-judgmental, and trusting environment, victims may be able to acknowledge abuse and violence they may have long denied or minimized, to identify themselves as victims, and to identify their lovers as batterers. In group, victims must be allowed to tell their stories again and again, if necessary.

Other group members may play a central role in a victim's healing process. They can point out, for example, how a victim is unfairly blaming himself for the violence, or behaving unnecessarily helplessly. As peers and fellow victims, group members can help foster insight and understanding in the victim that might take weeks or months to accomplish in individual therapy.

For many victims, a first step toward a life without abuse is to acknowledge, accept, and talk about the violence they have experienced, without guilt, self-blame, or minimization. Group support creates the opportunity for this to happen.

2. Groups help to reduce victim isolation. A support group can be tremendously helpful in reconnecting victims of domestic violence to people who understand their plight, thereby reducing the isolation associated with domestic violence.

This function of the group should not be underestimated, particularly in dealing with gay male victims. As gays in our society, as victims of domestic violence, and as part of the gay community that is uninformed about gay men's domestic violence, battered gay men may be totally isolated.

A support group can fill a huge gap in the lives of its members who have literally no other support or contact. Recognizing that they are not alone in their difficulties is empowering to all group members. They experience closeness in having shared similarly painful experiences and as a result begin to bond together, feeling stronger and less alone.

Del Martin, in *Battered Wives*, illustrating how groups can significantly counter isolation and benefit all members, writes, "For one who 'has borne . . . shame alone,' there is no more positive encouragement toward self-confidence and self-respect than the realization that others have suffered in the same way and that collectively they can find answers to their problems" (Martin, 1976, p. 162).

3. See "the victim role" in their lives. As weeks progress, victims gain increased courage to look at their victimization and generalize their learning. Victims may then be able to transfer their new understanding of victimization to other relationships in their lives. With group support they may be able to identify and acknowledge other areas in which they are victimized and how that role may not serve them well. As healing takes place, and their strength increases, victims may want to make changes in their lives that go beyond those made in their relationship. New nonvictim ways of relating to family, friends, and co-workers can be thought out, rehearsed, and role-played in the group.

4. Provide emotional support. Providing victims of gay men's domestic violence with emotional support may be the most important function the group serves. Group members can readily understand the fear, anger, sadness, guilt, loss, loneliness, and power-lessness that victims experience better than any of the victims' friends or relatives.

Support in the early stages of his new life can make the difference between a battered gay man who stays out of his relationship with an abusive man and one who goes back to more violence. Group members can provide time and willingness to listen and believe, encouraging words when needed, or shoulders to cry on, all of which support the empowerment of individual victims.

Emotional support can also help boost low self-esteem, charac-teristic of most victims of domestic violence. For example, a victim may realize that, "Even though these people know I've been abused, they still like and accept me." Such bolstering of self-es-teem is necessary and empowering, as victims learn to like and accept each other, and themselves.

5. *Exchange of helpful information.* Support groups for victims may also function as information exchanges for members who may be making dramatic changes in their lives. Help with both practical and emotional difficulties can abound in support groups. Keeping in mind that for many victims who suffer from Post-traumatic Stress Disorder after leaving their violent partners, the mere routine of daily life can be frightening. Everything from grocery shopping to visiting friends takes on new and dangerous dimensions for victims, making ideas and suggestions from understanding peers invaluable.

For example, members can provide each other with information on how and where to file restraining order papers; ways to deal with co-workers or family members; where to find cheap apartments or new furniture; how to make a new house feel "safe"; how to relate to aggressive men; how to combat loneliness or bouts of depression; and helpful books to read. The list is endless, and the benefits to group members significant. Victims learn that they can be helpful as well as needy, and still be liked and accepted. They can encour-age each other, share humorous stories, and relate to each others' difficulties. The emotional benefits for group members who ex-change helpful information are often as great as the practical bene-fits.

6. *The empowerment of group members.* The five factors de-

scribed above, individually and as a whole, work to facilitate the empowerment of victims of domestic violence. In group with other victims, an upward cycle of empowerment and strength begins to counter the learned helplessness that most victims of domestic violence experience. Members, supported by each other, gradually become stronger. With their new strength come gains in self-esteem and further healing. As healthier men they are able to regain control of their lives, piece by piece, further contributing to their sense of strength. The cycle continues, and by the end of the group, members report that feelings of weakness and powerlessness have been replaced by strength and control. Thus empowered by each other, members make their individual transitions from victims to ex-victims.

Minimum Outcome Measures.
A. Victims leave their abusive partners, or, those who have left stay out of their relationships.
B. Victims are able to identify themselves as victims of domestic violence and identify their lovers as batterers.
C. Victims reduce or eliminate minimizing comments in their descriptions of the violence they experience.
D. Victims report taking precautions for their safety, thereby demonstrating two things: (1) a realistic assessment of potential violence from the batterer; and (2) an appropriate recognition of the danger they may be in.
E. Victims report an understanding of the concept of "provocation" and are able to state that they do not deserve nor provoke violence from their batterer or from anyone.
F. Victims are able to acknowledge and identify other relationships or situations in their lives in which they behave like a "victim."

AVAILABILITY OF COMMUNITY SUPPORT SERVICES

Victims of gay men's domestic violence need community resources, services, and support. The federal, state, county, or city government should provide these services, advertise their availability, and place them in neighborhoods or districts where they are needed. In addition, individuals on their own in the gay community can establish such community agencies, because government funding for anything with the words "Lesbian and Gay" in it is often sparse or nonexistent.

What Victims Need

1. People Just to Talk to

The first person that a victim of gay men's domestic violence most often turns to is one who is a staff member of a community agency known to him, such as New York City's Anti-Violence Project. A gay man can walk in off the street to such an agency and find people who understand his terror. The victim is most likely still in a relationship with an abusive man and is currently suffering violence. The violence is also probably a secret and he has risked coming to the center, knowing that his abusive lover would not like it. He has an emergency need to talk to a person who will not diminish his concern or ridicule his state of agitation. Staff people to talk to who understand are the first and most important provision of a community agency.

2. Information

At the community agency (or as a result of its informational outreach program) the gay male victim finds information about gay men's domestic violence to help him understand the violence happening to him. Often the most important single piece of information is the agency flyer which, on one page, names the violence, describes the cycle of violence and suggests that the victim come in for help. The victim will learn here about the procedure and documents required for a restraining order, the criminal justice system, and what other legal assistance is available.

Most importantly, the community agency must publish a directory of services and referral sources with widespread distribution in the gay community and to employers and care providers, including the various hotline services in large metropolitan areas.

3. Referral

In the community agency are suggested courses of action for the just-emerging victim. Here, he can find the names, addresses and phone numbers of therapists, lawyers, and health care providers. The community agency should also function as the coordinator for matching up victims with lay helpers and safe houses.

4. Direct Assistance

At Community United Against Violence in San Francisco, the CUAV staff will provide crisis intervention counseling on the spot to help the victim calm down, if necessary. CUAV also has a packet of legal forms for victims, including blank forms for restraining orders. They will teach a victim how to fill out the forms and about the legal procedure which follows. The center should tell the victim how to best use the police when an episode of violence occurs. He should be instructed on what to say to the police on the telephone and after they arrive. The agency should instruct the victim on the current attitude in that locale of the police toward gays and gay domestic violence. The agency staff can help a victim rehearse what he is going to say to the police.

5. Temporary Safety

The community agency must have a policy that forbids batterers to set foot on the premises. Even when the victim and batterer request joint counseling (an action the community agency should strongly discourage and never provide) the victim must be assured that batterers are never allowed there. This policy is to ensure absolute safety and peace of mind at all times for *every* victim. The agency can never deviate from this policy. There may be times when a victim is pursued or threatened and finds that only the anti-violence agency is a safe haven for him.

6. Accessibility

In most large metropolitan areas, the community center for gay men's domestic violence should be open 24 hours a day. Night is the time when most domestic violence occurs. A victim who leaves his home to escape violence more often than not has nowhere to go. To be truly effective, the agency needs to be open when it is needed. The safe house network should include emergency shelters, private homes where an escaping victim can stay for one to three days and nights until a permanent safe house is found.

7. Long Term Support

A victim who learns how to use the services of a community center for gay men's domestic violence will find himself in contact with the agency for a period of months or even years. The role of the agency staff is ordinarily reduced to occasional supportive contact, encouraging the ex-victim to continue his work toward an abuse-free life and congratulating him on his accomplishments.

At other times the agency will recycle into periodic renewed involvement with the victim as he may need some of its services. Restraining orders, for instance, usually have a one-year or three-year term, and at renewal time the victim may once again need the services of the agency.

8. Group and Individual Counseling

The ideal agency set up to assist victims of gay domestic violence offers (and encourages victim participation in) individual and group therapy. The group and individual sessions can be conducted right on the premises and should be offered at times during the day and evening when victims can attend without missing work. The agency needs to assure victims and its funding community that *all* therapists associated with the project are victim advocates and adhere to all agency policies, including the philosophy that victims and batterers should never engage in couple counseling.

AVAILABILITY OF SAFE HOUSES
AND LAY HELPERS

The third and keystone element in the Treatment Model is the establishment of a large number of safe houses in every community in which large numbers of gay men live. For many victims leaving their abusive partners, living in a safe house is the only way they will successfully stay out of the relationship and away from the abuser.

A safe house is the new, temporary home for the new ex-victim. It is a dwelling that the abusive ex-lover does not know. The ex-victim must feel confident that the abuser does not know where he is. There must never be any publicity about safe houses, and their identity must always remain a closely guarded secret. The safe house must actually be physically safe with lockable windows and doors. Keys are to be given to only a few people. The house should be difficult for thieves or other intruders to gain entry into. An alarm system, if possible, should be in place. A garage for automobiles may be necessary.

The safe house should be big enough that the ex-victim guest can have his own space and storage areas. There should be no charge, except that which the ex-victim can comfortably contribute, certainly an amount no more than he was paying for his prior quarters. The ex-victim should be made to feel welcome and have access to all public areas of the house. The ex-victim should be allowed to stay for a more or less unlimited period of time, and the resident lay helper should realize that the stay may span several months.

The lay helper, ideally, is the primary resident of the safe house. It is under his care that the ex-victim will prosper and thrive. The lay helper certainly needs no special credentials or training, but he should be the kind of person who responds positively and quickly to the necessities of sensitive help outlined in Chapter VII. Certainly, the lay helper must not be an abusive person. There should be only one ex-victim in each safe house.

The coordinators at the community agency should screen ex-victims and match them with lay helpers and safe houses. Ex-victims must meet with the lay helper in the safe house to get acquainted and conduct the screening with the agency person before assignments are made. Of course, either party should be allowed the privilege of terminating the arrangement for whatever reason with no questions asked.

AVAILABILITY OF LAW ENFORCEMENT
AND JUSTICE SYSTEM SERVICES

The history of the involvement of the police, the courts, legislatures, and lawyers in domestic violence in the United States is not inspiring. Rampant lack of concern for the disastrous impact of domestic violence on families has led periodically to its de-criminalization by legislatures and a hands-off policy by authorities. For years police were improperly "trained," often mediating clumsily in family disputes and not arresting perpetrators. The home was thought of as the domain of the male occupant, where anything went—and often did. Pleas for help by battered family members went unheard or unanswered.

Legislatures and courts have failed to act decisively to protect victims. Legislators are more concerned now with stopping perhaps two dozen people from burning the flag than enacting laws to prevent untold millions of women and men from violence in their homes.

Courts have released batterers from jail too early, despite the impassioned and valid arguments by social workers, prosecutors, and victims that their violence would merely repeat and escalate. "Mandatory" counseling or rehabilitation programs accompanying arrests and convictions for domestic violence are disorganized and poorly monitored.

A study completed by the Auditor General of California revealed that the state's diversion program for domestic violence offenders is in disarray. Among the major problems cited, it was noted that courts in some counties grant diversion to defendants who are ineligible. (Diversion into batterer treatment programs is supposed to be reserved *only* for those men charged with misdemeanor acts of domestic violence.) Felony domestic violence charges often are reduced to misdemeanors, and batterers are diverted into "treatment." However, many divertees fail to attend treatment programs for domestic violence. Further, some so-called treatment programs require only a few counseling sessions, and even those are poorly monitored (Sjoberg, 1990, p. 1).

While some progress is being made for battered heterosexual women, it is still difficult for most to secure the protection, support, and concern from the legal and justice system that is needed. We know that it is certainly no better for gay men.

Since domestic violence is a crime, a victim of gay men's domestic violence will use the law enforcement and the justice system far more extensively than he ever imagined. As we and others around the country combine our voices to demand the enforcement of existing laws and the further criminalization of domestic violence, legislatures, law enforcement, lawyers, and the courts will play an increasingly important role in assisting victims of gay men's domestic violence to live abuse-free lives. It may seem unpleasant, difficult, slow, and even "unnecessary" at times to a victim, but the fact remains that in the vast majority of domestic violence situations, the law and the courts are or should be involved. No model treatment program will be complete without a significant portion of its foundation resting on the laws and the legal institutions of our country.

What Victims Need

1. The Police

In the last several years, more than half of the police departments in major cities across the country have established "pro-arrest" domestic violence policies. According to pro-arrest policies, police responding to domestic violence calls must arrest batterers on the scene. Further, arrests are *not* to be influenced by factors such as the marital status of the victim and batterer, the victim's history of prior complaints, or the victim's reluctance to have the batterer arrested. Every state except West Virginia has also adopted policies aimed at arresting perpetrators of domestic violence.

The law in California, passed in 1985, also stipulates that all sworn police officers receive eight and one-half hours of training on how to handle domestic violence calls. While this represents monumental progress in the appropriate further criminalization of domestic violence, it is unfortunately still insufficient.

Battering is the single largest cause of death to women in this country, exceeding rapes, muggings, and auto accidents (Randall, 1990, p. 939). And, battered women *are* involving the police. "In Kansas City, for example, a study of domestic violence homicides revealed that *85 percent* of the victims had called the police at least once before the murder occurred; in 50 percent of the cases, they had called *five times or more*" (Martin, S. and McNeill, M. 1988, p. II-6). Eight and one-half hours of training are not enough to teach police officers how to intervene effectively in the crime that is responsible for killing more American women than any other. Much more extensive educating and training is necessary and *must* include information on gay domestic violence.

In San Francisco, the police have a reasonably good record in responding to domestic violence calls. If the call is in response to gay domestic violence, however, the responses may vary greatly from quick intervention and arrest to ignoring the call altogether. Police are also known to further victimize gay male victims when arriving at the scene through their ignorant, homophobic, and bigoted attitudes. In cases involving two gay men, police should refrain from labeling the violence as "mutual combat" on their reports. Instead, they must classify it as domestic violence, and they must identify both a victim and a suspect. The police must be made to identify and label all domestic violence as a crime, regardless of the gender and the relationship of the victim and batterer. The police must eradicate the prejudice, bigotry, and stereotypes they too often hold toward gay men and substitute instead a concern for gay male victims of domestic violence, the same concern they show to victims of any other crime.

When the police properly do their part, the victim must follow suit. It does no good to call the police to a domestic violence emergency and then not tell the truth or not cooperate with the police. Victims must identify their abusers and cooperate fully in the prosecution of the batterer for his criminal conduct. This process begins with a victim insisting that police file incident reports and arrest the batterer. As a community, we must avoid blanket criticisms of the police. When they do something right, our community must support them. Progressive steps taken by police to respond correctly to domestic violence and gay bashing merit our praise and active support.

2. The Criminal Justice System

The police represent only one part, though significant, of the criminal justice system. All of the police training in the world will not help eradicate domestic violence unless the court system that prosecutes batterers is also brought up to par.

In San Francisco, the Family Violence Project, located within the District Attorney's office, has developed a comprehensive multi-level approach to the prosecution of domestic violence cases (Soler, 1988, pp. 3-5). This approach is a model for other cities to adopt and, with only slight changes, a model for the prosecution of domestic violence cases irrespective of the gender and/or the sexual orientation of the victim and batterer.

The approach used by the San Francisco Family Violence Project includes three major components, which we have elaborated on for application to gay men's domestic violence.

1. Victim advocacy. Successful prosecution of domestic violence cases often requires special services for victims, who need consistent contact, emotional support, and follow-up as they proceed through the criminal justice system. Advocates must provide this contact and support through services that include crisis intervention counseling; information and counseling related to victim's legal rights and options; referral services for help with shelter, finances, custody, and employment; and court accompaniment during the often lengthy and difficult criminal justice process. With education and training, advocates can effectively serve gay male victims, who as a group may be justifiably wary of the criminal justice process.

2. Vertical prosecution. This policy ensures that victims of domestic violence have only *one* attorney throughout the criminal proceedings, rather than a different attorney for all the various hearings. To serve gay male clients, attorneys must have not only experience and training in prosecuting domestic violence cases but also an understanding of the dynamics of gay men's domestic violence. The attorneys, too, must be effective advocates for battered gay men, who, in turn, will be better witnesses because they will be more likely to cooperate with an attorney who understands their plight.

3. Prosecution protocols. Both felony and misdemeanor prosecution protocols must contain sections that outline the psychological dynamics of gay men's domestic violence and the resulting issues and problems for prosecution. Emphasis must be placed on the gay male victim's fears and concerns regarding his case. These protocols must also focus on central elements of successful prosecution, including contact with the gay male victim within 72 hours of charging the batterer, the consideration of prior assaults, and the likelihood of future violence (Soler, 1988, pp. 3-5). The San Francisco Family Violence Project has made the criminal justice system more accountable and accessible to victims of domestic violence. This is exactly what needs to happen for gay male victims. All of the components detailed above are applicable to all victims of domestic violence, gender, and sexual orientation aside.

4. Prosecute all violations. Court orders prohibiting batterers from contacting victims (such as stay away orders, restraining orders, and emergency protection orders) should be, but are not, strictly enforced. These orders are designed to *protect* the victim from more violence. Theoretically, a violation of a court order results in an arrest, fines, revocation of probation, and jail time for an offender. In practice, however, the police and district attorney's office most often ignore what they call "technical" violations, such as harassment, threats, phone contacts, and letters. Illogically, then, victims must experience the violence the order is designed to protect them from before the police or district attorney will enforce the order! As a result, many victims experience months or years of harassment and are forced to file stacks of police reports for court order violations before the batterer is arrested or prosecuted.

We assert that every domestic violence misdemeanor charge should be prosecuted, because misdemeanor violations are what precede the felony assaults, attacks, and murders that the system later takes seriously. All domestic violence court order violations should result in warrants for arrest, arrests made, and the prosecution of offenders. By intervening at the misdemeanor level, domestic violence felonies can be prevented. Such a policy would coincide with known psychology of learning principles as applied to changing the behavior of adults.

Advocates, district attorneys, and judges must all be educated about gay domestic violence. (We believe that some judges should not even be sitting on benches. District Judge Jack Hampton of Dallas, Texas, for example, has been censured by his profession for his despicable action of giving a murderer a lighter sentence because the two victims were homosexual.) Through vertical prosecution, gay male victims should have the services of an educated and experienced attorney. Prosecution protocols must include language that specifically addresses the issue of gay male battering. And, cities across the country must adopt the no-nonsense, multi-level approach to the prosecution of gay men's domestic violence similar to the one described above.

Until we are sufficiently outraged by the heinous crimes of domestic violence, victims will continue to be assaulted, injured, maimed, and killed by batterers. One way to stop the violence is through effective use of the criminal justice system. Victims must be protected, and jail time for batterers sends a loud and powerful message to everyone.

ACTION

The four-part model described in this chapter does not yet exist anywhere. Pieces of it are operational in New York City, San Francisco, Minneapolis, and Seattle.

Exemplary prototypes of the model need to be set up and made operational in key cities. San Francisco is a likely place to start. The city has a concentrated, organized, and very large gay population. Gay men and women are in positions of political leadership and civic prominence. There are three widely read gay newspapers. Calls for money, action, and publicity work well.

Smaller scale working models can also be set up in any community where gays have visibly congregated. Portland, Oregon; Sacramento, California; Hartford, Connecticut; and Fort Lauderdale, Florida are but four of a long list of locations in the United States where concerned gay men can and should begin addressing domestic violence in their ranks with a planned program of response.

The challenge of appropriate response to victims of gay men's domestic violence is a large one. Its accomplishment rests on resources being applied to make available services in each of the four areas: therapy, community support, safe houses and lay helpers, and the law enforcement/criminal justice system. The time to act is now.

Chapter IX

The Unusual Psychology of Domestic Violence

THE NEIGHBORS CALL THE POLICE

It is a hot summer afternoon, and Stephen and I are in our San Francisco apartment having an argument. We are walking around the apartment, talking at first, then gradually getting louder and finally shouting. Stephen tells me to stop shouting, "or the neighbors will hear," and he's right. They might hear because it is a quiet, windless afternoon, and everyone has their windows open. Doubtless, someone can hear us. I, however, am not deterred by Stephen, and I continue shouting at the top of my lungs. My "noise" gets Stephen really angry, and as he moves around the apartment closing windows, he promises to "sort me out."

Within moments his fists are flying. I am flung against a wall. Stephen shouts, "Are you happy now? Now I'm really angry. Are you happy?" He is holding me by the shoulders, shaking me hard, in a rage. I shove him off me so hard he falls to the ground, and I make a mad dash to the front door, but not fast enough. Stephen grabs me from behind, and we struggle, ending up in the bedroom. My hands are on his shirt collar, and as I push him away, his shirt tears. He is livid now. The blow to my mouth comes fast and direct – POW! He hits me so hard he cuts both my lip and his knuckle; we are both bleeding. I turn my head quickly to avoid the next punch, and blood is smeared on the wall. We continue to struggle and grapple with each other, and Stephen is relentlessly punching me, in the face, in the stomach, on the side of my head, in the chest. It is all I can do to defend myself. I know that somehow I have to get out of the apartment. I literally throw him across the room, using

236

every ounce of my strength, and bolt for the front door. Next to the front door is a coat closet and its door is open. As I run for the front door, Stephen pushes me hard from behind, and I land face down in the closet on top of some suitcases with my legs sticking out into the hall.

Instantly Stephen is there behind me, kicking me in the shins. Kicking, kicking, kicking, with all his might, as hard as he can. From where I am I can see his face. For the first time I can see the expression on his face as he batters me. (Usually, I am defending myself with my hands in front of my face or turning my head away.) But now, I see him. The intensity, the deliberation, the concentration. I think, "Oh God, he is insane."

Then, suddenly, it is over. His rage has passed. The shouting and screaming that had been going on has stopped, and the apartment is quiet. Stephen walks away, going . . . I don't know where. I go into the bathroom and look at my lip. "It's a small cut," I think. "Maybe nobody will notice it." I feel my shins. I know they are bruised and will hurt even more later. And then I remember blood on a wall somewhere. I wet a facecloth, wipe my face and cut lip, and go into the bedroom to look for blood stains. As I'm wiping them off the wall, the doorbell rings. Stephen, looking out of a window, mutters, "Oh my God. There's a police car out front." Then he directs me, "Pull yourself together." Remarkably, he looks worse than I.

I listen from the bedroom as Stephen talks to the police. I hear only fragments. "No, no problems here. We were just having an argument, that's all. . . ." And then I hear the policewoman say something about "not leaving until we see the other party." Stephen politely calls out, "Patrick, will you come here please. They want to see you."

I quickly check my appearance in the mirror (I look okay. "Good enough," I think) and go to the door. "Everything is fine," I hear myself say. "We were just having an argument." I smile weakly.

The policeman responds, "Must have been a pretty big argument, because the people who called us live three buildings away." Stephen apologizes, "Sorry. Yes, it was loud. But we're fine now, really." I stand there, numbly staring at those two officers, wondering if they think I've been beating Stephen, because he looks absolutely terrified right now. I hear them say something about intervening, "if it gets physical." They leave.

Stephen and I stare at each other in disbelief for a moment. As he walks away, he wonders aloud about who could have possibly called, but I continue only to stare at the closed front door and the open closet door, thinking to myself that something is wrong here. Something is dreadfully wrong.

This narrative clearly illustrates several important concepts about domestic violence, primarily batterers' tremendous fear of authorities. We hypothesize that most batterers know that they are committing crimes for which they can be held accountable. It is only the "domestic" part of domestic violence that keeps them out of serious trouble. They do not want to be caught or arrested. When police arrive, the secret of their violence is scarily in danger of being known.

"Neighbors" also shows how reluctant a victim may be, even when the opportunity is present, to tell the police the truth about the violence and to file a complaint against the batterer. There are many reasons for victim reluctance. Fear is at the top of the list. Fear of recrimination from the batterer may prevent victims from saying anything to the police, particularly in the presence of the batterer. Gay male victims may also be understandably afraid of homohating police officers. Patrick has no way of knowing what the police may do if he identifies Stephen as a lover who beats him. They may decide the abuse is "mutual combat" and arrest them both. They may ridicule Patrick as a "fag" who deserves to get beaten up. They may tell both Patrick and Stephen that they are "sissies who should learn to fight like real men." (Both of the above scenarios were reported by victims of gay men's domestic violence when the San Francisco police arrived at their homes.) The police may also arrest Stephen and book him on spouse abuse, as they should, but Patrick has no way of knowing what they will do. At such times, victims may believe that silence about their experiences is their safest option.

The most important lesson of this narrative is about complicity. Patrick has now inadvertently joined Stephen as a "partner in crime." Patrick colluded with Stephen to lie to the police and to "cover up" the violence. They are now joined together as partners in violence against the world "out there," including the police. This act of complicity will make it even more difficult for Patrick to extricate himself from the relationship and much more difficult for him to convince Stephen that he wants no part of violence. (See "What! Have My Lover Arrested?" in this chapter.)

THE UNUSUAL PSYCHOLOGY
OF DOMESTIC VIOLENCE

One of the main objectives of this book is to help make domestic violence understandable to every reader. We believe that only when the shrouds of mystery are removed from domestic violence will people be willing and motivated to stop it. Making domestic violence comprehensible, however, is not so easy, because it seems inherently to defy logic and reason. Its unusual psychology baffles even the most astute observers.

Domestic violence is a phenomenon that involves a vast range of human issues, further adding to its complexity. While it is not a "relationship issue," it is a problem that occurs in relationships. It is a serious legal issue, a psychological issue, a power and control issue, and a political issue. By any measure it is both an extraordinarily unusual phenomenon and a dangerously common one.

We contend, however, that a little information goes a long way, especially about a phenomenon about which so little is known. In this chapter, then, we analyze some of the obvious though less talked about issues that domestic violence entails, such as the difficulties victims have calling the police on their lovers; the concept of provocation; AIDS; codependence; and gender. Taken individually, these are not hard-to-understand issues. In combination, however, they contribute to the unorthodox psychology of domestic violence and to its apparent incomprehensibility.

* * *

LET'S GET CLEAR ON THE CONCEPT
OF PROVOCATION

Say that you are walking down the sidewalk with your boyfriend, whereupon some bigot says something insulting and obscene to you such as: "Oh, look at those two! More fucking fags! I'll bet they like taking it up the ass!"

He does not brandish a weapon or otherwise appear to threaten you or your safety. He merely uses words.

In most areas of the United States, the law specifically prohibits you from a violent response to that bigot. You may neither threaten him nor actually physically harm him. If you do, you are in violation of the law, and you could be arrested and convicted for assault and battery. You would have become a perpetrator of violence, and the Neanderthal who insulted you would become a crime victim whom the law and the courts would rightfully protect from you. According to the law in most places in our country, you cannot and you may not hit someone just because of something nasty that they said to you, no matter how offensive the remark may have been.

California law is particularly definite about this concept. As a result, in criminal trials in California, juries are instructed as follows:

> No provocative act which does not amount to a threat or attempt to inflict physical injury, and no words, no matter how offensive or exasperating, are sufficient to justify a battery. (CALJIC 16.142, p. 307)

In civil cases in California, juries are instructed as follows:

> Words alone, no matter how objectionable or insulting, will not justify a battery against the person who utters them. (BAJI 7.53, p. 304)

This important legal principle is a central feature in understanding the unusual psychology of domestic violence. Millions of people (including the vast majority of men in America) do not understand that if someone only *says* something unkind, obscene, or insulting, our society does not allow the use of force in retaliation. This rule of law applies not only in public but also in the privacy of our own homes.

We estimate that a significant portion of gay men's domestic violence occurs because the assailant falsely believes (or wants to believe) he has a right to strike or threaten his mate in his home because of what his partner said to him. He falsely believes that he was provoked into the use of violence by the other person's words. He is wrong.

Our position is not a moral one, although the Judeo-Christian "turn the other cheek" credo supports civil law in this area. Our position is entirely a legal one. Gay men need to know what the laws of their states prescribe. Victims of domestic violence need to know it even more so.

The big problem here is a misunderstanding of the concept of provocation. Even if you say to your partner, "No! I don't want sex with you now! Get off me, you bastard! Get off me! I hate you!" you have not provoked your lover into the use of physical force. Words alone are not a justification, provocative as they may be. Laws protect you from violence, just as the bigot was protected in the earlier example, no matter how unkind you were in your choice of words to your lover. If your lover hits you because of what you said to him, he has committed a civil or criminal violation. His excuse that you provoked him to be violent and his attempts to blame you for his actions are false and are his own rationalizations.

So What Is Provocation, Then?

There are at least 100 synonyms for the words "provocation," "provoke," and "provoking." Instigating, inciting, agitating, stirring up, inflaming, aggravating, prodding, angering, starting, causing, and pushing are all substitutes for provocation. The word "provoke" really is loaded, especially for a man who does not understand that each and every action he takes is a choice. It is easy to see how a violent gay man could try to justify his violence as a response to being angered. How many times have you heard, "Well, *he* started it. *He* made me do it. I was just sitting there doing nothing and he called me a motherfucker! He *made me* hit him. I was provoked." Thus, abusive people use the word "provoke" and its synonyms as an excuse to justify battery. When a gay man claims that someone else "made" him do something it is a clear signal that he is attempting to deny responsibility for his own actions.

There is a difference between feelings and actions. Huge numbers of people do not understand that there is a difference between being caused to feel something and being caused to act. Someone's words may cause you to be hurt, angry, sad, or happy. People do cause others to have feelings, and other people's actions or words can be provocative. You feel angry when someone insults you. But no one makes you act. No one ever makes one person hit another by words alone. Each and every human being decides to perform every act, good or bad. You can cause me to be upset, *but only I can cause me to hit you.*

Provocation, then, is when another person's behavior causes you to feel some negative emotions. Yes, the provocateur may have stirred up feelings inside you. To act on the stirred up feelings, however, is to engage in behavior that you and you alone chose. Too many people falsely believe that others cause them to behave violently. These people, batterers among them, are unclear on the concept of provocation.

To keep clear on the concept of provocation, keep three things in mind:

1. Words alone are not a justification for battering.
2. Words can and do provoke feelings inside a person.
3. No one causes anyone to act. You and you alone are responsible for all of your actions. You choose and decide to act.

*   *   *

THE VICTIM'S PARADOX

Victims of domestic violence face an array of unusual and complex paradoxes that contribute to their inability to leave their violent partners. (A paradox is a situation that is or seems to be inherently self-contradictory. For example, "It takes money to make money.")

For victims of domestic violence, the confusion associated with their paradoxical situations can be debilitating and immobilizing. A brief examination of three victim paradoxes will, we hope, serve two major functions. First, it will educate all readers about the unusual psychology of domestic violence and further sensitize them to the plight victims face. Second, it will help victims to recognize that they truly may be in inherently paradoxical situations, problems that seem to have no solutions.

One significant paradox victims face involves leaving their batterers after an episode of violence. Simply stated, it is after a major battering incident when victims are most expected to leave their partners, most encouraged to leave their partners, and even most motivated to do so. It is also when they are *least able* to leave. Leaving after violence *is* a profound paradox to the victim. Leaving means making major life decisions and radical changes. Yet, after violence victims are often numb, dazed, and in shock. For hours or even days they may be completely disoriented, less capable than ever of making life decisions or changes. Leaving requires planning and organizing, activities requiring strength, perseverance, and a strong sense of self and independence. After violence, however, victims are shaken, nervous, afraid, even terrified. They report feelings of guilt, shame, worthlessness, and exhaustion. They probably also are physically injured. Strength and independence, which may already be foreign feelings to them, are virtually nonexistent after violence. Thus, all of the skills and qualities a victim needs in order to leave are the very same ones that are eroded or eliminated by repeated domestic violence and are particularly depleted after an acute battering incident. Paradoxically, violence becomes both the victim's primary motivation to leave the batterer and the force rendering him unable to do so.

A second and perhaps more subtle victim's paradox involves sources of comfort and support. For most victims, violence is a traumatic experience, and they are often in need of emotional support after a major battering incident. They need love and affection, calming and soothing words, and they need to be held and comforted. Given the isolation of most victims of domestic violence, however, usually the *only* person for them to turn to for support after violence is the person who battered them. Paradoxically, their source of comfort and support is also the source of their trauma. By seeking comfort from their batterers, victims may unwittingly facilitate the beginning of Phase III loving behavior, keeping the relentless cycle of domestic violence in motion. The cycle of violence guarantees that more violence will occur.

A third paradox victims of domestic violence face rests on the widely held and false proposition that by leaving the batterer the victim can put a stop to the violence. While this may sound like obvious common sense, research shows that it is simply not true. For many victims, periods of separation from their batterers are often extremely dangerous, because that is when batterers become even more frantic and violent in their attempts to find or get back *at* their victims. Rather than stopping the violence, leaving may mean more frequent, more severe, and even lethal violent attacks. The paradox the victims face, then, is that the best way for them to avoid severe violence may seem to be to stay with their battering partners and try to prevent it. This is an obviously bewildering situation for victims as they struggle to understand and put a stop to the violence in their lives. Leaving and staying become equally unappealing alternatives, paralyzing the victim into inaction and helplessness.

These are but three of many paradoxes that contribute to the unusual and complex psychology of domestic violence. They may be summarized as follows:

1. Violence is both the incentive for the victim to leave the relationship and the reason he may be unable to do so.
2. By accepting the comfort and support needed after violence from their batterers, victims may unwittingly perpetuate the cycle of violence.
3. Leaving a relationship with a violent man in order to stop the violence may have just the opposite effect, a further escalation of the violence.

For the friends and relatives of victims of domestic violence, an awareness of the victim's paradoxes can help make the confusion and immobilization of victims more understandable. For example, staying with the batterer can be understood as a coping strategy for the victim, rather than as pathology, denial, or masochism. It is our hope that friends and relatives will encourage and help victims to leave their batterers, while acknowledging the difficulties and potential dangers they face in doing so.

For therapists working with victims, the challenge of the victim's paradoxes is two-fold. First, therapists themselves must understand the dynamics of the paradoxes and recognize the forces that keep victims in relationships with abusive partners. Second, therapists must help their victim-clients to understand these forces and overcome the paradoxical situations. For example, victims can be coached to leave their partners *before* major battering incidents occur, thereby eliminating the loving and comforting behavior after violence.

For researchers, victims' paradoxes provide a wealth of possible research topics. Are most victims aware of the paradoxical nature of domestic violence? Can awareness alone help victims to resolve the paradoxes? What are the most effective resolutions? Do victims who seek comfort from sources outside the relationship experience less violence or leave their partners sooner?

Finally, for victims, the above discussion provides an all too rare acknowledgment of the paradoxical situations they face. Acknowledgment alone, however, is insufficient. It is our hope that victims will use their awareness to overcome their paradoxes and get out of relationships with violent men without further violence. Leaving the batterer may escalate attempts of violence, but staying is not the solution. Rather, it means precautions must be taken after leaving to prevent the occurrence of more violence. Victims must keep in mind that paradoxes, by definition, *seem* to be without solutions, but that does not mean that solutions do not exist.

*   *   *

WHAT! HAVE MY LOVER ARRESTED?

Call the police! Tell them to arrest your lover for committing crimes of domestic violence against you. It is the logical thing to do. Or, so people might think. Not so to the victim of gay men's domestic violence.

A puzzling phenomenon in domestic violence psychology is the reluctance of the victim to publicly denounce the abuser, have him arrested, and subject him to whatever punishment the justice system will mete out.

Reasons gay male victims do not call the police more frequently than they do include their valid fear of retaliation by an angry and humiliated lover and homophobic or abusive treatment by the police. But those are not the only reasons. An analysis of the American family also supplies a reason.

In a family, such as a gay couple, the members are bound to each other by emotional, economic, and psychological bonds. Solidarity develops, which explains why and how a family rallies to form a united front when a tragedy occurs. Old disputes are put aside and the family functions as "one" to overcome a problem or fight outside forces.

Solidarity also appears to be a central concept needed to explain family punishment practices. The way people go about punishing others is, in part, related to the amount of solidarity they feel toward them. When relationships are close, and solidarity is high, as it is in a family, punishment practices are more likely to be aimed at restoring and rebuilding than toward expelling or termination. High solidarity means personal closeness in which family members identify with each other and can easily put themselves in each other's shoes, and it means longstanding and strong emotional connections. High solidarity, then, resists family break-up.

Thus, even if they are the most adversely affected, kin and close friends are the least likely people to take legal action against an abusive friend or family member, such as calling the police on their batterers.

Furthermore, in gay relationships solidarity may be abnormally high. Living in a homohating society such as the United States, many gays, cut off from family, church, and other traditional forms of societal support, may place a greater value on their own relationship. Often gay couples hold an "us against the world" view, obviously intensifying the solidarity between the members of the couple. Homophobia may also play a more direct role in increasing solidarity in gay couples. Gay couples with children may understandably fear police involvement and the accompanying heterosexist custody laws that may destroy their families. Fear of bigotry and police brutality may unite victims and batterers on one side, as members of an oppressed and hated minority, and police on the other side, as oppressors and gay-haters. For many gay men of color, trusting the police may simply be out of the question.

Ironically, domestic violence itself can also heighten solidarity and cement victims and batterers together. For example, often only the victim and batterer know about the violence. It is their shared secret, and they are bound by shame, guilt, and a conspiracy of silence. Isolation, too, may increase their solidarity, as batterers become increasingly dependent on victims to satisfy all their needs.

While solidarity may be the force at work in victim reluctance to call the police, it is not the only force binding batterers to their victims. Batterers experience a pathological emotional dependence on and obsession with their victims that, though appearing to be solidarity, is actually an unhealthy and potentially dangerous cementing force. The phrase, "I love you so much I'll never let you go," is a perfect example of batterer obsession and his overwhelming fear of abandonment. The desire to possess, control, and keep the victim is the dominating force at work for batterers, not love or solidarity. Love may "set you free," but a batterer will punch, slap, kick, and degrade you until you are unable or too afraid to leave. Thus, the positive connotations associated with solidarity, such as dedication, commitment, and unity, may not apply to batterers nearly as much as they do to victims.

This discussion of solidarity has important messages for victims. First, it is important for gay victims to understand that their reluctance to turn in their batterers may have its roots in a healthy and normal human phenomenon: high solidarity with family. However, in relationships with violent men, high solidarity can be lethal, inhibiting victims from effectively dealing with a life-threatening situation. Victims must acknowledge, then put aside, their feelings of solidarity in order to survive.

Second, a batterer's pathological dependence may have the illusion of solidarity, but much more is involved, and their dependence should be recognized as extremely unhealthy. In fact, acknowledging batterer obsession may help victims put aside their own feelings of solidarity, as they see the disparity between the two forces.

* * *

ALCOHOL AND DRUGS

Alcohol does not cause traffic fatalities. Drunk drivers do. For seventy-five grief-filled years we erroneously blamed alcohol for the slaughter on our nation's highways. But finally during the 1980s, due in large part to the inspired activism of Mothers Against Drunk Driving (MADD), we forced ourselves to face an unpleasant cause-and-effect truth: decent, sane people were committing auto-related crimes while under the influence, but they were not being held sufficiently accountable for their conduct because "alcohol was involved." Our country's sad history of denying drunk driver accountability is a perfect example of misattribution of "cause" to mere means to excuse misconduct.

People in our society have long used drugs and alcohol as excuses to avoid full responsibility for their conduct. It is an old ploy, and some people and some lawmakers still fall for it. Unfortunately, such faulty logic insinuates its way into discussions about domestic violence, especially when evaluating perpetrator behavior. Batterers, of course, would prefer everyone (especially themselves) to believe that they are less responsible for their conduct when they have been drinking, but such an excuse is unacceptable today. After all, the drinker's decision to drink precedes the drunkenness. Drugs and alcohol never reduce user responsibility or accountability.

Functions of Alcohol

Drugs and alcohol certainly play a part in domestic violence. For one thing, abusers who have been drinking are more careless in their attacks on victims. Whereas a sober perpetrator will be careful to strike a victim on the stomach, chest, groin, back, or back of the head where bruises or cuts are generally not as visible to outsiders, a perpetrator who has been drinking will be more sloppy in her or his attacks, leaving evidence of the abuse more readily visible. Since alcohol is expected to and actually does relax inhibitions, the perpetrator may also attack more strongly and viciously than when sober, causing more serious injury to victims.

Alcohol consumption by the victim may play a crucial role in legitimizing violence in the eyes of society. More specifically, a victim who drinks may be inappropriately blamed for a perpetrator's violence because (a) a victim's drinking in and of itself may be deemed a "provocative" act, and (b) alcohol consumption is perceived to be associated with "aggressive behaviors or other socially inappropriate behaviors that may 'provoke' aggression" and violence (Dent and Arias, 1990, pp. 186; 191).

Societal permissiveness about drinking and gives rise to two related psychological phenomena: Abusers themselves believe they are less accountable for what they do, and they also expect others to hold them less accountable. Studies of batterers in treatment show that many batterers actually decide to batter *before* they decide to drink (Sinclair, May, 1990). The decision to drink serves to prepare the batterer to batter, an obvious self-delusion, and serves as a premeditated strategy designed to elicit leniency from others, if they ever find out about the abuse. Such self-deception and lying to authorities is flagrantly apparent. Gelles and Straus (1988, p. 46) report that a high proportion (over 80 percent) of batterers who say they are drunk in fact are not drunk.

A common misconception about domestic violence and alcohol is the notion that batterers who drink must be drunk at the time of the assaults on their mates, or that only heavy drinkers are batterers. Not so. Gelles and Straus (1988, p. 46) report that moderate drinking, not heavy drinking, is most closely associated with domestic violence, further evidence that alcohol serves as a permission-giving device for the batterer. Undoubtedly, drinking alcohol also serves to prop-up a failed masculine self-image in the batterer.

Alcohol is also assumed by most people to be involved in virtually all incidents of domestic violence. Again, this is not the case, as corroborated by victims in a West Harlem police study, which found that "only ten percent of domestic violence complainants alleged that the accused was drunk" (Martin, 1976, p. 57).

It has also been widely documented that the men who batter will do so whether or not they are under the influence (Sonkin, Martin and Walker, 1985, p. 49; Walker, 1979, p. 25; Browne, 1987, p. 73). Not only, then, will men batter when sober, but, according to Hamish Sinclair, a treatment provider for male batterers, domestic violence often increases when perpetrators stop drinking (May, 1990). The myth that alcohol causes battering remains just that, a myth, and the men who batter only when they are drunk are just as fully responsible for their violent and abusive behavior as the men who never drink. What becomes clear, however, is that men who batter will continue to be violent and abusive, regardless of their alcohol consumption, until they do something about their *battering disorder.*

Two Separate Problems

People who are abusive and who have a substance abuse problem have at least two separate, serious problems. The problems are related only in that drinking is used inappropriately as an excuse for, or a self-delusion about the cause of, battering. The two problems must be dealt with separately, with the drinking problem handled first. It is common for people to have two separate problems that need separate treatments. We in the gay men's domestic violence movement must strongly resist the current, trendy tendency to link together all psychological problems. We advocate the absolute necessity for authorities and interventionists, who have contact with gay male batterers in particular, to separate and keep separate the problems of their drinking (or other substance abuse) and their battering.

Logic precludes any claim that alcohol causes domestic violence. In summary, alcohol is merely an unacceptable excuse for violence, a permission-giving preparation for battering, and a denial of actual intent to harm. In its worst form, it is a premeditated deception, designed to elicit a softer judgment from an alcohol-consuming society. Batterers cause domestic violence, and if they have a substance abuse problem also, then they have at least two compelling reasons to obtain help.

*   *   *

AIDS IS NO EXCUSE

Is AIDS causing all the domestic violence that the gay community is starting to hear about? Is the stress of AIDS making gay men abusive and violent? Do gay men batter out of the anger and sorrow associated with AIDS?

The answer to these questions is "No." Yet many people in our community believe that because of AIDS more and more gay men are battering their lovers. As with alcohol or drugs, AIDS is seen as the cause of domestic violence, the reason why a gay man is violent. There are also people who think that domestic violence is "understandable" given the pressure that AIDS puts on gay men in general, and on gay couples in particular. In response to this, the newest excuse for domestic violence, it is important to remember that, in terms of responsibility, the only cause of gay men's domestic violence is violent men.

More Gay Men Coupling

While there is no research on the relationship between AIDS and battering, it is possible that, in this age of AIDS, domestic violence is occurring at a higher rate in the gay male community than ever before. This possibility is based on two assumptions about gay men. The first is that more gay men are coupling now than they were before the epidemic started. The second is that gay men are staying in their relationships longer than they were pre-AIDS. These two factors could have impact on the rate of gay men's domestic violence. For domestic violence to occur, gay men must be coupled, so more gay couples means the possibility of domestic violence occurring increases. In addition, the longer a couple is together the more likely a victim will stay once domestic violence starts. Therefore, if gay men are staying in their relationships longer, the possibility increases that domestic violence will start, that the victim will remain, and that the violence will continue and become more serious. If AIDS is having any impact on domestic violence in the gay male community, it is because more violent men are in relationships now than ever before.

Victims and Batterers with AIDS

While having AIDS, or having a lover with AIDS, cannot be used as an excuse for domestic violence, it is important to understand that for many gay men involved with violent partners, AIDS adds tremendous complications to their relationships. For example, gay male victims of domestic violence face even greater difficulties attempting to leave their relationships after their batterer is diagnosed with AIDS. Commitment, caretaking, guilt, and abandonment are just four of the many issues these victims must face. ("How can I leave? Who will take care of him? He needs me now more than ever. How can I stay here with all this violence? If I stay I'll end up in the hospital, too. And nobody even believes he can be violent now, because he's sick.") Imagine leaving a violent lover who is also a person living with AIDS, only to face a community that knows little about domestic violence and understands even less.

And what about the victims of domestic violence who are diagnosed with and/or who are sick with AIDS? Where can those men go? We know of one victim of domestic violence who had AIDS, was quite sick, and was stabbed by his lover. This victim desperately wanted his batterer to be let out of jail because he was so dependent on him. The batterer was this man's sole source of financial and emotional support and was his caretaker. The victim was perfectly able to acknowledge that he was living in an extremely dangerous situation, but it was a situation that he knew. That familiar setting was preferable to the unknown, particularly since this man believed that leaving his violent partner and facing the unknown meant "dying on the street." Thus, the unusual psychology of domestic violence is here further complicated by AIDS.

Providing Options and Support

It is necessary to be mindful of the way that AIDS is talked about in relation to domestic violence. It is now being used as an excuse or cause of domestic violence, and it is an excuse that many people are ready to accept. As is the case with alcohol or drugs, or job stress, or wrecking the car, AIDS is just another item on a long list of excuses that removes responsibility for violence from the men who commit it. This must not continue.

Support must be provided to those men who are affected by both AIDS and domestic violence. They must be helped to see and take advantage of the other options and services that are available. Staying with a violent lover must never be a victim's "only choice," regardless of the health of the victim or the batterer. Victims who say their lovers are violent and abusive must be believed, no matter how frail or "weak" their lovers may look.

AIDS is not responsible for one single incident of domestic violence. The violent men who cause domestic violence will be abusive under the best of life situations and under the worst. While AIDS may indeed be one of the worst catastrophes gay men have had to face, it is no excuse for violence.

*   *   *

GENDER

No one knows for sure what causes some men and some women to become batterers. This book, in part, outlines our perspective on the question. Theories abound that attempt to explain the development of people who are abusive, and there is heated disagreement among professionals regarding the cogency and sufficiency of the various theories. One of the disagreements surrounds the claim by some theorists that battering is gender-based. That is, they believe that only males (and a few females who perversely adopt malevolent male roles) are the perpetrators of domestic violence.

A major difficulty that bars agreement on causation is that domestic violence spans a very wide range of conduct: psychological abuse, physical and sexual violence, and property destruction. Further, batterers target not just spouses or mates, but children, parents, relatives, roommates, and people whom a batterer is dating. Targets frequently are also people with whom the batterer formerly had a relationship of some kind. Adding gay male and lesbian categories, the entire spectrum of domestic violence is complete.

When evaluating the efficacy of theories to explain the causes of this entire range of abusive conduct, it is important to establish basic standards of judgment. The theories must first explain the origin of all types of abusive conduct and, second, they must be able to explain equally well the inverse: the development of nonbatterers.

Both men and women are domestic batterers. While most authorities agree that abusive men overwhelmingly outnumber abusive women in the heterosexual, spousal abuse category, the proportions of women to men perpetrators in child abuse and elder abuse cases are much more evenly balanced. Further, when causes of domestic violence are described, most people mention (or infer) only physical and sexual abuse. Psychological abuse, property destruction, neglect, and exploitation are each significant, integral components of the larger picture of domestic violence. There are no data to suggest that these other, important categories of abusive behavior are the exclusive domain of males. Females are just as capable of and just as likely to commit psychological abuse, child neglect, all categories of abuse of elders, exploitation of children, and property destruction as are males. Finally, of course, there is lesbian battering.

Thus, any theory that claims that only males are perpetrators of domestic violence is at the very least severely flawed. In fact, we think it is simply wrong.

Domestic violence remains best explained as caused by perpetrators, of either gender, who have serious psychological problems, as well as problems with power and control. It is *a person* with the proclivity to perform batterer behavior who becomes a batterer, and any person in America, male or female, lesbian or gay, can have learned how to be a batterer.

Social learning, sociopolitical, and gender-economic theories are adequate to explain the mechanisms by which some individuals acquire the controlling, manipulating, intimidating, and exploitative attitudes and behavior descriptive of batterers. But it is absurd to apply these theories only to males. An abusive person tries to control and manipulate the other people on whom he or she believes control will work. Logically, abusive mothers batter children for the same reasons that abusive husbands batter wives: as disturbed persons, they intend to control other beings. They do it because they can, not because of their gender. They "can" because you and I do not stop them. We in effect sanction and approve their behavior through our inactions. The stereotypical sex roles our culture ordinarily assigns to males and females are not adequate to explain the occurrence or the dynamics of lesbian and gay male domestic violence and other forms of domestic violence other than wife abuse.

It is also impossible to apply these same sociological, gender-based, anti-male theories to all people. Everyone grows up and develops in the same general culture. The theories, which purport to show how violent men develop, are simply unable to show how anyone else, man or woman, let alone a majority of both, ends up as nonviolent.

All theories that claim that society is the sole cause of violent behavior must be subjected to this test of *inverse application:* If the theory cannot explain how *non*violent men and women emerge from the same culture as violent women and men, then that theory is flawed. In fact it, too, is wrong. The characteristics of the batterer, not the batterer's gender, are the best predictors of whether or not a child will become a victim of child abuse or an adult will become a victim of partner abuse.

Finally, we believe that while neither male nor female victims share a personality profile, there is considerable evidence that male and female batterers have many characteristics in common, and that their differences (gender, specifically) are less important than their similarities in predicting their abusive proclivities.

Domestic violence is *not* a gender issue.

* * *

DOMESTIC VIOLENCE IS NOT CODEPENDENCY

"Codependency," that vague and overused label in pop psychology today, has been applied to everything from alcoholism, to rebellious teenagers, to workaholics. This trendy way of viewing the world and of understanding relationships may be effective when applied to such so-called "compulsive disorders." Codependency, however, is totally inappropriate, ineffective, and even dangerous when used in an attempt to understand or label domestic violence.

What is codependency anyway? Even Melody Beattie, best-selling codependent guru, has trouble with that question. Despite providing readers with a whopping 234-item list of codependent "characteristics," in *Codependent No More*, Beattie admits, "Codependency has a fuzzy definition because it is a gray, fuzzy condition" (1987, p. 31). She adds, "Codependency is part of treatment jargon, professional slang that's probably unintelligible to some people outside the profession and gibberish to some inside the trade" (1987, p. 27). The codependent, according to Beattie, "is one who has let another person's behavior affect him or her, and who is obsessed with controlling that person's behavior" (1987, p. 31). Unfortunately, this "fuzzy . . . gibberish" is at times applied to victims of domestic violence, and the consequences are often dire.

Separate Problems

There is nothing gray or fuzzy about domestic violence. Battering is brutally clear to most people. Also clear is that domestic violence is not a "co-" problem. Phyllis Frank, author of *Confront-*

ing The Batterer, writes in the Domestic Abuse Couple Counseling Policy Statement, "Battering . . . is a violent criminal act, not a marital or relationship problem" (1989, p. 1). Domestic violence occurs because one member of a couple is abusive and violent. It is neither the victim, nor the victim's relationship with the batterer, that causes or perpetuates the violence. The sole source and cause of the abuse in domestic violence is inside the batterer. Victims, while obviously adversely affected by batterers' behavior, are *not* codependent. Frank explains that, "The batterer and the victim have two different problems. The batterer's problem is violent behavior. The victim's problem is that he or she is coupled with a batterer. These [are] two distinct problems" (1989, p. 3).

Some alcohol and drug abuse programs may contribute to batterers' failure to accept sole responsibility for their violence. Describing this phenomenon in male heterosexual batterers, researchers Hamberger and Hastings state that though batterer programs "place total responsibility for the violence on the male perpetrator, his alcohol and drug program may be focusing on family issues such as his partner's codependence and how she needs to stop enabling his behavior . . . such incompatible messages may be confusing to the batterer who may, in turn, resolve the conflict by adopting a systems approach to understanding his violence, thus sabatoging his domestic violence intervention" (1990, p. 168).

Victim Survival Skills

Unlike the codependent "caretakers" of Beattie's books, victims of domestic violence develop sets of behaviors in their relationships that ensure *their own* survival. Lenore Walker, in her book, *The Battered Woman*, explains that these "unusual actions which may help them to survive in the battering relationship have been taken out of context by unenlightened medical or mental health workers" (1979, p. 21). The coping skills victims employ are designed to "protect them from further violence" (Walker, 1979, p. 229), not, as in codependency, to prop up, or "enable," their batterers.

One coping skill used by many victims of domestic violence is to stay with their abusive partner and try to prevent more violence, having learned that attempts to escape are most often met with more severe violence. In an article drafted for publication in a professional journal, Gail K. Golden and co-author Phyllis Frank point out that when applied to victims of domestic violence, the label codependent carries "a very strong implication that if a victim were healthy, he would not be coupled with a man who beats him. Codependency suggests that his staying is due to some early deficit . . . in himself. It even intimates that he finds or even seeks out a violent partner who he may continue to try to please, to change, to protect, and whom he may not leave" (1990, p. 2, cited with permission of the authors, who also gave permission to change the feminine pronouns to masculine, so as to make clear that victims are either men or women).

All of these assumptions and implications have absolutely no basis in fact, and are contradictory to the abundant research that has been done on victims of domestic violence. Victims are strong, healthy, sane people surviving in chronically dangerous environments. And, as Golden and Frank point out, "It is critical to remember that more victims of domestic violence are killed leaving their abusive mates than staying" (1990, p. 3). For many victims, staying means surviving; it does not mean codependency.

The behavior of victims of domestic violence can be understood only when examined in the context of the violent and life-threatening situations in which they live. Codependency literature fails to take these violent situations into account.

Target of the Disorder

Codependency notions grew out of work in the mental health profession with alcoholic and drug-abusing clients. These disorders, as well as many others in the codependency world, are inherently *self*-abusive, *self*-indulgent, and *self*-destructive. The "co-" person in these disorders is not the primary target of the disorder. Rather, the target of the disorder is the person with the disorder.

In domestic violence, the dynamics are exactly opposite, and the target of the disorder is *another* person. The violent behavior of the batterer is intended to harm and control the victim, not the batterer. For the codependency "jargon" to apply, victims of domestic violence would have to be addicted to, and the caretakers of, batterers

who are violent to *themselves*. The hospitals, shelters, and morgues
of this country are not being filled by men who are battering themselves, but by their victims. It is both ignorant and insulting to use
codependency when describing domestic violence. The label "codependent" implies that domestic violence is a "relationship problem," it illogically links victims to the psychology of their abusive
partners, and it fails to acknowledge the strength and skills that
victims possess to survive.

Inadequate Conceptual Model

At this time, the ideas surrounding codependency are poorly
thought out, inadequately researched, and so vague as to be mean-
ingless. We doubt that codependency as a concept serves any useful
purpose in diagnosing anyone's psychological condition. It certainly explains nothing about the dynamics of domestic violence.

* * *

SEPARATE PSYCHOLOGIES

Batterers and victims exhibit what we call "Separate Psychologies." This means that just before, during, and right after domestic
violence there is no close union between the mental functioning of
the two men. A glimpse into the head of each man would reveal a
vastly different mental scenario. Observers, and victims and batterers themselves, often falsely conclude that they are relying on
each other psychologically. This is not true.

Seeing their psychologies as separate is difficult for two reasons:
misunderstanding and misinterpreting provocation, and mislabeling
victims as self-defeating personalities.

Provocation

Though many actions are provocative, no one can "provoke"
anyone into action. Behavior is always a choice. Batterers looking
to abuse someone rely on either a deliberate or an ignorant misinter-
pretation of provocation in order to give themselves permission to
be violent. The eventual trigger for violence is almost always unre-

lated to the stressors acting on the batterer. Batterers decide to be violent.

Victims Are Not Self-Defeating Personalities

Victims do not seek out batterers. Once victims have left batterers and received treatment, they rarely enter into a relationship with another violent man (Walker, 1984, p. 15). Batterers may seek new partners to victimize, but victims (with rare exceptions) are not self-defeating.

Illustrating the separate psychologies is best accomplished by listing the thoughts and concerns common to each man separately just before, during, and right after violence.

Sample Victim Thoughts

I am afraid. Walk on eggs. What did I do? Escape. Get out of here. Stop this violence. Protect myself. Avoid violence. Run. Placate. No, not again. What happened this time? How can I stop this? What's wrong with me? I don't like this. I don't need this. Watch out.

Sample Batterer Thoughts

I am angry. That fucker. I'm going to get my way. Agree with me, damn it. He'll pay for this. I'm going to explode. Intimidate. Threaten. Why doesn't he just give in? Why doesn't he meet my needs? Here I go again. I guess I'll have to teach him a lesson. He better not try to get away. He asked for it. He deserves this.

Sample Treatment Objectives

The vastly different and unrelated psychologies of victim and batterer require vastly different and separate treatment objectives.

Victim

Empower the victim to leave the relationship and stay away from the batterer. Teach the victim that the violence is not his fault, that he did not and could not have provoked the batterer's conduct, and that he does not deserve any violence. Help the victim to develop safety guidelines and other strategies to take charge of his own well-being. Advocate legal action against the batterer. Help the victim to get grounded and stay focused on his task of getting out and staying out. Assist the victim to plan activities he must undertake and to handle the feelings that accompany those actions.

Batterer

Teach the batterer immediate alternate behaviors to battering. Teach the batterer that his behavior is a crime and that he could be arrested. Help the batterer learn how to name what he is doing as criminal violence. Help the batterer broaden his social support network so that he has someone other than the victim to turn to for support. Teach the batterer how to identify new behavior, reinforce it, and adopt it on his own. Teach the batterer that he and he alone is accountable and responsible for every act he takes. Teach the batterer that he cannot blame one other person, or society, for his actions. Teach the batterer that he is choosing violence, deciding to harm, and premeditatively inflicting abuse.

The task facing friends, relatives, therapists, community workers, neighbors, and anyone else hearing about the violence brought into a relationship by a battering partner is not to work at seeing the two individuals as having intertwined psychologies but rather to work at seeing the individuals as having entirely separate psychologies. They are, in fact, two individuals in a relationship together having entirely different experiences of the relationship.

*   *   *

END PIECE

New answers emerge here to the question of "Why does he stay?" Solidarity works both for and against the victim. The law really is clear about provocation. The victims' paradoxes complicate their already difficult lives. AIDS and alcohol are revealed as excuses for violence. Domestic violence is clearly not just a male problem. Victims, far from being codependent, evidence an entirely separate psychology from that of their abusive partners. Being gay and being abused has to be a double jeopardy answer for a question almost no one knows how to phrase properly, but it is,

"What is the biggest unprotected group of victims in America today?" Don't lose sight of some fundamentals:

1. Domestic violence, gay and straight, is first and foremost a crime, and batterers, not victims, cause all of it to happen.
2. Our society is unbelievably easy on batterers and unbelievably insensitive to victims.
3. Domestic violence has historical roots in patriarchy and social custom, but that fact does not let one single gay male batterer off the hook of accountability. It is the individual who must be held accountable for his decision to be violent.
4. It's everyone's attitude about domestic violence that needs a big fix.
5. No one ever provokes anyone to do anything.
6. More often than not, a victim feels he is damned if he does (get out) and damned if he doesn't (get out).
7. There is only one rule that operates correctly 100% of the time for victims of gay men's domestic violence: *Get out.*

Chapter X

How to Stop the Violence

MUTUAL FRIENDS

Once I left Stephen, and ended two years of abuse, I was faced with the task of trying to explain to friends and to my family what had really happened between us. The facade of the "happy couple" that Stephen and I worked hard to create over the years, I managed to destroy in a single day by leaving him. Thus, the friends we shared at the time found it difficult, if not impossible, to believe what I told them about the violence. I have since lost all of our mutual friends, except for a few. Most of the people we knew as a couple chose to believe Stephen's claim that he was a helpless man whom I had suddenly abandoned, leaving him without a job, without money, and worse yet, without even giving him the chance to explain himself. Few people believed what I had to say, and I tried to explain myself to them just once. After that, my policy was that if people believe me, great, and if not, it doesn't matter. I would let the chips fall where they may.

The weeks and months that passed proved to be, for me, an almost continuous encounter with the "blame the victim" attitude that so pervades reactions to domestic violence situations. Most of our friends held me accountable for destroying a "good" relationship. The following examples help illustrate not only how readily people blame victims of domestic violence for the violence and all things bad in the relationship, but also how difficult it was for people to see me, a man, as a victim of domestic violence.

First, there was Michael, a fairly close friend whom I ran into on the street about three weeks after I left Stephen. Having been under so much stress, and having distanced myself from everybody, I was delighted to see Michael. He, however, did not share my enthusiasm.

"I heard what you did to Stephen, Patrick. I heard it and I couldn't believe it!"

"Wait a second, Michael," I protested. "You don't understand what was. . . . "

He cut me off. "Like hell I don't. Stephen told me the whole story and I want to know one thing: Who the hell do you think you are?!" Leaving him like that! No job! No money! And, bringing the police to your apartment?! What the hell did you do that for?! Then he grabbed me by the shoulders and shouted again, "Who the hell do you think you are?!"

I was shocked and totally confused by this. I could not believe how the tables had turned. Stephen hit me! I'm the one who put up with the beatings for so long . . . and now Michael is mad at me for leaving?! It made no sense.

I shook my head and said, calmly, "Michael, you don't understand a thing," and walked off.

Then there was Keith, a good friend whom Stephen and I were both close to. Keith and I had dinner about two months after I left Stephen, and Keith quietly admitted that he was surprised by what I "had done to Stephen." In his characteristically gentle manner, Keith said, "Well, I know you were unhappy, honey, but really—a restraining order? I don't know. Actually, I'm not surprised. I know what a drama queen you can be, and **this** *is typically dramatic." When I explained that violence had been going on for over two years, he said, "Oh, come on Patrick. You're upset now, but surely it wasn't that bad. I just can't believe that Stephen would . . . do those things." I realized then that I was getting nowhere. Keith did not believe me and probably never would.*

Before I left Stephen, we both did volunteer work for an organization in San Francisco, where several people knew us as a couple. As mentioned earlier, after I left Stephen, I stopped doing volunteer work for several months. Upon returning, I encountered hostility from several people who had heard (from Stephen) about "how stubborn" I was being by not going back to him, by not seeing him, and even by refusing to talk to him. One woman, Kristi, was particularly vocal about her resentment of me.

"I don't know why you're being like this, Patrick. Why can't you just work it out with him? Stephen is such a nice guy, and he cares about you. You know he does. Can't you just work it out with him?"

My response was to ask her if she would encourage a battered woman to go back to her husband. When she said, "No, of course not," I asked, "Then, why are you encouraging me?" Kristi never brought up the subject again. In fact, she avoided me completely.

*There were other accusations and comments dropped into conversations over the next year or so, as I slowly began initiating contact with friends again. Remarks such as, ". . . and Stephen told me you even took the sheets, Patrick"; "I can't believe you were stupid enough to stay so long!" and, "Oh, **you're** the battered wife, huh?" were made again and again. I was blamed for leaving and ridiculed for staying.*

In fact, 15 months after I left Stephen, two friends were still encouraging me to go back to him. They just could not seem to fathom the idea that I was a victim and Stephen was a batterer. My friend Ken, for example, finally said, "Can't you just get together and talk with him, Patrick? He misses you; he really misses you. I know you guys fought a lot, but that's over now. He just wants to talk. God, aren't you civilized enough to sit down and talk?"

I thought immediately of Sarah's house and erupted in anger at Ken, "The time to talk is over! And, don't ever encourage me to meet with him, Ken. Ever!" About a week later I gave Ken an article that had been written about me as a victim of gay men's domestic violence in a San Francisco gay newspaper. Reading that seems to have helped him, as he no longer advocates Stephen and my "getting together to talk." Somehow, reading it in black and white was more convincing to Ken than hearing it directly from me.

As "Mutual Friends" clearly shows, mutual friends of a now-divorced couple often make quick judgments, are typically uninformed about facts, and can be painfully unsupportive. When a couple divorces, it is more common than not that friends take sides, choose one member of the couple to "believe," and stay with that person as a friend. It is virtually impossible for a friend to remain neutral about a split couple when the stories that are told are almost always contradictory. No one can believe two different versions of something at the same time. So friends make choices, and, as a victim sometimes learns all too fast, many friends choose to believe and remain in contact with the batterer.

There are several different, though related, reasons why people choose to believe a batterer's "version" of a couple's break-up. One reason is that batterers almost always trivialize or deny their violent behavior, making their story easier to believe. To a friend who does not know otherwise, it is easier to believe, "Patrick is exaggerating. I hit him once, but he hit me right back," than it is to believe "Stephen has been battering me for two years." The batterer's story is certainly easier and a lot less painful to believe.

Believing the victim also means that friends must admit that violence had been happening and they were unable to detect it. They would like to believe that if Stephen has been violent with Patrick, surely they would have noticed it. By admitting they were unable to detect it, they may feel foolish, blind, or even guilty ("How could I have not known? How could I not see it?"). Friends tend to both overestimate their ability to know things, and underestimate a couple's ability to hide traces of domestic violence.

And why are victims' stories harder to believe? Not only are they often gruesome and unpleasant, but they also reveal information about the batterer that friends do not want to believe. Believing the victim means facing the fact that someone they love, trust, and may have known for years is a violent and abusive man. Keith sums up this notion perfectly when he states, "I just can't believe that Stephen would . . . do those things." Keith does not believe Patrick because he does not want to believe that what he is hearing about Stephen is true.

This narrative also describes classic examples of "blame the victim." Where does "blame the victim" as a way of responding originate? How do people come to react this way? Three elements in our culture are primarily responsible. First is school. In school, when one was bad, one learned how to blame someone else or some circumstance for the bad behavior. ("Bobby, stop talking to John." "But John asked me a question.") Some children learn not to take responsibility for their own behavior in school. Thus, many people adopt, to some extent, a perpetrator's position and want to deny responsibility ("The devil made me do it"), making it easier to blame a victim than ourselves for what happens to him. Second is comedy. Jokes abound about how people humiliate others and make

victims the butt of their actions. Ridiculing a victim is a cornerstone
of comedy. Third is the family. Many people who grew up in a
home with brothers and sisters learned to blame their victims (siblings) and to not take responsibility for their own behavior.

While having its roots in childhood, blaming the victim serves an
important and unfortunate function in adulthood. Simply stated, it
allows us to take no action whatsoever to help the people we blame,
or to hold anyone else accountable for their predicament. Thus, the
rape victim "asked for it"; the molested 12-year old "seduced the
molester"; and battered women or men "caused" or "provoked"
the violence done to them. This psychological safety mechanism
allows us to remain inactive and to separate ourselves from "those
people" who are raped, molested, and battered.

This narrative is also a small but important demonstration of the
lack of information about domestic violence in the lesbian and gay
community. People more knowledgeable about domestic violence
would recognize Patrick as a victim of domestic violence when he
describes what he has experienced. Ignorance about the phenomenon makes the denial and trivialization of it easy, and uninformed
people freely dismiss the whole issue as "not a problem." Clearly,
we need to educate ourselves and our community, so that when
victims of gay men's domestic violence come forward, we will
show them the support, compassion, and understanding they need
and deserve.

THE PREVENTION OF DOMESTIC VIOLENCE

Public response to gay men's domestic violence today is obviously in its most primitive form. Little research exists about the
problem. Treatment programs for victims and batterers are virtually
nonexistent. Public concern is apparently just now emerging, as
people begin to learn about this widespread gay men's problem.
The gay male community, comprised of at least 12 million American males, a population roughly equal to that of the entire continent
of Australia, must now contend with its own domestic violence.
Police do not yet understand, as so many in law enforcement are
homophobic and ignorant about domestic violence. Victims are terrified, injured, isolated and without a place to go or support from
the community. Ordinarily well-meaning friends and relatives criti-

cize victims for staying with abusive partners and criticize them when they leave. The situation could not be more chaotic.

We believe that things have to change. In this chapter we outline a Prevention Model for the eradication of gay men's domestic violence. The model addresses the entire national problem of domestic violence, gay and straight, with special provisions for minority groups, such as gay men. There are two components in the model: Legislative Response, and Public and Private Action. Legislative Response requires government to conduct hearings, sponsor and enact laws, and oversee their enforcement. Legislative Response also requires appropriation of significant funding and its allocation to create agencies, various programs, and services on domestic violence. Public and Private Action itemizes six action programs: Education, Publicity, Training, Outreach, Services, and Research.

This two-part Prevention Model needs to be applied throughout every level of government — federal, state, county, and municipal — and it needs to be visible and operational all the way from the neighborhoods where gay men's domestic violence occurs to the White House, where a concerned president should put force and dignity behind efforts to provide services to victims and to condemn and eradicate the crimes of domestic violence in America.

THE PREVENTION MODEL
PART ONE: LEGISLATIVE RESPONSE

Even though heterosexual domestic violence has been in the public eye for about 15 years, very little comprehensive government activity has occurred to stop it. A coordinated, interlinked 50-state program of reform and action is needed now. The federal government should lead the way, and our elected officials, including the President of the United States, must provide the leadership.

The Legislative Agenda

Domestic violence needs to be further criminalized. New federal and state legislation on many aspects of domestic violence should be drafted and enacted. Existing legislation needs revision and adaptation to current needs. The general purposes of the new legislation and revised laws are to:

1. Broaden the criminalization of domestic violence, specify its enforcement and increase the severity of punishment for offenders. Current arrest and prosecution criteria, using California and New York as standards, are to be maintained or increased for the next 20 years.
2. Broaden the language in all domestic violence laws to ensure that all victims are equally protected regardless of gender or sexual orientation. (See Appendix for the San Francisco Police Department Policy excerpts.)
3. Provide that all victims of domestic violence are eligible for compensation for injuries, for damage suffered, and for costs of shelter, treatment, and recovery, and provide that all victims have the right to sue the assailant for civil damages.
4. Set up a domestic violence agency network, coordinated by state and federal offices, with adequate funding to carry out locally the mandates of the new legislation.
5. Provide for simultaneous, though entirely separate, treatment services, including psychotherapy, for victims and batterers.

Necessary Legislation: Criminal Statutes

Many states have taken significant, correct steps to further criminalize domestic violence. These states have recognized that domestic violence is a crime and perpetrators need to be prosecuted. We believe that all states need to take action, including but not limited to all of the following suggestions.

1. Pass laws that require each law enforcement agency to have a pro-arrest policy in domestic violence cases, and specify that all victims will have the right to have their cases heard in court within 15 days.
2. Pass laws that require the prosecution of all misdemeanor domestic violence charges, and that specifically prohibit repeat offenders from diversion programs.
3. Enact measures which clarify and tighten the statutory scheme for protecting victims of domestic violence and expand and strengthen available preliminary relief and enforcement mechanisms.
4. Pass laws to provide that victims of domestic violence,

though related to the offender through some form of relationship, are eligible for compensation to the same extent as unrelated crime victims, and include specific language to clarify and specify the compensation rights for same-sex domestic partners and cohabitants, irrespective of existing domestic partner law.

5. Pass laws clarifying that the arrest of a perpetrator for violation of a restraining order does not preclude the victim from filing a criminal accusatory instrument instead of a restraining order violation instrument.

6. Establish policies that provide reimbursement from the offender or the State for the cost of all victim rehabilitation, medical treatment, psychological treatment, and other expenses of recovery from victimization, including job retraining.

7. Establish policies which provide reimbursement to the providers for the cost of safe-house or shelter stays for victims of domestic violence.

8. Pass laws that permit court proceedings to be initiated in whatever county the victim has sought refuge from violence.

9. Enact measures that provide that upon conviction for any offense the court may enter a restraining order to be in effect for up to five years beyond the date of the maximum prison term that may be imposed on the perpetrator.

10. Pass laws requiring all police or law enforcement officers investigating domestic violence to give the victim notice of all appropriate community services and all available legal rights and remedies, including the nearest community antiviolence agencies.

11. Pass laws to mandate perpetrator treatment with specific behavioral outcome requirements and to further mandate increasingly severe penalties and prison terms for recurring convictions of any domestic violence offense.

12. Pass laws to empower police to issue five-day temporary restraining orders in the field without judicial approval.

13. Enact a more standardized definition of domestic violence nationwide. (This nation's officials and social service providers must cease referring to domestic violence as "spousal

abuse." That terminology is heterosexist and unacceptable to all other adult victims of domestic violence who are not spouses. Further, the term "spousal abuse" implies an equality of blame for the violence between victim and offender, a condition that never exists.)

14. Require, for all law enforcement officers, a minimum of 24 hours per year of domestic violence training, including at least four hours in gay domestic violence.

15. Pass laws to tighten and strengthen enforcement of restraining order violations, requiring district attorney-initiated criminal proceedings against the offender to begin after one violation. Specifically, every misdemeanor violation of restraining order violations must be prosecuted.

16. Pass laws to prohibit the mental incompetence (insanity) defense for perpetrators, except in the rarest of instances where there is overwhelming just cause to suspect the presence of real mental incompetence; and to prohibit plea bargains in all domestic violence cases.

17. Pass laws specifying mandatory sentencing for specific domestic violence criminal convictions in which bodily injury has resulted.

18. Prohibit violence on television as a matter of public policy. (Stratton, 1988; Digirolamo, 1986, pp. 3-17)

Necessary Legislation: Civil Statutes

Civil law permits a plaintiff to sue a defendant for monetary damages resulting from the conduct of the defendant. Gay male victims of domestic violence should, when appropriate, bring suit against their abusive partners for damages done to their person, psyche, and property.

1. Civil law in most states needs to be revised to specify damages recovery rights for victims of domestic violence from the defendant to include as a minimum: intentional infliction of emotional distress, medical and mental health expenses, loss of earnings, loss of earning capacity, pain and suffering, false imprisonment, property damage, costs of repairing or replacing property, and loss of use of property.

2. Civil law needs to be revised to comply, where necessary, in spirit and language with newly written or revised criminal codes regarding domestic violence.

Necessary Funding: State Level

1. Legislative action, or executive order is needed in every state to create an agency, similar, at a minimum, in mission and power to New York State's Office for the Prevention of Domestic Violence.
2. Each county in each state and each city of 250,000 people or more should be required to create its own agency for the Prevention of Domestic Violence.
3. Each of the state, county, and municipal domestic violence agencies must have a gay and lesbian component with a specifically worded outreach and services mission to the gay and lesbian communities.
4. Funds for the operation of these agencies must be appropriated and allocated by the various legislative bodies or executive orders. When legislation is insufficient, grants from other governmental entities must be made available for the operation of these new domestic violence prevention agencies. Guaranteed funding for battered men's and women's shelters in each county and in each city of 250,000 must be provided.
5. Appropriations for state and local gay men and women's domestic violence agency operations must specify a percentage dollar allocation to be applied to: staff; educational and outreach materials and programs; publicity and advertising programs; seminar and training budgets; therapy reimbursement or staff therapist salaries; safe house (shelter) monies; and emergency discretionary funds to use as grants to victims, when necessary, to pay for life necessities, medical bills, legal services, and job retraining.
6. Funding must be provided to District Attorneys' offices for the sole purpose of prosecuting all domestic violence offenses, including, specifically, violations to restraining order provisions.

Federal Legislative Response

It's time that the federal government take responsibility for a concerted national response to domestic violence in America.

Grass roots organizations, such as the National Coalition for the Prevention of Domestic Violence, which monitors the 1,200 programs offering some form of assistance to female heterosexual domestic violence victims, and the National Woman Abuse Prevention Project, have for too long played the major role in stimulating our elected officials to pay attention to the problems of heterosexual battering. It is only through the work and research of these volunteer organizations that we now know that battering is the major source of injury and death to women in the United States (Randall, 1990, p. 939).

While the federal government has responded with the federal Victims of Crime Act and made some funds available through its appropriations and also through specific budget line items from the Department of Health and Human Services, it is clear that the federal response is woefully inadequate. The United States Congress must move beyond a mere Select Committee on the Family, Youth and Children and its pitiful National Institute of Justice grants, to a major commitment to the prevention of domestic violence.

A New Federal Agency

The job of preventing domestic violence and responding to its terrible aftermath is too big and too important for the states to handle in 50 different (or indifferent) ways. Because of the sheer scope and enormous consequence of the problem of domestic violence in America, we believe that the federal government must not ignore its duty any longer. Ten percent of the entire population of the United States (equivalent, for instance, to all the people who live in California) is affected by domestic violence. Because gay men and lesbians are proportionately involved in domestic violence and because gay people of color are proportionately involved as well, the federal government has compelling constitutional grounds for its necessary involvement. Therefore, a federal agency, under the Secretary of Health and Human Services, must be created to initiate, coordinate, and oversee federal efforts to prevent domestic violence and provide services for victims and perpetrators.

This new United States Office for the Prevention of Domestic Violence will have numerous duties and responsibilities to all Americans.

1. Federal legislation and funding. The new United States Office for the Prevention of Domestic Violence will do research for, initiate, oversee, draft, testify at hearings for, and monitor the national legislative agenda on domestic violence. It will also oversee, manage, and administer the distribution and granting of federal funds, including those for research, exemplary programs, and supplemental assistance to those cities or regions where local funding is inadequate.
2. State coordination. The United States Office for the Prevention of Domestic Violence would oversee federal funds for, and coordinate and monitor, federally funded state domestic violence programs and services.
3. Education, Training, and Publicity. The new United States Office for the Prevention of Domestic Violence would have national responsibility for developing curricula and implementing educational programs for public schools, grades K-12, training programs in government agencies, and a 10-year national publicity campaign to teach the general public (and government officials, including judges) about domestic violence.
4. Leadership. The primary function of the new United States Office for the Prevention of Domestic Violence would unquestionably be to focus the attention of the entire country on the problem of domestic violence. Of special importance will be the need for this agency to make sure that the needs and rights of all people, gay and straight, are met through federal programs to prevent domestic violence and respond to its consequences.
5. Clearinghouse. The new United States Office for the Prevention of Domestic Violence will provide the academic, mental health and medical communities, all government agencies in all of the states (including law enforcement), the media, grass

roots advocacy organizations, private organizations, and any interested group or person with state-of-the-art information, statistics, methods, and research findings to facilitate any and all efforts made by anyone to combat and eradicate the problem of domestic violence in America.

Legislative and Commission Hearings

Hearings should be held on a variety of topics in every state and at the federal level. Topics for the hearings include, at a minimum:

1. Incidence and severity of domestic violence among minorities, especially among gay men and women.
2. Cost to society in lost work, medical care, child neglect, police time, and other direct financial consequences to society.
3. Services, treatment, education, training, publicity, and research needs.
4. The best types of public response to alleviate the aftermath effects on victims and their loved ones.
5. The best national approach to eradicate domestic violence in all of its forms against all people and especially minority groups such as gays and lesbians.
6. Criminal code revisions to strengthen criminalization of domestic violence, provide punishment guidelines, and provide funding for prosecution.
7. Methods to mandate, enforce, oversee, and promulgate the results of sophisticated reporting mechanisms for occurrence and extent of domestic violence in America.

THE PREVENTION MODEL
PART TWO: PRIVATE AND PUBLIC ACTION

Education and Training: Combating Incompetence, Ignorance and Homophobia

Domestic violence is a problem in our society that is perpetuated, in part, because not enough people know enough about the phenomenon to stop it. As part of the Prevention Model, we believe that an educational campaign about gay domestic violence, with the right target audiences, will help to alter the status quo. The target audiences include all of the following:

1. Social services providers (including social workers, MFCC's, psychiatrists, and psychologists);
2. Hospital and health care providers;
3. Police and law enforcement workers;
4. The entire gay community.

Armed with an understanding of gay issues and information about gay domestic violence, these target audiences can help to reduce, eliminate, and prevent further domestic violence in gay relationships.

Health Care Professionals

The first two groups, comprised of social service and hospital and health care personnel, include any and all medical and mental health care professionals and para-professionals who might come in contact with victims of gay domestic violence. Therapists, counselors, social workers, hot-line staffs, shelter workers, doctors, nurses, and emergency room personnel are all part of this group. These people may be the first and only contact a victim has with health care professionals, making their education crucial.

A recent series of studies, published in the *Journal of the American Medical Association,* reveal that health care professionals fail abysmally to meet the needs of domestic violence victims. "Despite the widespread presence of domestic violence, and its major role in women's health, the medical community has yet to identify victims of domestic violence and extend treatment beyond the physical manifestations" of the violence (Randall, 1990, p. 939). Even though many hospitals have domestic violence protocols, such as providing victims with information, referrals, and addressing their safety needs, these protocols are rarely if ever carried out. As a result, "victims of domestic abuse are discharged without any arrangements made for their safety, to return to the same abusive (partner) that caused their injuries" (Randall, 1990, p. 939).

Medical personnel need to know about, understand, and be able to recognize signs of domestic violence. Intervention beyond the treatment of injuries is absolutely essential, and must begin immediately.

Stereotypes about male and female roles need to be put to rest, and myths about domestic violence, gay and straight, need to be replaced with facts. Women do batter. Men are victims. All victims of domestic violence need to be able to turn to health care professionals in all capacities and be treated with understanding and compassion.

We insist that accurate information about gay domestic violence should be included in the training programs of all health care personnel. Everyone from physicians to suicide hot-line workers needs to be made more sensitive to the phenomenon. Further, domestic violence should be given a more prominent place in the general curricula of colleges and universities today. Everyone, it seems, knows something about alcoholism as it adversely affects so many millions of Americans, and about AA. Yet, although a heterosexual woman is battered every 15 seconds, a gay man is abused by his lover every 90 seconds, and four heterosexual women are killed by their batterers *every day*, nobody seems to know very much about domestic violence. Thus, widespread education about domestic violence, straight and gay, is necessary before any progress will be made in stopping it. We believe that the colleges, universities, and training institutions for health care professionals are required places to start.

Police and Law Enforcement Workers

This category includes, but is not limited to: prosecutors, district attorneys, public defenders, probation officers, all jail and prison personnel, sheriffs, judges, police training personnel, attorneys general, highway patrol officers, state police, military police, and the FBI. While the police, obviously, need the education and training discussed above, their role in domestic violence intervention calls for a separate discussion here. Difficult and homophobic as they may be to deal with, the police can play a central role in eradicating domestic violence by arresting batterers and protecting victims. Thus, for any appropriate police intervention to occur, the police must be aware of and be able to identify gay domestic violence when they see it.

Years of training in the San Francisco Police Department are beginning to pay off, as police now increasingly identify and report cases of gay domestic violence. The San Francisco Police Department General Order of October 26, 1986 (see Appendix), sets forth policies and procedures for domestic violence. Of particular and noteworthy importance is language in the definitions portion of the General Provisions, which specifically include "former spouses, *gay relationships* (our emphasis), or boyfriend-girlfriends" in the "wide range of relationships" to which the definition of domestic violence applies. Further, under Policy, this general order requires that "Officers shall convey the attitude that violence in the home is criminal behavior and will not be tolerated." If all cases of police-reported "mutual combat" were accurately labeled "domestic violence," there would be both a better understanding of the magnitude of the problem and a channel through which to do outreach to victims and batterers.

Police training, then, should emphasize the criminal aspects of domestic violence, as well as address myths that exist about domestic violence, straight, and gay. The police also need to develop increased sensitivity toward gay male victims of domestic violence who may have experienced considerable abuse before police arrive.

The Gay Community

One would think that the gay community would be easy to educate about gay domestic violence. However, gay people know as little about domestic violence as anyone else in our society. In fact, based on the false assumption that domestic violence is a "heterosexual problem" gays may know even less about domestic violence than the average American.

The time for the gay community to fully address domestic violence is now. We would like to see a series of articles about domestic violence written in every single gay newspaper across the country. We would like to see in-depth analyses of what needs to be done in our community to help victims and batterers. We would like to see gay leaders, gay politicians, and all gay people everywhere speak out about and condemn gay domestic violence. The problem needs to be brought out of the closet of the gay community.

Homophobia

In addition to information about domestic violence, all of the above-mentioned groups need accurate information about homosexuality and about the lifestyles of gay men today. Despite years of progress and "a generation of pride" in gay America, much of society still clings to myths and stereotypes about homosexuals. An anti-homophobia campaign and an educational campaign need to be implemented on a national level, aimed in part at blitzing the first three target audiences (Kirk and Madsen, 1989).

Research: Filling Up the Knowledge Void

The fact that the most definitive survey ever done on gay men's lifestyles was conducted by a newspaper indicates a sorry state of affairs. But the truth hurts, and the *San Francisco Examiner*'s nationwide survey of gay men in the Spring of 1989 remains the most authoritative large-scale study of gay men to date (Yollin, 1989). While we thank the *Examiner* for its rather well-researched series, we also take the opportunity to observe how much gay America is in need of sophisticated research. The need is urgent and compelling to shed light on the dynamics of and solutions for gay domestic violence. The proper places for the necessary research activity are in the graduate schools of our universities and the research industry of the private sector. Gay men's domestic violence ought to be the subject of research at the highest level, from master's theses, to doctoral dissertations, to significant, large-scale studies conducted by the most sophisticated private research firms. To stimulate interest and indicate direction, we offer a sampler of ideas for research to help advance the body of knowledge about gay men's domestic violence from the speculative and anecdotal to validated facts.

Survey Research

Survey research needs to be conducted on the entire spectrum of gay men's domestic violence issues. A nationwide sampling of gay men should be surveyed to determine definitively the scope and depth of the incidence of gay men's domestic violence. We need to know if physical abuse is more prevalent than psychological and if severity increases, as suspected, over time. How does learned helplessness overtake a male victim as time passes? Answers to these questions are needed to convince legislative bodies to allocate funds for the eradication of domestic violence. We *know* the problem is severe, but we need data and facts to show in order to obtain resources to combat the problem.

The same kinds of questions can be surveyed within smaller segments of the gay community. Proper sampling methods can be applied to tap the gay populations in New Orleans, for instance, to determine prevalence and severity statistics there. The results can then be compared to those of similar studies conducted in, say, Minneapolis and to national surveys to pin down closer approximates of true incidence and severity.

Attitudes toward domestic violence in the gay community also must be measured using survey techniques. How important do gay men think this problem is and what do they think needs to be done about it? The results of educational and publicity programs on gay men's attitudes toward and knowledge issues in domestic violence can be measured over time to see if efforts to educate the gay community are paying off.

Case Studies

Individual cases of domestic violence need to be studied in depth. The only ways to discover the psychology and the mechanisms of gay men's domestic violence is to study victims and batterers as individuals, in depth. Successfully rehabilitated victims need the most careful study, since it is in understanding their recovery that treatment can be specified for others. It is especially important to conduct individual case studies to continue to affirm the need for psychologists and social workers to *unlink* the psychology of the victim and perpetrator, rather than to continue to think of them as interlinked in a "psychology of family violence." Finally, through the combined efforts of thousands of case studies, we will zero in, in yet another way, on prevalence, severity, reinforcers, and other elements in the theories outlined in Chapters II, III and IV.

Research on Treatment and Outcome

Therapists and agencies, which sponsor treatment to victims and batterers of gay men's domestic violence, should participate in well-planned research studies to determine the efficacy of their treatment. For instance, can treatment outcome objectives be reached in six weeks or does it take six months?

Different types of groups can be run with victims to determine which group treatment works better. Will support therapy work to achieve outcome objectives just as well as a gestalt therapy model, for instance? And, of individual therapy approaches, which seem to result in fastest recovery from Post-Traumatic Stress Disorder? Are groups better than individual treatment for batterers? What can be done to lower the dropout rate in treatment groups for batterers? Do men who reside in safe houses with lay helpers make a faster recovery than those who do not? There are countless research questions to be asked and answered about treatment modalities for the recovery of victims of gay men's domestic violence.

Services

The domestic violence service organizations called for in this prevention model were described in detail in Chapter VIII. To summarize, organizations offering services to gay male victims should provide the following:

1. People to talk to
2. Information about domestic violence
3. Referrals: therapists, lawyers, health care providers
4. Direct Assistance: crisis intervention, help with legal system
5. Temporary safety for victims
6. Accessibility: 24-hour service
7. Long term support
8. Individual and group counseling and support.

Without question, services for victims and batterers must be kept completely separate. Furthermore, victim safety, both real and "perceived" must be of predominant importance to every organization working with victims or batterers.

Similar to other aspects of this model, the need for organized and comprehensive services is urgent. Thousands of victims and batterers all over the country would seek help at gay anti-violence projects, on crisis hot lines, and with individual and group therapists if they existed.

Service organizations for gay domestic violence must also be adaptable. As more is learned about gay domestic violence over the next decade, service organizations need to adapt to current knowledge and treatment. The results of research need to be incorporated into the policies and practices of those working with victims and batterers.

Outreach: Finding Victims and Batterers

The majority of gay male victims and batterers do not know if help is available to them. The topic has had no publicity, and virtually no outreach has been done. We believe that a widespread and creative outreach program will not only alert victims and batterers to available resources but will also serve as an educational and publicity tool about gay men's domestic violence within the gay community.

First, ads need to appear in all gay newspapers specifically naming "Gay Domestic Violence" and providing the names and telephone numbers of appropriate service agencies and therapists. These ads will serve as outreach to the thousands of gay male victims who scour bookstores and newspapers searching for some information about or acknowledgement of their problem.

Second, telephone books and resource books need to list the heading "Gay Domestic Violence," with appropriate resources following. It should be made easy for batterers and victims to locate agencies to help them. At present, however, it is impossible. In order to contact help, even through gay phone directories, victims need already to know the names of specific organizations for which they are looking. Similar to "AIDS Resources," and "Substance Abuse Resources," domestic violence needs its own listing. The few services that *are* available should not be hard to locate, but they are. For example, *Gaybook*, a San Francisco lesbian and gay resource/telephone book, has twenty listings under the heading "Parents and Parenting'' (*Gaybook* 9, Winter 1990). But there is no listing or heading for gay domestic violence. It is easier to find out how you and your lover can adopt a child than it is to find out where to go when that same lover beats you senseless. The available resources need to be easily located together under one appropriately titled section.

Third, every street fair, parade, festival, health conference, anti-violence conference, and other community event, should have booths set up providing information about gay domestic violence. The huge cross section of the gay community attending these events provides an ideal target audience for an outreach program. For example, small cards with lists of physically and psychologically abusive acts, a definition of domestic violence, and local phone numbers to call for information or help could be handed out to hundreds of thousands of lesbians and gay men on Gay Day Parades. The right people are already gathering together for parades all over America. All we need to do is make information about domestic violence available to them.

Fourth, flyers need to be posted telling people about lesbian and gay domestic violence and where they can get help. Gay neighborhoods, community centers, gyms, churches, political organizations, mental health organizations, laundromats, public bulletin boards, and bookstores should all have domestic violence flyers posted. They should be as common as flyers advertising T-dances at local bars and gay candidates in local elections. Flyers are cheap, effective, can be utilized in a thousand different locations, and they are a safe and anonymous way for victims or batterers to learn about the phenomenon of domestic violence. Further, their power should not be underestimated. The words "GAY DOMESTIC VIOLENCE" on a small sheet of paper stapled to a telephone pole can help save a person's life.

Newspaper ads, phone book and resource book listings, booths at parades and conferences, and flyers are four simple ways to do outreach to millions of lesbians and gay men. This is, of course, by no means a comprehensive list of outreach strategies. Rather, it is a start. Variety and creativity are necessary. We realize that gay communities differ all over America, and the best ways to reach the gay men in your community are probably best known to you. We do know, however, that victims and batterers are in your communities, and most do not know where to turn. Outreach programs can help to get help where it is needed.

Publicity: Galvanizing the Gay Community

A little bit of publicity would help. A lot of publicity would help even more. We need to get the word out on domestic violence and fast. The word needs to be spread in newspapers, on billboards, in 60-second TV spots, in books, articles, and videotapes. In short, the methods used to sell beer and underwear need to be employed for domestic violence to get the attention of the gay community, the straight community, and those who hold the purse strings and make the laws. The time for silence and timidity is over. Now is the time to put up some flashing neon signs for everyone to see about the menace of gay men's domestic violence.

Publicity about gay men's domestic violence will wake up gay and straight America to the third most severe health problem facing gay men today. We can teach people in a 30-second TV spot that the number of gay men in America is the same number of people who live in the entire Northwest quarter of America (equal to the combined populations of Washington, Oregon, Idaho, Montana, Wyoming, North and South Dakota and Nebraska). And of those gay men, a number equal to the entire population of the city of Seattle are abused each year, battered by a number of gay men equal to the entire population of Wyoming.

The right publicity campaign can, in a few seconds, teach people that assault (the threat of violence) is a crime inside the home as well as outside it. Or, that victims do not provoke violence. Or, that perpetrators choose to be violent.

A sign on the back of 10,000 buses in cities all over America could ask: "Does the hand that holds you in public strike you in private?" At the bottom of this sign could be the inscription, "This message was brought to you by your local gay men's domestic violence project."

Every single gay newspaper in America should donate a little space in every edition to advertise the message that domestic violence is unacceptable in the gay community, and should provide a telephone number for victims to call.

Space on billboards can be purchased to advertise the message: "Are You a Victim of Domestic Violence? Does Your Lover Hit You? Are You Harassed and Afraid? Call 1-800-VICTIMS." Gay porn promoters could substitute, on occasion, their usual ads with a serious message condemning domestic violence.

But television, most of all television! How about a gay candidate, when running for office, putting out a pro-family, domestic tranquility, anti-violence ad on TV instead of his face?

Publicity, we need publicity about this problem. What Mothers Against Drunk Driving did 10 years ago, we can do about gay men's domestic violence in the 1990s. They got mad and they got publicity. They got little news clips at night on the evening news. They appeared at courtrooms and talked to reporters. They made news. We can make news about gay men's domestic violence. And we need to do it today.

A FINAL WORD

Patrick:

It has been three years since I ran down the fire escape of my old apartment building and left behind a life of abuse and violence. Three years, but it is still not over. Stephen is still around and still harassing me. I continue to file police incident reports. I continue to put pressure on the District Attorney's office to issue a warrant for his arrest. They tell me I complain too much, and that my case "is not worth the taxpayer's money." They say that since Stephen has not harassed me since the last (eleventh) incident, I should "just let sleeping dogs lie." I do not let them deter me. I deserve protection under the law. I will get that warrant. Meanwhile, I continue to look over my shoulder.

There is little in my life now that resembles my life on September 7, 1987. I am back at school and will soon be working on a PhD. I have new friends, a new job, and more supportive people in my life than ever before. I have a great apartment and roommate. I work out, travel, do political work, and date cute men every now and then. The healing, too, continues. I have nightmares about violence only every so often now. I do not startle nearly as often or as dramatically as I used to. I am much less apprehensive when I am out and about in San Francisco. Everything is back to normal now, almost. But I am not safe yet. I still must take precautions to protect myself from more violence from Stephen. I do not want to become one of those people we all read about in the newspaper who is killed by an angry ex-lover.

Gay men's domestic violence is hard to face. It is a brutal and ugly problem. It is a painful reminder that some gay men abuse, injure, and kill the men they love. As a community, we often do not want to believe that this happens. But it does. Since you began reading these final comments, 10 women in this country were beaten by their husbands, and by the time you finish, a gay man will have been beaten by his lover. How many more bruises, screams in the night, or trips to the hospital are we willing to tolerate before we take gay men's domestic violence seriously?

To all gay men who batter their lovers, I say, "Get treatment for your disorder." You, too, deserve lives free of abuse and violence. When you stop battering, gay men's domestic violence will cease to exist.

To all of the men who have been victims, I say, "Speak out!" Tell your stories. Let our community know what you have experienced. Your needs are, in part, what will shape the movement to stop gay men's domestic violence. Your voices will educate all of us and provide the outrage necessary to stop the violence.

* * *

David:

By now, you're undoubtedly clear about how we feel about gay men's domestic violence. It's damned stupid, unacceptable behavior that should not be tolerated by America's gay community. One more time though, we gay men have to do something about it, just like we are attempting to do for AIDS, because the dominant culture, so pathologically obsessed with its hatred and fear of us, won't. We should get started today and give ourselves 10 years to eradicate this disgusting and embarrassing phenomenon from our community.

Domestic violence in the gay community will stop only when batterers own up to their responsibility (with us holding them accountable), obtain treatment and stop their battering. By their intentionally abusive conduct, batterers show evidence of a progressive, curable mental disorder, and most of them are also criminals. Victims are injured, isolated and in serious need of help. But, the rest of us are also the problem – victims and potential victims included – because we all tolerate batterers, their unconscionable behavior and their wimpy excuses.

And so we challenge you with the publication of this book. Educate yourselves, gay America. Intervene in the lives of your friends who are abusive or victims of abuse. Push the politicians, the police, and the publicists. Get the word out. Get the programs going. Get mad. The health of our brothers is at stake. And, if you don't get moving fast, you just won't sleep well tonight when you go home after dinner at your favorite restaurant, where you noticed that the handsome waiter who took your order had bruises on his neck. Because now you know how he got them.

References

American Psychiatric Association: Diagnostic and Statistical Manual of Mental Disorders, Third Edition, Revised. Washington, D.C., American Psychiatric Association, 1987.

Bartolomeo, N. Domestic violence: A serious problem lacking in resources. *The Washington Blade*, July 27, 1990, p. 7.

Battered Lovers. *The Advocate*, March 4, 1986, pp. 42-45; 46.

Beattie, M. *Codependent no more*. New York: Harper & Row, 1987.

Book of approved jury instructions (7th ed.). St. Paul: West Publishing, 1986.

Browne, A. *When battered women kill*. New York: The Free Press, 1987.

California jury instructions, criminal (5th ed.). St. Paul: West Publishing, 1988.

Dent, D. Z. & Arias, I. Effects of alcohol, gender, and role of spouses on attributions and evaluations of marital violence scenarios. *Violence and Victims*, 1990, *5,* 185-193.

Digirolomo, K. First report to the Governor and legislature. Albany: New York State Governor's Commission on Domestic Violence, September 1986.

Donat, H. Domestic violence strikes gay relationships. San Francisco: *Sentinel*, August 2, 1990, p. 5.

Dutton, D. G. Profiling wife assaulters: Preliminary evidence for a trimodal analysis. *Violence and victims,* 1988, *3,* pp. 5-29.

Farley, N. *Same-sex domestic violence*. Paper presented at the 12th National Lesbian and Gay Health Conference, Washington, D.C., July 1990.

Frank, P. B. Domestic abuse couple counseling policy statement. New City, New York: Volunteer Counseling Service of Rockland County, Inc., 1989.

Frank, P. B., & Engelken, C. *The case against couple counseling when dealing with domestic abuse*. Paper presented at the 12th National Lesbian and Gay Health Conference, Washington, D.C., July 1990.

Frank, P. B., & Houghton, B. D. *Confronting the batterer: A guide to creating the spouse abuse educational workshop.* New City, New York: Volunteer Counseling Service of Rockland County, Inc., 1987.

Gathright, A. The Cycles of Abuse. *San Jose Mercury News,* March 13, 1990, p. 1D.

Gaybook 9. San Francisco: Rainbow Ventures, Inc., Winter 1990.

Gelles, R. J., & Straus, M. A. *Intimate violence.* New York: Simon & Schuster, 1988.

Golden, G. K., & Frank, P. B. Blaming by naming: Battered women and the epidemic of co-dependence. Unpublished manuscript submitted for publication, August 1990.

Gondolf, E. W. *Men who batter: An integrated approach for stopping wife abuse.* Holmes Beach, FL: Learning Publications, 1985.

Gondolf, E. W. *Research on men who batter: An overview, bibliography and resource guide.* Bradenton, FL: Human Services Institute, 1988.

Hamberger, L. K. & Hastings, J. E. Characteristics of male spouse abusers consistent with personality disorders. *Hospital and Community Psychiatry,* 1988, *39,* pp. 763-770.

Hamberger, L. K. & Hastings, J. E. Recidivism following spouse abuse abatement counseling: Treatment program implications. *Violence and Victims,* 1990, *5,* pp. 157-170.

Kingston, T. Breaking the silence: Gay domestic violence. San Francisco: *Coming Up!,* February 1989, pp. 10-11.

Kingston, T. The truth behind mutual combat. San Francisco: *Coming Up!,* December 1987, pp. 12-13.

Kirk, M., & Madsen, H. *After the ball: How America will conquer its fear and hatred of gays in the 90's.* New York: Doubleday, 1989.

Lobel, K. (Ed.) *Naming the violence: Speaking out about lesbian battering.* Seattle: Seal Press, 1986.

Martin, D. *Battered wives.* New York: Simon & Schuster, 1976.

Martin, S. & McNeill, M. Law enforcement intervention. *Domestic violence: A training curriculum for law enforcement* (Vol. 1). San Francisco: Family Violence Project, 1988, p. II-6.

Moore, E., & Bundy, A. *Battery between gay men: An exploratory study of domestic violence in the San Francisco gay men's com-*

munity. Unpublished master's research project, San Francisco State University, 1983.

NiCarthy, G. *The ones who got away: Women who left abusive partners*. Seattle: Seal Press, 1987.

Randall, T. Domestic violence begets other problems of which physicians must be aware. *Journal of the American Medical Association*, 1990, *264,* 940; 943-944.

Randall, T. Domestic violence intervention calls for more than treating injuries. *Journal of the American Medical Association*, 1990, *264,* 940; 939-940.

Reed, Pierce J. Naming and confronting gay male battering. Boston: *Gay Community News*, April 16-22, 1989.

Sinclair, H. *Not her, him*. Paper presented to the San Francisco District Attorney's Office and General Works, San Francisco, May 1990.

Sjoberg, K. R. *The administration of the state's domestic violence diversion program could be improved*. Sacramento: State of California Office of the Auditor General, 1990.

Soler, E. The San Francisco family violence project: An overview. *Domestic violence: A training curriculum for law enforcement* (Vol. 1). San Francisco: San Francisco: Family Violence Project, 1988, pp. 3-5.

Sonkin, D. J., Martin, D., & Walker, L. E. *The male batterer: A treatment approach*. New York: Springer, 1985.

Stratton, N. R. M. *How will California handle spousal abuse incidents by the year 2000?* Walnut Creek, CA: California Commission on Peace Officer Standards and Training, 1988.

Walker, L. E. *The battered woman*. New York: Harper & Row, 1979.

Walker, L. E. *The battered woman syndrome*. New York: Springer, 1984.

Webb, D. The other closet. *Dallas Observer*, February 8, 1990, pp. 12; 14.

Yollin, P. Lesbians come of age. *San Francisco Examiner* (Gay in America Series), June 6, 1989, p. 17-18.1.

Zemsky, B., & Gilbert, L. Gay and lesbian domestic violence institute. Paper presented at the 12th National Lesbian and Gay Health Conference, Washington, D.C., July 1990.

Appendix

Domestic Violence

The purpose of this order is to set forth policies and procedures for domestic violence cases, restraining orders, and stay away orders. These policies and procedures are the result of California State mandates governing law enforcement response to domestic violence (Penal Code Sections 13519 and 13700 *et. seq.*).

I. GENERAL PROVISIONS

A. Definitions

1. "DOMESTIC VIOLENCE" is abuse committed against an adult or fully emancipated minor who is a spouse, former spouse, cohabitant, former cohabitant, or a person with whom the suspect has had a child or has had a dating or engagement relationship.
2. "ABUSE" means intentionally or recklessly causing or attempting to cause bodily injury, or placing another person in reasonable apprehension of imminent serious bodily injury to himself/herself, or another.
3. "OFFICER" means Law Enforcement officer employed by a local police department or sheriff's office, consistent with Section 830.I.P.C.
4. "VICTIM" means a person who is a victim of domestic violence.

Note: The above definitions include:

a. *Only* adults or fully emancipated minors;
b. A wide range of relationships such as former spouses, gay relationships, or boyfriend-girlfriends;
c. Threats as well as criminal activity.

B. Policy

1. Officers shall treat all acts of violence identified as "domestic violence" as criminal conduct. Domestic violence incidents shall be treated the same as all other requests for police assistance in cases where there has been physical violence or the threat thereof.
2. It is the policy of this department that arrests shall be made in domestic violence situations when the elements of a crime exist. Dispute mediation or other police intervention techniques shall not be used as a substitute to arrest.
3. Officers shall convey the attitude that violence in the home is criminal behavior and will not be tolerated.
4. The existence of the elements of a crime and/or the willingness of the victim to sign a Citizen's Arrest Card shall be the sole factors that determine the proper method of handling the incident. The following factors, for example, are *not* to influence the officer's course of action in domestic violence incidents:
   a. The marital status of the suspect and the victims;
   b. Whether or not the suspect lives on the premises with the victim;
   c. The existence or lack of a restraining order or stay away order;
   d. The potential financial consequences of arrest;
   e. The victim's history of prior complaints;
   f. Verbal assurances that the violence will cease;
   g. The victim's emotional state;
   h. Injuries not visible;
   i. The location of the incident (i.e., public or private);

j. Speculation that the victim may not follow through with the prosecution, or that the arrest may not lead to a conviction;

k. The victim's initial reluctance regarding an officer-initiated arrest.

CALIFORNIA JURY INSTRUCTIONS FOR BATTERY

Battery. Every person who, willfully uses any force or violence upon the person of another, is guilty of misdemeanor battery, a violation of Penal Code S242. (CALJIC 16.140, p. 304)

As used in the foregoing instruction, the words force and violence are synonymous and mean any application of physical force against the person of another, even though it causes no pain or bodily harm or leaves no mark and even though only the feelings of such person are injured by the act. The slightest unlawful touching, if done in an insolent, rude, or an angry manner is sufficient. (CALJIC 16.141, p. 305)

Battery—definition of. A battery is any intentional, unlawful and harmful contact by one person with the person of another. The intent necessary to constitute battery is not intent to cause harm, but an intent to do the act which causes the harm. (BAJI 7.51, p. 302)

These are the words in the standard instructions that juries must follow in California when deciding civil and criminal violence cases involving battery.

Here are what these jury instructions mean in ordinary language:

1. Battery is a crime.
2. A crime of battery has been committed even if no harm to the victim's body has occurred, or, even if no malice or anger was present, or, even if the person was not touched.
3. A battery is also a civil wrong, meaning a victim can collect monetary damages from someone who commits battery on him.
4. A civil battery has occurred even if the perpetrator only intended to commit the act (but not intended to harm).

RECOMMENDED READINGS

In addition to all of the works cited on the reference list, we recommend the following books on domestic violence:

NiCarthy, G. *Getting free: A handbook for women in abusive relationships* (2nd Ed.). Seattle: Seal Press, 1986.
NiCarthy, G., and Davidson, S. *You can be free: An easy to read handbook for abused women*. Seattle: Seal Press, 1989.
Ohlin, L., & Tonry, M. (Eds.). *Family violence*. Chicago: University of Chicago Press, 1989.
Sonkin, D. J., & Durphy, M. *Learning to live without violence: A handbook for men*. Volcano, CA: Volcano Press, 1989.
Walker, L. E. *Terrifying love: Why battered women kill and how society responds*. New York: Harper & Row, 1989.
White, E. C. *Chain chain change: For black women dealing with physical and emotional abuse*. Seattle: Seal Press, 1985.

For general information about domestic violence, contact:

The National Coalition Against Domestic Violence
2401 Virginia Avenue, N. W., Suite 306
Washington, D. C. 20037
(202) 638-6388

RESOURCES

For information about services available to gay male batterers and victims of domestic violence, contact:

The Community United
 Against Violence
Gay Men's Domestic Violence
 Project
(Services for Victims)
514 Castro Street
San Francisco, CA 94114
(415) 864-3112 Office
(415) 864-7233 24-hour hotline

New York City Gay and Lesbian
 Anti-Violence Project
(Services for Victims and
 Batterers)
1208 West 13th Street
New York, NY 10011
(212) 807-6761 Office
(212) 807-0197 Hotline

Seattle Counseling Service for
 Sexual Minorities
(Services for Victims and
 Batterers)
200 West Mercer, Suite 300
Seattle, WA 98119
(206) 282-9314 Office
(206) 282-9307 Services

Community University Health
 Care Center
(Services for Victims)
2016 16th Avenue South
Minneapolis, MN 55402
(612) 627-4774
(612) 340-7444

Men Overcoming Violence
(Services for Batterers)
54 Mint Street, Suite 300
San Francisco, CA 94103
(415) 626-6683

Home Again
(Services for Victims)
P.O. Box 14248
San Francisco, CA 94114
(415) 626-4067

Family Violence Project
(Services for Victims)
District Attorney's Office
850 Bryant St., 3rd Floor
San Francisco, CA 94103
(415) 552-7550
(415) 821-4553

Index

Accountability, 52,60-61,83-85,130,
    247-250
AIDS, 19,212,250-252
Alcohol and drugs, 18-19,247-250
American Psychiatric Association,
    68-76,112,113,114
Anti-social personality disorder,
    73-74
Arrest policy, San Francisco Police
    Department, 290-292
Assault, 56-57

Batterers
    and AIDS, 251-252
    and alcohol and drugs, 247-250
    as criminals, 55-58,85,150,204,
        230-231
    as mentally ill, 49,58-64,69-76
    as not "crazy," 40,54-55,58-59,
        270
    as source of comfort to victims, 7,
        34-35,243,244
    characteristics of, 11-12,18,31,44,
        49,58-60,76-81,96-97,127,
        145,158-168,238,255
    confusion about masculinity,
        49-53
    dependence on victims, 79,
        246-247
    development of, 64-68,253-255
    "failed macho complex" of, 51,
        249
    indicators of potential for
        violence, 158-166
    intent to harm, 25,31,40,58,78,
        249
    minimizing violence, 78,83,265

personality profile of, (*see*
    characteristics of)
prosecution of, 233-235
tenacity of, 79,96-98,104,
    144-145,150,151-152,
    166-168
theories of development, 64-68
treatment objectives and programs
    for, 63,81-83,259-260
Battering
    as a decision, 40,78,249
    as a mental health issue, 54-55,
        58-60,61-64,68-83
    causes of, 62-68,76,80,138,
        247-250,250-252
    mental disorders of, 68-76,76-81,
        143,249,257
    the progressive mental disorder
        of, 40,45,58-59,76-81
    see also incidence
Battery
    defined, 292
    see also California state penal
        codes
Beattie, M., 255
Blaming the victim
    see victim, blaming the
Book of approved jury instructions,
    240,292
Borderline personality disorder, 73
Browne, A., 94,96,97,158-159,195,
    249

California jury instructions,
    criminal, 240,292
California state penal codes, 56-57
    see also battery
Codependency, 24,255-258

Lay helper for victims
  basic guidelines for, 173-183
  confidentiality of, 175-176
  defined, 147-148
  finding one, 147-148
  role as advocate, 174-175
  safe house guidelines for,
    183-190,229-230
  special advice for, 190-198
Learned helplessness, 95-96,99,
  101-102,109,146
Leaving a violent partner, 22-24,40,
  43,44,93-104,108,123-127,
  146-147,208,242-245
  legal help for, 178-180
  preparation for, 123-143
  recovery after, 118-122
  victim response to, 112-118
  see also staying away from a
    violent partner
Lesbian battering, 8,62,99-101,202
Living without abuse, 156-158,
  222-223
Lobel, K., 100,101,103

Martin, D., 94,95,96,97,98,150,
  223,249
Martin, S. & McNeill, M., 232
Masculinity, 49-53
  comparisons between nonviolent
    men and batterers, 52-53
Material destruction, 17,18,25-28,
  41,47-49,56-57,78,108
Mediation
  dangers of, 169-171
  not as a substitute for arrest, 291
Men as victims, 15-16,21,101-103,
  129-132,215,253-255
Men Overcoming Violence, 35-36,
  294
Mental disorder, 40,45,58-60,60-61,
  62-63
  arguments against, for batterers,
    59-60
  defined, 70

  need for diagnostic categories for
    batterers, 58-59, 70-72
  victimization and, 112-117
  see also battering; *DSM-III-R*
Mental disorders of battering, 68-76,
  76-81
Mental health
  accountability and, 83-85
  battering and, 61-62
Mental health professionals
  role in prevention, 275-276
  role in stopping domestic
    violence, 60-61,63-64,71
  treating victims, 148-150
  see also therapists
Mental map, 127,135
Misdemeanor charges, 234,268
Moore, E. & Bundy, A., 36
Myths, and gay male battering,
  15-24

National Woman Abuse Prevention
  Project, 272
National Coalition Against Domestic
  Violence, 99-100,293
National Coalition for the Prevention
  of Domestic Violence, 272
New relationships, 193-194
  screening partners for, 158-166
New York City Gay and Lesbian
  Anti-Violence Project, 9,12,
  35,226,294
New York State Office for the
  Prevention of Domestic
  Violence, 13,271
NiCarthy, G., 94,95,100,158
Nonviolent individuals, development
  of, 254-255
Normalcy, defined, 61-62
Nowhere to go, 97-98,100-101,
  103-104,133-135
  see also victims